GRAND SLAM

GRAND SLAM

THE STORY OF THE
FIVE NATIONS
CHAMPIONSHIP

Miles Harrison

AURUM PRESS

First published in Great Britain
1999 by Aurum Press Ltd
25 Bedford Avenue, London WC1B 3AT

A catalogue record for this book is available from the British Library.

ISBN 1 85410 653 8

1 3 5 7 9 10 8 6 4 2
1999 2001 2003 2002 2000

Design by Don Macpherson
Typeset by York House Typographic, London
Printed and bound in Great Britain by
MPG Books Ltd, Bodmin

I dedicate this book to my wife Helen

CONTENTS

FOREWORD

Having provided television commentary on rugby union for a number of years, one is well acquainted with the vast amount of preparation required towards being fully equipped for the process of helping viewers to enjoy and understand what is taking place on the pitch. And as a keen admirer of Miles Harrison's television commentary style one is in no doubt that he has brought to the production of this splendid record the same attention to detail, accurate information and unfettered enthusiasm that are so evident in his television method.

The Five Nations championship, as the jewel in the northern hemisphere crown, has been in operation for the best part of one hundred years and has spawned not only some wonderfully thrilling elements of play, both collective and individual, but also a huge fund of stories from a host of characters and personalities for which the rugby union game is justly famous. In modern times, when rugby union has become a serious business, it lifts the spirit to read of the fun and frolic that were so much part and parcel of the great game in its amateur days.

In putting together such a fascinating tome, Miles Harrison has covered an amalgam of great feats on the field and that wonderful element of humour, light and shade in the rugby union game. It is a work that will provide for the devotees of the game, but also for those not quite so committed, a fascinating insight into one of the great rugby union competitions that has been the envy of the rest of the rugby union world for all those years.

Here is a riveting story that underlines the author's deep love and knowledge of the rugby union game and that is, in every sense, a treasured addition to its literature.

Bill McLaren
Hawick, 1999

ACKNOWLEDGEMENTS

Most of the research for this book was conducted through interviews with the players who have been directly quoted in the text. I am also grateful to Dr Tony O'Reilly for permission to quote from his contribution to *The Wit of Rugby*, edited by L.W.H. Paul.

The other major sources of information were the following rugby histories: *The International Rugby Championship 1883–1983* by Terry Godwin; *The Complete Who's Who of International Rugby* by Terry Godwin; *The Book of English International Rugby* by John Griffiths; *The Encyclopedia of Rugby Union* by Donald Sommerville (Aurum Press 1998); *Rothmans Rugby Yearbook* 1972 to date.

Back copies of newspapers from the National Newspaper Library at Colindale and magazines from my own collection have also proved invaluable including: *First XV*, *Rugby Journal*, *Rugby Monthly*, *Rugby News* and *Rugby World*.

I must also thank the Westgate Sports Agency, API Consulting and Advantage for supplying their information and interviews to the media through their excellent Infoline.

This book is a journey through a great rugby tournament, as seen through the eyes of those who have made it so special. The generosity and ease with which people have given up their time to enable me to include their stories comes as no surprise – this sport has always brought out the best in human qualities. I thank everybody for their contributions and goodwill. Of course, for a rugby fan, this project has been a magnificent excuse to talk to those heroes who make us all go misty-eyed. My wife, Helen, would return home from work to enquire about the progress I had made on the book. 'Well, who did you speak to today?' she would ask. When you can reply, 'Oh, Barry John and Jack Kyle,' you know it has been a pretty good day at the office!

Special thanks go to Bill McLaren for writing the Foreword. Some sports commentators over-use the word 'great' – Bill never has but, if I may say so, he is! His record of covering Five Nations games since the early 1950s is unparalleled, and I am honoured that he has contributed to this project. Equally, I am very grateful to Ian McGeechan for providing his thoughtful analysis in the Conclusion and taking on the unenviable task of picking an all-time Five Nations team.

I must also thank another Scot, my publisher, Bill McCreadie, who after our previous foray into print has once again proved a pleasure to work and play golf with. Bill knows a lot more about books and fairways than I ever will! Also at Aurum Press, the dedication and skill of Graham Coster have been invaluable.

Finally, a note of indulgence: when I watched my first Five Nations game in the early 1970s, I never thought that one day I would be in a position to write a history of the championship. It has been an immense privilege to do so, and I hope that you have as much enjoyment reading this as I had putting it together.

Miles Harrison
Berkhamsted, 1999

The author and publishers would like to thank the following for their kind permission to reproduce the photographs in this book:

Illustrated London News Picture Library (page 1); Hulton Getty (page 2); Vivian Jenkins (page 3, TOP); *Western Mail* (page 3, BOTTOM; page 5, BOTTOM; page 6, TOP; page 8); Museum of Rugby, Twickenham (page 4); Irish Rugby Football Union (page 5, TOP); Colorsport (page 6, BOTTOM; page 7, page 9, BOTTOM; page 10, page 11, page 12, page 13, page 14, TOP and BOTTOM LEFT; page 15, TOP and BOTTOM LEFT; page 16, TOP); Allsport (page 9, TOP; page 14, BOTTOM RIGHT; page 15, BOTTOM RIGHT); Huw Evans (page 16, BOTTOM).

INTRODUCTION

The Five Nations championship is the most basic of sporting concepts but has proved to be one of the most successful, in any sport at any time. It is amazing to think now that the winning of the tournament was only recognised by the game's administrators in the 1990s, when a trophy was finally awarded to the champion country. Before then, the so-called 'championship' was nominally shared when two or more teams ended the season with the same number of points. Indeed, for many years, the annual matches were seen as one-off contests with no official table being compiled, and it was left to the newspapers to print the unofficial tables and to devise such terms as the wooden spoon, Triple Crown and Grand Slam. It is believed that the origin of the wooden spoon – a metaphorical booby-prize given to the nation with the worst record of play in any one season – dates back to the 1820s when Cambridge University students taking examinations were grouped into three classes of honours. The bottom group was called the 'wooden wedge', which subsequently became the wooden spoon. The Triple Crown – awarded to England, Ireland, Scotland or Wales if they should beat the other three in a year – had been created by the end of the nineteenth century, long before France's inclusion in the championship in 1910. The Grand Slam came later, and it was not until the 1950s that the expression, describing a clean sweep of wins against all four opposing nations, was first used in *The Times* newspaper.

As we go into the new millennium, Italy become the first country to join the championship for ninety years, bringing to it their own rugby culture and another hangover, albeit one earned on excellent red wine! In the Conclusion of this book, the state of the Five Nations is reviewed, and the most successful coach in the northern hemisphere, the forward-thinking Ian McGeechan, examines what place the Six Nations will have in modern rugby. It is clear that in the fast moving world of the professional game the championship must evolve, but that in recent times it has been jeopardised by the power games bedevilling the sport since professionalism became a reality should serve as a warning to us all. It is too important to be used as a pawn, and recent events have tarnished the crown of one of sport's great institutions.

On a lighter note, Ian McGeechan also selects his all-time Five Nations team – see how your selection would compare. To assist you in making your choice, the statistical evidence is provided at the back of the book – an Appendix giving the results of every Five Nations game, team records and the championship roll of honour.

But this was never intended to be a book of figures – such detail is provided superbly elsewhere. No, the aim here is to combine the facts with the stories. All the Five Nations games have been mentioned in the text in some way (however cryptically) and, from the wealth of tales available, I have tried to select the ones which represent all aspects of the tournament's development. There are many individuals whose reflections could also have been included, but with space limited I wanted to concentrate not only on the great stars but also on the lesser lights who had briefer moments of Five Nations fame. Whether as a player, official, supporter or even broadcaster, we all have our personal recollections. By using the anecdotes of others, I hope to spark your own memories, be they of great tries, wins or lost weekends.

In modern rugby, I feel it is important that the past lives on – current championship games, however exciting, are made even more meaningful because of what has gone before. In the final year of the Five Nations, the oldest surviving participant in the tournament, Ireland's Tommy Wallis, who played in the early 1920s, recalled his favourite player: fellow countryman Dicky Lloyd. 'Nobody will know the name now...but what a player! If it had not been for the Great War he would have been a legend – look him up in the books.' This work remembers such individuals, young and old – and above all, it is the exploits of the players that have made this particular sporting story so special.

PART ONE

1910–1939

The memories of the last weekend of the final Five Nations championship should live with us for many years. Mighty England stood on the verge of a whitewash of the rest. But in the warm April sunshine, in their own backyard, they were ambushed by a Welsh team who struck a blow for rugby equality. Scott Gibbs's bullocking run and swallow-dive for the English line at Wembley, a mixture of the brutal and the balletic, opened the way for Wales's Celtic cousins Scotland to win the championship. A day earlier, the Scots had magnificently put the French to the sword and, after two Grand Slam years, France had conceded over 100 points in a season for the first time.

It was 48 hours that proved the old adage, 'What goes around, comes around.' For France's previous worst defensive performance we have, remarkably, to go all the way back to 1910. This was the year the home unions took the step that produced one of the twentieth century's most successful sporting competitions, by inviting France, a rugby nation still in its infancy, to play annual internationals against England, Ireland, Scotland and Wales. Thus was born the Five Nations championship.

Prior to this, an unofficial 'British and Irish championship' had been in existence for the best part of three decades, although in some years not all fixtures were fulfilled. England made the initial impact, but the Celts all had their moments – it was the shape of things to come. This was a time when rugby was still establishing its laws, never mind traditions, but by now the sport had spread worldwide and for the home unions regular matches against their neighbour France seemed an inevitable progression. The Scottish required the most persuading but, after four years of procrastination during which the others all at some stage took on the French, finally agreed to join in.

As the tournament began to take shape the games were soon played in an established sequence. In the early years of the Five Nations, however, even a number of newspapers took some convincing as to the credibility of the competition, and when they printed championship tables France were often omitted. Ironically, though, the French were never far from the news. In 1914, just before the break-out of World War I, Scotland refused to play them, such had been the violence directed at the Scottish team and the match referee at the end of the previous year's encounter. After the war France returned to the championship and recorded some notable victories, but before long there was new controversy. It was France's thriving club competition that fired the fans' imagination – the majority of French supporters lived in the south, which made travelling to any Five Nations game a long, drawn-out experience – and when the clubs broke away from their Union in the early 1930s this led to France's expulsion from the championship between 1932 and 1939. For eight seasons the most the other nations could achieve was to beat their three home rivals and win the Triple Crown: there could be no Grand Slam.

This disagreement highlighted the issue of alleged payment, a cloud that had hung over rugby union ever since the split between union and league in the 1890s, when a number of clubs in Yorkshire and Lancashire had wanted to compensate their players for wages lost while playing rugby. When the English Rugby Football Union refused, the clubs had created the Northern Union, which in time became the Rugby Football League. The word 'competition' was frowned on in union circles, and extraordinary measures were taken to preserve the amateur ethos – with the constant threat of expulsion from the sport for those who became 'professionalised'. If a player even took part in a game that included another who had at some point been professional, that amateur was forever tainted.

Against this background and the inevitable loss of players to rugby league, the Five Nations was able to establish itself as rugby's major annual contest. From 1910 to 1939 the English enjoyed great success, winning six Grand Slams and two Triple Crowns in an era dominated by the development of forward play. During the 1920s, England had, in their captain Wavell Wakefield, one of the game's great innovators and tacticians. Wales had been a strong side from the turn of the century and had even more success when they won the Grand Slam in 1911, but unfortunately could not repeat the feat before World War II. Economic decline hit the Welsh hard as rugby in the Principality had always been the working-man's game; the deepening recession prompted a migration to better employment prospects in England, a dip in gate receipts and an inevitable drift to rugby league. Wales had some great players and some famous wins between the wars, but the depression was not confined to the coal-fields: it hit the nation's rugby as well.

Of course Ireland had major political problems, but here at least, ever since 1879 when its two unions north and south of the border had come together as the Irish Rugby Football Union, rugby was a unifying force and internationals were played in both Belfast and Dublin. The Ireland team frequently came close to glory between 1910 and 1939 but never once won a Triple Crown, let alone a Grand Slam. Over the water in Scotland the most conservative of governing bodies acted as the ultimate protector of the amateur principle. Even numbering of the Scottish jerseys was outlawed until 1933 – when asked why by King George V, the head of the Scottish Rugby Union, James Aikman Smith, apparently replied, 'This is a rugby match, not a cattle auction!' On the field, Scotland were more progressive, and with mould-breaking back-line play they had their fair share of success, with a Grand Slam in 1925 and Triple Crowns in 1933 and 1938.

1910–1914

1910 – England's championship
1911 – Wales's GRAND SLAM
1912 – England and Ireland share championship
1913 – England's GRAND SLAM
1914 – England's GRAND SLAM

Unsurprisingly, France made a poor start to the Five Nations. They were a raw side while their Welsh opponents included a number of rugby greats: full-back Jack Bancroft, following in the footsteps of his legendary brother Billy; the versatile back Billy Trew, less than ten stone but a little genius; and half-back Dicky Owen, the first master of the reverse pass. It was little wonder, then, that in Swansea on New Year's Day Wales scored what was for them a new record international total of 49 points, with Bancroft landing eight conversions – a record set on the new championship's very first day which has still not been surpassed.

Next, the victorious Welsh played England in the first international to be staged at Twickenham. Previously a market-garden site, the ground had been purchased by the RFU in 1907 on the advice of committee member Billy Williams. Affectionately known thereafter as 'Billy Williams' Cabbage Patch', the venue was a far cry from today's majestic arena. Spectators stood on heaps of straw to get a better view as England celebrated at their new home with a try almost straight after the kick-off from winger Fred Chapman. However, they could have been helped by Wales's less than ideal pre-match preparation – because of traffic congestion the team arrived only five minutes before the scheduled start. Even though the Redruth back Barney Solomon scored a try in the match, he still felt that the distance from Cornwall to London was too far to travel for internationals, and this was his first and last championship appearance.

The victory over Wales was the beginning of an unbeaten season for the English, and only a scoreless draw against Ireland prevented the first Grand Slam of the Five Nations. England's captain for their first two matches that year was fly-half Adrian Stoop of Harlequins, whose Stoop Memorial Ground is named in homage to a great sporting family. Against Scotland the brothers Adrian and Frank Stoop played together in the English back line for the first time. Adrian's apparent insistence on playing with the same ball used in the Scottish win over France two months earlier was an eccentric but effective move, as English victory made sure of the title and the Calcutta Cup. The cup had been donated by the Calcutta Football Club when it folded back in the 1870s, the remaining rupees in its coffers having been melted down to create the trophy which is awarded to this day after England-Scotland encounters.

The Scots were now playing their home matches at Inverleith in Edinburgh, a ground owned, like Twickenham, by the Union. Although Scotland had decided not to award caps for that international against the French they did deign to wear white jerseys to avoid a clash of colour – a positively revolutionary move on their part. The closest France could come to a win in their first year in the Five Nations was when they narrowly lost at home to Ireland, who had previously been beaten by Scotland. After their loss to England, Wales recovered to win their two remaining games, and when winger Johnny Williams scored a hat-trick in Dublin the future looked brighter for the men in red.

Sure enough, the following year Wales went one better than England and won the first-ever Grand Slam. The term was not yet in use in 1911, but the achievement, of beating all the four other nations, remains the same. Furthermore, in only two seasons they had scored the huge total of 39 tries. It was a team full of talent, and in loose forward Ivor Morgan they had the perfect link between the pack and the backs – an increasingly important role. Skipper Billy Trew led his team to victory over England but was less confident about the game against France – handing over the captaincy to Johnny Williams because Trew could not speak French! France lost that game to Wales, but had previously discovered a new word for their rugby vocabulary – 'victory' – in beating Scotland in Paris. They were soon back to square one, however – thrashed by England at Twickenham with winger Douglas Lambert scoring 22 points, a match record which still stands. Ireland had a better year, winning three games – a fitting send-off to captain George Hamlet, one of the greatest forwards ever to wear the green jersey. Defeat at Twickenham rounded off a miserable season to consign Scotland to the wooden spoon. Their captain and half-back, Pat Munro, left to take up an administrative post in the Sudan – giving one of his caps to a tribal chief who proceeded to wear it on all official occasions, preferring it to his fez!

It was Wales and England who were dominating the early years of the championship but the Scots, now led by forward J.C. MacCallum, had the satisfaction of foiling a first English Grand Slam in 1912 by winning in Edinburgh. In turn, England's win over Ireland prevented an Irish Grand Slam, but France, losing all four of their matches, clearly still had some catching up to do. The championship was not yet established as an important event – Welshmen Owen and Trew opted to tour Devon with their club Swansea rather than play against France in Newport. The famous half-back pairing's final match together was therefore the earlier victory over Scotland on their home ground, St Helen's, where the crowd had shown their appreciation by hoisting them high on their shoulders.

In 1913 and 1914 England swept majestically to eight straight wins over the other nations to record the first back-to-back Grand Slams, the side further reinforced by the introduction of such notable sportsmen as winger Cyril Lowe and fly-half W.J.A. Davies. But it was 'Cherry' Pillman, the most capped member of the pack, who above all others that 1913 season was instrumental in his side's amazing defence, which saw them concede no tries in any of their four matches. The season did not start so well, however, for an English referee, John Baxter, who required a police escort to protect him from irate supporters at the Parc des Princes following Scotland's win over France, during which he had awarded numerous penalties against the home side. Scotland's reaction was to cancel the following year's fixture against the French and Wales, after their victory over the Scots, called in police reinforcements for their trip to Paris. When the guards encroached onto the Welsh goal-line during the match, the referee, Mr Miles of England, much to the delight of the crowd, ordered them back – but the spectators did not cheer the Welsh victory.

After defeat in Scotland, the Scottish winger W.A. Stewart scoring four tries, the famous Irish scrum-half, Harry Read, announced his retirement. It was sad that he should go out on a losing note, because he and his partner, Dicky Lloyd, are remembered for setting a new trend in rugby by establishing definitive half-back roles, where previously it had been the fashion to interchange between fly-half and scrum-half during a game. Lloyd's drop-goal (he was the master of them) was in fact the only score the English let past them that season. The new-look Irish team went on to lose to Wales, but a resounding victory over France in Cork on the morning of Easter Monday saved them from the wooden spoon.

One of the features of the championship at the time was a tendency for players to take the law into their own hands. Accounts of these early matches frequently refer to off-the-ball activities which simply would not be tolerated by the referees of today. Ireland's defeat to Wales in 1914 has been described as one of the roughest-ever games in the Five Nations. Apparently the gauntlet for this infamous confrontation had been rather jokingly laid down on the Friday night before the game, when the Irish pack leader, Dr William Tyrrell, and the other members of the team met with the Welsh forwards, known as the 'Terrible Eight'. When the match began, nobody took a backward step – least of all the leader of the Welsh team and pack, the Reverend Alban Davies – doctors and vicars, whatever next! Fights broke out, sometimes involving nearly all the players, and late tackles were the order of the day.

In 1914, England went from strength to strength, scoring twenty more tries. After a narrow win over Wales, they returned to

Twickenham a month later to beat Ireland at home, in a match famous for taking place while debate was raging in Parliament over Home Rule. A win by one point over Scotland kept centre Ronnie Poulton's team on course for the Grand Slam. In that match Cyril Lowe came up against fellow Cambridge University flyer, the Scot George Will, and between them they scored five tries. The brilliant Lowe, a player who typified the freedom of spirit in this blossoming English team, went on to get three more in England's crushing win over France, to become the first man to score consecutive international hat-tricks. Wales and Ireland both beat Scotland and France but England seemed unstoppable – only one thing could halt their progress. World War I began, and the championship was suspended for five seasons.

1920–1924

1920 – England, Scotland and Wales share Championship
1921 – England's GRAND SLAM
1922 – Wales's championship
1923 – England's GRAND SLAM
1924 – England's GRAND SLAM

The war took its toll on all human life, and rugby suffered the loss of many who had and could have worn their country's jersey. Its continuing impact was clear when the championship restarted in 1920: Frenchman Marcel-Frederic Lubin-Lebrère and his opposing forward, Jock Wemyss of Scotland, who played in the first game, had each lost an eye in the conflict. But some things had not changed, as France lost. Even a move of stadium from the old Parc des Princes to the Stade Colombes could not alter their luck, as Wales beat them too. Twickenham had been a further setback and, despite producing players with the flair of winger Adolphe Jauréguy, French play was still disorganised – the referee for the Welsh game, Colonel Craven of England, was so unhappy with the French put-in to the scrum that he did it himself! At least a win over Ireland in their final match enabled France to avoid the wooden spoon: that went to the Irish, who had suffered a wretched run of four defeats.

England made a losing start to the post-war age against Wales, and for winger W.M. Lowry the game was doubly disappointing. In what would have been his first international he was photographed with the team before the kick-off at Swansea, but because of the heavy ground was dropped and replaced at the last minute by H.L.V. Day. At least Lowry was awarded his cap, and he became the first man to have been given that honour without taking the field. He did start the next game against France. Also beginning his career was one of the greatest forwards of all time, Wavell Wakefield. Wakefield played in every English international between 1920 and 1926 and was central to the development of the art of forward play. In 1920 it was his fellow pack member, 'Jenny' Greenwood, who captained his side to three victories. Scotland also won three games, including their match against Wales, when forward Charles Usher, who had earlier cut short his honeymoon to play in Paris, was rewarded with the captaincy. Usher helped Scotland to their first-ever share of the championship, as England and Wales joined them at the top of the table.

It was now only France who had failed to end a season as champions, but they were improving and the following year won two matches – a first victory in Scotland and a win at home to Ireland. The Five Nations was becoming increasingly popular, and when over 50,000 crammed into the ground at Swansea to see a Welsh side that had previously lost to England take on Scotland they spilled onto the pitch, and at one point the game was nearly abandoned. Scotland won that day but lost all their other matches, while Wales had to be content with two wins and Ireland just one. Back to their pre-war form, England won their third Grand Slam after victory over France in Paris, with their half-backs, W.J.A. Davies and his partner Cecil Kershaw, outstanding. The first half of the 1920s was becoming a golden era for English rugby.

Wales did challenge English dominance with an emphatic victory at the start of 1922 when they scored eight tries in a breathtaking display. The spectators found their heroes easier to spot, as for the first time both sets of players wore numbered jerseys. Wales went on to become champions with a draw against Scotland their only blemish. For the Scots, winger and supreme athlete Eric Liddell made his debut in the draw with France at the Stade Colombes, the stadium where two years later he would set a new world record in winning the 440 yards Olympic title – an achievement which inspired the hit film *Chariots of Fire*. As the movie memorably recalled, Liddell, a profoundly religious man, refused to run the heats of the 100 yards sprint because they were held on a Sunday. After his Olympic triumph and just two seasons in a Scottish jersey, he became a missionary in China. In 1922, despite only losing once, to England, Scotland could only finish in mid-table. After their draw against the Scots, France almost won at Twickenham, but were denied by a late try from the English forward Tommy Voyce. Defeat to Ireland in their final game was a familiar end to France's season, and a desperately-needed win for the Irish after losing their other three games.

Ireland's poor run continued in 1923 and, despite the continuing presence of talented centre George Stephenson, whose brother Harry also played with distinction in the Irish backs during the 1920s, they managed to win just once, at home to Wales. The only Welsh victory was over France in another violent game featuring numerous scrapes and scraps, the referee, Jack McGowan, feeling compelled to call the secretary of the French Federation onto the field so he could translate a warning to his team. Meanwhile, Scotland were having a better season, winning three games, with their captain and centre, Archie Gracie, an influential figure. In an unfortunate episode during the win in Cardiff Gracie scored a brilliant try but, in crossing the dead-ball line, accidentally kicked a boy in the crowd, who subsequently lost some teeth. England took their match against Ireland to Leicester, and beat them to pave the way to another Grand Slam, but the crowd of under 20,000 was not considered large enough and England returned to Twickenham for all their Five Nations games until the end of the century. In the Grand Slam match in Paris W.J.A. Davies, playing his last international, emulated Charles Usher by interrupting his honeymoon for the game. The Welsh-born Davies, whose England career spanned the war, never lost a Five Nations match.

Another great England player, Cyril Lowe, also retired after another successful season, but the impact of his loss was lessened by the emergence of a winger from Percy Park, Carston Catcheside, who in 1924 stepped into Lowe's famous shoes with amazing results. In another Grand Slam year for his team Catcheside scored the first-ever 'Grand Slam' of tries – that is, a try against all the other nations in a single championship season, just as Gregor Townsend would do 75 years later. What made Catcheside's feat even more remarkable was that he was winning his first caps. Scotland finished second in the table after three victories, including an impressive eight tries against Wales, but France lost all of their matches and their loyal servant and captain, centre René Crabos, broke his leg in Dublin in a sad end to his championship career. In contrast, Irishman Frank Hewitt, at nearly seventeen and a half, became the youngest-ever player in the championship during a rare win for Ireland in Cardiff. Frank's older brother, fellow back Tom, also made his debut in that game and both scored a try. In the 1950s and 1960s the next generation of the Hewitt family would continue the association with the Five Nations.

If there was one factor that dominated these times it was the rigid amateur code, on which the governing unions issued firm directives. An example of the constraints imposed on players is the scandal of the Welsh full-back Ossie Male. During the 1924 season Male was already at Paddington Station en route to play France, when the Welsh Rugby Union discovered he had played for his club the week before the international – something strictly forbidden. He was sent home. At the end of the season the Welsh created the 'Big Five', a committee charged with co-ordinating the selection procedure, but it was three years before Male was selected again.

1925–1929

1925 – Scotland's GRAND SLAM
1926 – Ireland and Scotland share championship
1927 – Ireland and Scotland share championship
1928 – England's GRAND SLAM
1929 – Scotland's championship

The 1925 championship season had an unusual beginning, the French aviator, D'Oisy, who had recently flown solo from Paris to Tokyo, being given the honour of kicking off the match against Ireland. But neither this nor the fact that the game was being played on a Thursday did much for French fortunes as Ireland won. They were captained by one of the championship's most colourful characters, full-back Ernie Crawford. With a strong Belfast accent never dulled despite his spending much time in Dublin, and a reputation for gamesmanship both on and off the field, Crawford despised authority. Ironically, in later years he became President of the IRFU! But in his playing days, according to Irish rugby historian Sean Diffley, Crawford coined the word now applied to those in rugby officialdom - 'Alikadoos':

The term originated on a train trip to London [writes Diffley in *The Men in Green – the Story of Irish Rugby*] when Ernie failed to entice some other player to join the ritual game of poker. His colleague preferred to read a book which was about some oriental potentate. Ernie growled his displeasure: 'You and your bloody Ali Khadu!' After that, anyone who strayed from Ernie's conception of the proper order of affairs became an Alikadoo.

Crawford's Ireland went on to draw with England and beat Wales but, in between, lost to Scotland, as did all the other nations that season. This was a vintage year for Scottish rugby as they scored seventeen tries on the way to their first Grand Slam, profiting from a sparkling back line which had its roots down south. Full-back Daniel Drysdale and half-backs J.B. Nelson and Herbert Waddell were joined by four students from Oxford University – captain Phil Macpherson, his centre partner George Aitken, and wingers Johnny Wallace and Ian Smith, otherwise known as the 'Flying Scotsman'. The 'southern connection' went even further afield than Oxford, because in 1921 Aitken had led the All Blacks against South Africa and Wallace would return to the United Kingdom as captain of the Australian Waratahs in 1927. Smith had also been born down under, but his Scottish parents had brought him 'home', subsequently to carve himself a permanent place in Scotland's Five Nations history. In 1925 Smith's impact was astounding as he scored four tries in his team's win over France and four more against Wales. Scotland's Oxford University quartet proved that scouring the world for international talent is not just a modern phenomenon.

Scotland's Grand Slam was only won after an epic battle with England, who had already beaten Wales and would go on to defeat France. It was the first Five Nations game to be played at Murrayfield, on a piece of land purchased from the Edinburgh Polo Club three years earlier. A debenture issue had raised the capital to construct a purpose-built rugby stadium, with room for more than 70,000, a significant increase on the capacity of Inverleith. The two teams christened the venue with a marvellous spectacle, the lead changing hands three times. But controversy surrounds the try which hauled the Scots back into the game – England's Wavell Wakefield and Tommy Voyce, it has been claimed, tackling Ian Smith out of play short of the line. The try was scored by Johnny Wallace who, like England's Catcheside the year before, had performed the Grand Slam of tries. In *International Rugby Union – a Compendium of Scotland's Matches*, his history of Scottish rugby, John McI. Davidson responds to suggestions that the try should not have stood:

> There is, of course, no doubt that the scorer was Johnny Wallace. He had been given an overlap inside the 25 and sprinted for the corner where he dived under Holliday's tackle to touch down just over the line. The photograph...shows that the corner flag was still upright and the next nearest Englishman still some two yards away. The nearest Scot, G.P.S. Macpherson, was following up in support about five yards away, ready for a possible inside pass and I know that he had no doubts about the try.

England full-back 'Toff' Holliday still had a chance to win the game but missed a last minute drop-goal, and both sets of players staggered from the field in exhaustion. At the after-match dinner the notoriously spendthrift SRU, the story goes, treated both sides to champagne – yet their generosity stopped short of paying for fires to be made up in the players' hotel rooms. There was a warmer response from the Scottish team, who gathered to give three cheers to the beaten English as they departed from Waverley Station.

The following season Scotland maintained their good form, but had to share the championship with Ireland, both countries winning three matches and Ireland taking the game at Murrayfield. It was a typical Irish team, based on a fiery pack, and none burning brighter than flanker 'Jammie' Clinch, the son of 'Coo' Clinch who had played in the 1890s. In the backs, Crawford and George Stephenson were joined by winger Denis Cussen, a national sprint record holder over one hundred yards, and the half-backs Eugene O'D. Davy and Mark Sugden, a pairing as good as any in the 1920s. But in Swansea their Grand Slam ambitions were undone, when against Wales they could not repeat the thrilling performance of their victory over England and Tom Hewitt's late drop-goal went agonisingly wide. Wales themselves had drawn with England and beaten the French and could have been champions, but their loss to Scotland cost them the title. Poor France lost the lot for a third season in a row.

1927 was almost an exact replica of the previous year, with Ireland and Scotland sharing the title again with three wins each. After starting the season with three losses France, however, beat England for the first time, but sadly their great forward, Aimé Cassayet, who had been through the hard times, losing 22 out of 26 Five Nations matches, missed the game through serious illness and died shortly afterwards. The Paris defeat was the last game for England's Wavell Wakefield. The English, it seemed, were no longer the dominant force of the early 1920s, and their only victories that season came at home, against Wales and Ireland, as Scotland beat them at Murrayfield.

A year later, however, forward Ronnie Cove-Smith took up the English captaincy and presided over the sixth Grand Slam for his country since 1910. Ireland threatened, winning three games and narrowly losing to England by a point in Dublin, but the other three nations were left to play out a mini-championship among themselves: Scotland beat the French, Wales triumphed over Scotland, and France won against Wales for the first time, another important milestone. For the Welsh these were the 'breadline days', as a report in the *Western Mail* on 12 January 1929, quoted by John Billot in his *History of Welsh International Rugby*, illustrates:

> Three members of Aberavon RFC left the town on Friday for Weston-super-Mare, where they have obtained employment. It was alleged that they were answering advertisements displayed in a window of the Port Talbot Labour Exchange. This said, 'Weston-super-Mare local offices are requested to forward particulars in respect of good rugby footballers. Wing and centre three-quarters preferred. The men should be good, heavy labourers, hewers or colliers' helpers, and not more than 25 years of age. Successful applicants will be found employment with the local Urban District Council, with possession of a permanent job.

It was a battle to hold on to players in the tough economic climate, and with the ever-present lure of rugby league the sport in Wales was at a low ebb.

France were knocked back down to earth in the 1929 Five Nations season and lost all their games. Club rugby was thriving, but the continuing failure of the national side was a destabilising influence on the sport there. Unusually, that year's championship actually began in 1928, with France playing their first match against Ireland on 30 December. A disillusioned Welsh public were relieved that their side's defeat at Twickenham in January was the only reverse of the season, but the Irish went one better, gaining their first victory at England's headquarters in a match dubbed 'the Battle of the Cushions' after

Ireland's supporters threw their seat covers into the air on the final whistle in spontaneous joy. A draw between the Irish and the Welsh meant both had to be content with a share of second place. It was Scotland who took the title with just one defeat against Wales. As England went down in front of yet another huge Murrayfield crowd captain J.M. Bannerman, a towering figure in the pack for the whole decade, was able to leave the championship on the perfect note with his team's third and final victory.

1930–1934

1930 – England's championship
1931 – Wales's championship
1932 – England, Ireland and Wales share championship
1933 – Scotland's Triple Crown and championship
1934 – England's Triple Crown and championship

Although France had not won two matches in a championship season for nine years, they began the 1930s in promising fashion. Ably led by forward Eugene Ribère, they beat Scotland and Ireland, only to lose to England at Twickenham. When England beat Wales Bristol hooker Sam Tucker was called up as a late replacement and flew from his home town to Cardiff on the morning of the game. Tucker kept his place and captained the side in a nil-nil draw at home to Scotland and in taking the title England were only defeated by Ireland. That season the Celtic nations said goodbye to three of the championship's biggest names from the inter-war period, Wales's flanker Ivor Jones, Scotland's Herbert Waddell, who won his final game against the Welsh with a late drop-goal, and Ireland's George Stephenson, who missed out on a Triple Crown with a loss to Wales on his last appearance. But while standards of play were increasingly sophisticated, there remained a tendency for games to boil over. So appalled was the Secretary of the French Federation, Cyril Rutherford, by what was going on in the closing match of the championship, a Welsh victory in Paris, that he actually ran onto the pitch to point out a misdemeanour by one of his players so that a penalty could be reversed against France!

A year later, France had more to worry about, as they were dramatically heading out of the championship. The home unions' long-held doubts over the amateur status of the French game were apparently confirmed by the decision of twelve clubs to break away from the French Federation to set up a competition of their own. Playing their 1931 games under the threat of expulsion France still beat Ireland and England, but just when it appeared they were a growing force in the game, they were ejected. In the subsequent period of isolation, regular internationals against Germany, Italy and Romania could do little to improve French rugby standards. Eventually, by the end of the 1930s, France promised to get its affairs in the order that the home unions required and its team was readmitted into the competition, though a whole generation of Five Nations involvement had been lost. In 1931 England, too, had problems and they slumped to the wooden spoon for the first time, their only point coming from a draw against Wales. The Irish win at Twickenham was followed by victory over a Scottish team grateful for their opening win over France. It was Wales who took the title, however, with three wins confirming a much-needed recovery in the valleys.

The 1932 championship started on the back of a South African tour of the British Isles and Ireland. The tour had a great impact, with all four Home Nations losing to the Springboks, who had arrived full of fresh ideas, and especially the kick to touch, a skill not yet fully exploited in the northern hemisphere. England began the Five Nations with a defeat in Wales, signalling the need for team changes for the game against Ireland. It heralded a call-up for scrum-half Bernard Gadney, who had played for the Midlands in the only defeat for the Springboks on that tour, performing well against the great Danie Craven, a man who went on to fulfil just about every possible role in South African rugby administration (and as a player, quite remarkably, played in four different positions in four consecutive internationals). Nevertheless, the news of Gadney's England selection came as a complete surprise. 'I was working at a residential school,' recalls England's oldest-surviving rugby captain, 'and one night after I had gone to my room I was awoken by a call to attend the senior headmaster's office. I thought the worst – perhaps somebody had died? But when I arrived a bottle was out on the table and I was asked if I wanted a drink – they had heard on the wireless that I'd been chosen to play for England!'

Gadney took part in an English victory in Dublin over an Irish side led by his Leicester colleague, George Beamish. The Ireland pack also contained the excellent Jimmy Farrell, in his last season, and two emerging forwards who would have a major role to play in Irish rugby, Victor Pike and Jack Siggins. England then comfortably beat Scotland at Twickenham, two experienced and talented Scottish backs, Phil Macpherson and William Simmers, disappointingly ending their careers in a side which that year lost all three games. With Ireland beating Wales and France absent, the title was shared by three of the four remaining nations. Gadney's abiding memory of his debut season was the spartan facilities at Twickenham: 'In the changing-room, there were three white kitchen tables, and on them were fifteen jerseys and fifteen pairs of stockings which needed cutting at the top. My first thought was, "I do hope there's some running water in this place!" Before the match, the Secretary came in to remind us that we must hand in our jerseys at the end of the game, but we saw them as fair loot because we were proud to swap and get one from the opposition.'

Such frugal measures from the authorities reflected the hard times off the field, with the domestic economy under the strain of a world depression. Regardless, the amateur ethos in rugby union was in full cry and any contact with the professional code was frowned upon and seen as treason. But Bernard Gadney believes that to portray the amateur players of this era as carefree and undedicated is wholly wrong. 'Whether it's better to have a lot of money or very little money in rugby I don't know, but I want to correct one thing: the idea that we didn't care about winning or bother to train is nonsense. We were training at night and did our best. We were all holding down jobs, if we were lucky enough to have them, although of course some of my friends were out of work. When I was crocked rather badly, I was invited by Herbert Chapman of the Arsenal to go down there whenever I wanted. They used to roar with laughter at how rugby footballers trained, but if you were supposed to be doing a job it wasn't very easy to have a timetable like theirs.' In those days Saturday was part of the working week – when Gadney used to play against Swansea, he recalls, most of their players had been down the pit on the morning of the game. Bradford, he adds, heart of the woollen industry, had one of the great rugby union sides of the time, but if they had to travel to play, the team missed their Friday afternoon and Saturday shifts: 'I don't blame the boys for going their own way and joining rugby league, because they were not being paid for broken time. I dare say I would have done the same.'

As in rugby league, this was a period when union's ruling bodies continued to experiment with the laws of their game. One area of constant flux was the scrum – in 1932 it was decreed that the front-row had to comprise three players, a move which hit New Zealand hardest, since they were used to a two-man front-row with both men termed 'hookers'. Throughout the world many other formations had already been tried for packing down. In Britain, the norm was a 3–2–3 pattern, but for some time the South Africans had been using 3–4–1, a method which allowed their flankers to leave the scrummage more quickly. To further complicate matters, 1933 saw the introduction of a law making it compulsory for the first forwards to arrive at the breakdown to be first into the scrummage. Understandably it proved unpopular, and the law was soon revoked.

Under the leadership of forward Watcyn Thomas the Welsh went to Twickenham on the opening day of the 1933 season with two backs, Vivian Jenkins and A.H. Jones, who had been at Llandovery School together, winning their first caps. For full-back Jenkins, still an imposing figure in his 88th year, the day should have been the fulfilment of a long-held dream. 'But on the eve of the game I had the flu and a temperature of 103 degrees. I remember waking up in the morning, taking the clothes off the bed and a cloud of steam went up – I thought, "Oh, hell!"' 'For God's sake, play!' he remembers his old schoolmate, with whom he was sharing a room, urging him: 'if you don't, you'll probably never get another chance.' 'But I didn't really improve and I should not have played. When I was being introduced to the Prince of Wales before kick-off, I was still shaking with the flu.' Jenkins got through the match, but afterwards was so ill he had to stay at the hotel until the following Thursday and missed Wales's next match.

But the stricken Jenkins had played his part in an historic day for Welsh rugby. It was the tenth time Wales had made the trip to England's home, and at last they were able to leave with a win. Winger Ronnie Boon got all the points, recalls Jenkins: 'We used to call him "Cocky" Boon – he was very fast, a sprint champion and could have played anywhere, even fly-half.' Wales had been trailing by a try on 'a slippery sort of day,' Jenkins goes on, when the ball went loose near the England line and the English captain, Carl Aarvold, in his last game on their wing, went to fly-kick the ball into touch. 'But it came off the side of his foot, across the field and straight to Boon. He was in front of the posts with an open field on his right. I remember thinking, "Have a go," meaning, run for the corner, as with his speed he had to make it. But suddenly he took a pot at goal and I thought, "Oh, no!" – but being Ronnie it went over!'

Boon added a try to his assured drop-goal and Wales were four points in front. Vivian Jenkins' conversion went just outside the right-hand upright – but while one touch-judge was signalling no goal the other put his flag up and the scoreboard was changed to 9–3, which meant England would have to score twice to win. It was twenty minutes before the error was corrected, and not long afterwards the law was changed to introduce a drop-out re-start after a failed conversion.

Another man who made his debut in that game was Welsh centre Wilf Wooller, tall and fast and a great all-round sportsman who would go on to lead Glamorgan County Cricket Club with distinction after the war, and in 1933 was still at school waiting for a place at Cambridge University. But that year Scotland proved too much for Wooller's Wales. Winger Ian Smith, one of the original Oxford University quartet, was now the proud Scottish captain and in his final season celebrated a famous double achievement – the championship and the Triple Crown. For the only time this century the title rested on Scotland's game against Ireland. Snow and gales had postponed the match from its customary earlier position to April – in February, the Scots' boat had waited outside Dublin Bay for sixteen hours before being able to dock, and the game was called off. When it was eventually played, two drop-goals, worth four points in those days, from Ken Jackson and fellow back Harry Lind, were enough to beat two Irish tries from backs Paul Murray and Morgan Crowe. England had also beaten Ireland, and the Irish had won against Wales, but it was Scotland's year. Bennie Osler of the touring Springboks had adroitly demonstrated how to kick strategically, and this was now influencing play to the extent that Scotland's Triple Crown had been attained with only three tries scored.

Tries had not become altogether extinct, however: in 1934, when they won back the title and the Triple Crown, England managed to touch down eight times. Crucial in breaking down the opposition were the speed of service away from set-piece, and the strength of the scrum-half, and in Bernard Gadney England had one of the best. By the time the English played against Ireland – the final match for the great Irish back, Eugene O'D. Davy – he had been appointed as captain. The canny O'Davy would have admired Gadney's tactic that secured the Triple Crown at Twickenham. The visitors, Scotland, fresh from a victory over Ireland, were trailing by three points to six after another try from winger Graham Meikle, who had now scored in all three championship games. But with the brilliant back, Wilson Shaw, having scored for Scotland, the game was not safe for England. Late in the game England had a scrum in the corner on the Scottish line, and when the ball came out Gadney kicked it into touch. The crowd did not appreciate his move very much – 'They thought it was a very rude and common thing to do,' he recalls, unrepentant, 'but I happened to know that time was running out, and it was far better to win than to go and muck the whole thing up!'

Though it was England's season the Welsh, who had also beaten Scotland, were looking to finish well. They returned home to meet Ireland eager to play a running game, and on the morning of the match the conditions seemed set fair: 'We had all walked up and down Swansea bay in the sun,' Vivian Jenkins explains – 'we thought our backs were going to sew up the Irish. Then, underneath the stand in the changing-room, we heard the rain coming down – sheets of it, as it only can on the edge of the Atlantic there.' The match still had a historic outcome for the Welsh full-back. After catching a sliced Irish kick inside his own 25-yard line, he took the ball to the open-side and gave it to Cliff Jones, in his first season and, says Jenkins, the finest fly-half he has ever seen. Jones went with the three-quarters – first Idwal Rees and then Arthur Bassett, who set off hell-for-leather for the corner flag with Jenkins following up just behind. 'But somehow Ireland got back and, as Arthur was going into touch, he slipped the ball to me and all I had to do was scoop it up and fall over the line. My first try for Wales was from a yard and a half!' Wales's enterprise had paid off, and Jenkins had scored the first-ever try by a Welsh full-back – it would be 33 years before Keith Jarrett scored the next.

1935–1939

1935 – Ireland's championship
1936 – Wales's championship
1937 – England's Triple Crown and championship
1938 – Scotland's Triple Crown and championship
1939 – England, Ireland and Wales share championship

In 1935, Vivian Jenkins confirmed his ability to be in the right place at the right time. After a draw with England at Twickenham, the mercurial skills of Cliff Jones had inspired Wales's victory over winger Ken Fyfe's inexperienced Scottish team in Cardiff. 'It was the worst match I played for Wales and the best write-up I'd ever had,' says Jenkins, who should know, as he later became the rugby correspondent of the *Sunday Times*. 'I had "boobed," you see. When Scotland suddenly attacked, they passed the ball very quickly to the outside centre and Charles Dick cross-kicked back towards his forwards. Jock Beattie, a big Border man from Hawick, was probably the best all-round forward in Britain at that time. He got the ball – I was running back flat-out trying to get to him and he jinked inside me to set up a score.' But at the end of the game Jenkins had a chance to redeem himself for earlier aberrations, when he got the ball forty yards from Scotland's posts. 'I tried to go past Dick but I didn't have the speed. I turned inside and he grabbed me by the left ankle. In haste, I took a drop at goal with the ball falling down horizontal. It was a terrible kick, but when it got to the Scottish posts it leapt up suddenly and over it went – amazing really!'

Wales failed to win the championship, however, as they lost to Ireland in Belfast. The Irish lost their winger, Joe O'Connor, who had earlier scored tries in his team's defeat by England and victory over Scotland, with a broken collar-bone and, with no replacements allowed, their having to fight on with only fourteen men makes their achievement even more commendable. The match was the final appearance for Welsh scrum-half Wick Powell, who had developed a reputation for a long, if sometimes erratic, pass – an ability that, in a period when space on the field was becoming increasingly limited, had helped to give more time to his back line. Ireland took the championship, Scotland, despite a final-day win over England, the wooden spoon.

Ireland's six tries in 1935 and England's eight the year before had temporarily silenced any complaints about a lack of running rugby in the Five Nations. In 1936 all the chatter concerned the try-scoring of one man – Alexander Obolensky, a dashing Russian prince who was studying at Oxford University. In the January of 1936 'Obo', as he was affectionately known, graced Twickenham with two incredible scores on his England debut to give the English victory over the All Blacks for the first time. On the opposite side of the field, also making his debut that day, was Hal Sever. 'I always say that I was the other wing to Obolensky,' says the sprightly Sever, who retains a vivid memory of the game. 'He was a quiet, withdrawn, modest bloke – very pleasant.'

The second of Obolensky's tries has assumed the greater fame, but Sever wonders if the first try was not even better – 'he got the ball out on the wing, swerved around the full-back and scored. For the second one he was rather in the wilderness on the right-hand side. He could see the whole way was blocked, so he started running to the left and, quite frankly, I don't think he really knew where he was going. But he came round behind the scrum and sort of looped each of the opposition in turn – the stand-off, the first centre and the second centre. Then I thought he was going to pass the ball to me but, oh, no, he ran around my wing and the full-back as well to score.'

A star had been born and, after such success, it seemed there would be no stopping England winning the Triple Crown. But Wales had also beaten New Zealand and had other ideas. Having never played against Obolensky, their increasingly influential full-back, Vivian Jenkins, had done his homework on England's new hero. There was no television to watch a match on in those days, of course, so Jenkins paid a shilling and bought a ticket at the little news cinema at the bottom of the Strand. After he had sat through a lot of cartoons, on came a newsreel of England's game against New Zealand. 'Obolensky was fast, strong and went like the wind,' remembers Jenkins. It was the first try that really interested him, when the Russian prince rounded the New Zealand full-back, Gilbert. 'I saw that he beat him in a classical way, veering in and then taking him on the outside – but the news film finished, just like that, so I had to wait another hour watching all those damn cartoons to see it again. In fact, I spent four hours in that booth to work out exactly what to do if I was confronted by him in our first championship game in Swansea.'

Armed with what must have been the earliest-ever video analysis of a match, Jenkins shared what he had learnt with his colleagues. 'I said to Cliff Jones and Wilf Wooller, "If he comes up to me, I'll go for the outside break, but I'll have to go so fast that if he comes on the inside you'll have to get him." Sure enough, come match day he tried to beat me on the outside, and I remember thinking, "Keep going, don't stop for his inside fake," because if he did I knew Cliff and Wilf would be there. Just as I thought, he tried to emulate his first try against New Zealand, veered in and then went out again. I ran right into him and hit him up into the straw bales in front of the stand.' Jenkins ended up in the straw, but Obolensky had not scored.

In fact, neither side scored, a testament to their defences but also a great disappointment after what they had achieved against New Zealand. It was certainly a physical match, as Eddie Long, a wing forward from Swansea winning his first cap, let the England captain know at the very first scrum. 'As the ball came out on the England side,' Vivian Jenkins remembers, 'he hit Bernard Gadney with the biggest right hook you've ever seen, just to say, "Take that to start with!" Poor old Bernard was a gentleman and didn't expect this real clonker right on the chin. The look on his face when he was clouted for nothing was a picture! I don't know how old Eddie stayed on the field but he did and the Swansea crowd roared their approval. The players used to do this kind of thing without any malice at all – it was just part of it.'

For his part, Alex Obolensky found the supply to the wing cut as defences started to get on top again. He never scored another try for his country, failing to cross the line in his team's defeat by Ireland and victory over Scotland. That game signalled the end of a short but memorable England career, and tragically the flying wing from St Petersburg was to become the first international player to lose his life during World War II when he was killed in an RAF training accident. His memory lives on, though, in a restaurant at Twickenham named in his honour. His captain on the field of play, Bernard Gadney, fondly recalls the only Russian ever to play for England: 'I often think of Obo. He ran beautifully and could tackle so well. I don't think he would ever have pretended to be a Wilson Shaw or Eugene Davy – or the modern chaps, for that matter. But Alex did run in the true sense.'

Ireland had discovered another quality back, Larry McMahon, who scored a try in their win over a Scottish team previously defeated by the Welsh, and their travels led them to Wales looking for a first Triple Crown. The fans flocked to the Arms Park – the gates on Westgate Street had to be closed two hours before kick-off. The official attendance was 56,000, but many believe it was more like 70,000 people who crammed in that day. The referee himself, Cyril Gadney of England, brother of Bernard, was shut out of the ground. 'When he said, "But I'm the referee,"' recalls Vivian Jenkins, 'they replied, "We've had half a dozen of those already."' The fire brigade turned their hoses on fans who rushed the gates; some were hurt in the crush. Inside the ground the crowd came right up to the touch-lines. 'There was a hell of an excitement that day,' says Jenkins – 'they would have been up all night queuing to get in, with people singing chapel hymns to keep themselves warm. And for us, it was almost like going to church, not playing rugby.' The home side denied Ireland their Triple Crown, with a Jenkins penalty the only score of the game. It had been a season that had promised so much, but in the end only three tries and sixteen points won the title for Wales.

'I just hope that one side doesn't win by a drop-goal to a try,' commented Hal Sever's father prophetically in the car park at Twickenham before England's match against Wales at the start of the 1937 championship season. When Wales had a penalty inside their own 25-yard line Vivian Jenkins did not want to kick for touch, and his great pal, forward Arthur Rees, did not want to run the ball. They had been each other's best man, but on this occasion neither was prepared to say 'I do'! 'Vivian kicked the ball and it went to our forward Robin Prescott,' says Hal Sever, by now an integral part of the England side. 'It bounced off his right shoulder and I was standing beside him and caught it. The whole of the Welsh side was there and it was a question of – what do I do now? I was not an Obolensky who could run right across the field, so I just took the opportunity and dropped a goal. Nobody was more surprised than I was when it went over.' Worth four points, the kick outscored Wilf Wooller's three-point try to give England the win.

England, now led by full-back 'Tuppy' Owen-Smith, returned to Twickenham to play Ireland and Sever was again key to the victory. About ten minutes from time his team were losing 8–3 when centre Peter Cranmer kicked a penalty-goal to make it 8–6. Then from a scrum the ball was passed out to Sever, still 75 yards from the try-line. 'I ran up to half-way,' he remembers, 'and I managed to hand off the Irish full-back, George Malcolmson, and then Vesey Boyle, their left wing, came right across the field to tackle me and I cut inside him. The ground was slippy and he fell on his backside – that left me forty yards to go. Wing-forwards were fast approaching and I remember thinking, "I must keep away from the touch-line, because if they tackle me they may take me into the corner flag."' Tackle him they did, but Sever got the ball down, the touch-judge awarded the try, and England had won by nine points to eight. 'Nowadays, we would see replay after replay to check it was a good score,' says Sever, 'but unfortunately that try has never been pictured on screen – not even on the *Pathé Gazette*, because it was so late in the game they had all gone home to get the film out.'

The Scots, meanwhile, had already beaten Wales, on a day when the Edinburgh Wanderers club had supplied both captains – Idwal Rees and Scottish scrum-half Ross Logan – and then lost to Ireland. At Murrayfield, England's prolific Sever scored yet another try to seal the Triple Crown. 'I don't think we attached the same importance to winning the Triple Crown in those days as they do today,' reveals Sever. 'Every match was played as a match. Actually, the feeling was that we must win at Murrayfield because we had never won there before.' The score was 6–3 – so in three matches, England had scored only five points more than the opposition, and had won them all!

'Against the Welsh I finished the game with the ball in my hands, so naturally I kept it and took it home,' says Sever, undoubtedly England's star of the 1937 season. 'After the Irish win "Jenny" Greenwood, the President of the RFU, gave me one of the touch-flags – they were very nice things, a long bamboo cane and a silk flag with the English rose on one side and the opposition crest on the other.' That was two mementoes, and after the victory in Scotland he was keen to get another. His opportunity came at the after-match reception, when the piper who piped in the haggis got very drunk. Sever takes up the story: 'After the meal, Peter Cranmer got hold of his dirk and took that away, and I got his glengarry and wore it for the rest of the evening – I had a bit of an argy bargy with a Yorkshireman who wanted to get it off me but he didn't.' Sever went to bed absolutely thrilled that he had his three souvenirs. 'Anyway, at eight o'clock the following morning Doug Prentice, the English selector, rang round and said the piper had returned back to barracks less a few of his regalia, and did anybody know anything about it? So we all had to return our prizes and I never did get my memento of the Scottish game.'

Certainly one of the most surprising aspects of Sever's remarkable year is that he was never once asked a question by the media. The Welsh team, beaten in all three matches just a year after they had won the title, were also mercifully free from interrogation. The post-match inquisition was for a later date, with newspaper reports in the inter-war years concentrating on factual detail, not quotes or opinion. Newsprint was supplemented by the radio coverage being pioneered by former Harlequins captain H.B.T. Wakelam. The first live commentary on a championship match had been in 1927 when England played Wales, and by the 1930s radio had become an established way of following the game. It was, however, a style of broadcasting that would be unrecognizable today – first the commentator would call out the number of a square on a grid printed in the *Radio Times* to help identify the location of the play: then he would describe the action. Television coverage began at the end of the 1938 season with the England-Scotland encounter. At this time, a young Scot was discovering a love for the game, and he would go on to play a major role in bringing the championship to the attention of the millions who have watched as the Five Nations and television have developed hand-in-hand. Bill McLaren's own burgeoning rugby career was cut short by illness but, having now covered it for fifty years, he has become synonymous with the tournament.

As if aware of their increasing audience, the players provided tries in abundance during 1938. Wales scored two in their victory over the English, with forward Walter Vickery making his first appearance for the Welsh even though his father had been capped by England. In the next game against Scotland another member of the Welsh pack, Harry Rees, was involved in the critical moment which led to a Scottish victory. A matter of seconds from time a penalty was given against Wales. 'I awarded the penalty,' the referee, Cyril Gadney, is quoted as saying, 'because the Welshman lettered J (Harry Rees) was lying on the ball in a scrummage. It was a horrible thing to have to do at that time of the game. To me, it was almost as bad as taking a man's life.' In fact Rees was dazed and unable to move, and also smothering another concussed player, his team-mate and scrum-half, Haydn Tanner. Later his fellow players confirmed that Rees was muttering about aeroplanes! The forward W.H. Crawford kicked the penalty, and the Scots won by eight points to six.

The next two matches of the championship saw it raining tries: seven for England in their win over Ireland, who responded with four of their own. The Irish scored four more against Scotland, but again ended on the losing side. They lost their third match to Wales in a game which signalled the retirement through injury of Cliff Jones at the young age of 24, and also of Claude Davey in the centre, whose power tackling had complemented Jones's artistry. Most impressive that season, though, were Scotland – their captain, Wilson Shaw, was in majestic form at fly-half and, importantly, he had found attacking allies in centres Charles Dick and Duncan Macrae, to form a midfield trio that fitted together perfectly. Could they supply another win against the English for a Triple Crown at Twickenham?

In 1938 the amateur ethos was still being upheld to absurd extremes, as Duncan Macrae recalls. The day before the game, Charles Dick had arrived at the team hotel from Guy's Hospital where he was a doctor to ask where they were training, and be told that they were not allowed to go out for a run – the Scottish authorities considered such practice professionalism. 'What?' he replied. 'I've been in hospital all week – I've got to go out.' So Macrae and Dick went off in the doctor's car to his ground at Guy's and spent an hour and half training there – 'and that was it,' says Macrae: 'the rest of the team didn't do anything. Looking back on it now, it was an appalling state of affairs.'

On his arrival at Twickenham Macrae was uplifted by what he saw. 'I've never forgotten how good the ground looked that day. The grass had been cut and it was just like Wimbledon tennis courts – a beautiful sight on a sunny afternoon, everything was perfect. It was a fantastic match, back and fro, the lead was changing hands. England's full-back, G.W. Parker, started kicking goals and we simply could not get the ball in the scrum. But somehow we still managed to score five tries.' England's Hal Sever, playing in his last championship game, remembers one of those scores as particularly crucial. 'Two years previously against Ireland I'd scored a try by picking up the ball from the forwards and going bang through the middle of the pack. Exactly the same situation arose in the Scottish match and I went through seventy-five per cent of their pack. I got near enough to the line but I couldn't put it down. If we'd scored then, we would have been well in front with the conversion to come. About three minutes later, we had a scrum around their twenty-five, it came out on their side and Wilson Shaw ran the whole length of the field to score. He was quite a small fellow and I can still see his legs going all the way up the field. Suddenly the game had turned around.'

The purring display of Shaw was the main reason for Scotland's win. He scored another try and had a hand in at least one more. 'Wilson was made for our running game,' says Duncan Macrae. 'He didn't kick, he hadn't learnt to – "To hell, boys, let's have a go," was his attitude, wherever you were.' On the day Macrae and Dick had also put the previous day's hastily-arranged training session to good use. 'At Guy's, Charles and I had raced each other and he was always two yards ahead of me,' explains Macrae. Finding an open field in front of him with the full-back coming up, he says, 'I thought, "Well, come on, Charles, you're faster than I am – it's your try.'"

The Scottish strategy had worked: forward Laurie Duff's pack had withstood the pressure from an English eight under the guidance of their much respected hooker and new captain, Bert Toft, and their backs had run England off their feet. Scotland had gone to their second Triple Crown of the decade – not that this gave the players instant recognition. In the Twickenham tea-room after the match, the story goes, an exhausted Wilson Shaw turned to the elderly man next to him and remarked, 'Pretty hard going out there today.' 'Yes,' agreed his neighbour. 'You must be glad you weren't playing.'

Scotland's famous midfield never played together in the championship again. They had been a lucky talisman for the side, and perhaps their break-up was one reason why in 1939 the Scots followed their 1938 Triple Crown with three defeats and the wooden spoon. England beat Wales in their first match but then lost to Ireland. Led by scrum-half George Morgan, the Irish followed their Twickenham win with victory over Scotland in Dublin and Wales again stood in the way of a first Triple Crown. But in Belfast Welsh fly-half Willie Davies dropped a goal – the last in the championship to merit four points – and scored a try, and Wales had thwarted Irish Triple Crown hopes.

The total of ten tries in 1939 was a record low for the championship, but the settling of the dispute between the French Federation and the home unions was paving the way for the return of those entertainers-by-instinct, France. But then World War II brought the championship to an abrupt halt. For the young centre from Instonians, Harry McKibbin, who had been kicking the goals for Ireland during that 1939 season, rugby had always managed to overcome the territorial difficulties that so affected his country's politics: 'I remember playing in the centre with Desmond Torrens – he was some sort of second cousin of mine and from the south, but there was never any difficulty. There has always been a great unity in Irish rugby, and the atmosphere was every bit as good in Belfast as it was in Dublin. As a schoolboy, I used to travel down on the train to Dublin to watch matches, and there was quite a number of people who regularly travelled the other way for games in the north.' Now he was left to rue the intervention of a war caused by issues of boundaries and borders. 'I joined up right away – that was the end of my rugby. It ended so many careers, a calamity in that sense, but I suppose one of those things.' Between 1940 and 1946 there would be no more championship games.

PART TWO

1947–1969

After World War II, Celtic rugby was on a high. In 1948 Ireland at last won their first Grand Slam, in a season cherished to this day as the finest in Irish rugby history. They followed this triumph with the Triple Crown a year later. Wales too tasted success, winning the Grand Slam in 1950 and again in 1952. Unlike Ireland, however, they were able to maintain their run of form through the 1950s; though Welsh fortunes began to decline as the decade closed, the second half of the 1960s saw Wales come back strongly and, by establishing a national coaching structure, an innovation in the Five Nations, sow the seeds of even greater success.

Meanwhile, France had re-joined the Five Nations, and were a different proposition, winning their first championship title outright in 1959. Their backs had always had the capacity to thrill, but now the forwards had started to combine discipline with new techniques, proving themselves to be comfortable with the ball in hand. Where they had previously been the followers, now they were the leaders. It all culminated in a first Grand Slam in 1968. France were now at the heart of the championship and, although some suspicions remained over French claims to be amateur, their team had earned the right to be respected.

England's only Grand Slam of this period came in 1957 after their Triple Crown success three years earlier. In following years their battle with the French for European supremacy was hindered by an alarming turnover of players at the whims of the selectors – a trend which became a hallmark of English rugby. For Scotland it was a period with almost no tangible reward, apart from a share of the title in 1964. At the start of the 1950s they lost fifteen consecutive championship matches.

The laws of the game were continuing to evolve. From 1949, the value of the drop-goal was reduced from four points to three, but the temptation to kick for touch in broken play remained strong. After a Scotland-Wales game in 1963 that contained more than a hundred line-outs, it became obvious the laws would have to be changed. It was not until the end of the 1960s, however, that the legislators accepted the 'Australian dispensation' – the concept that a player could only kick directly into touch from behind his own 25-yard line, a variation tried in the southern hemisphere as early as the 1920s. Other moves to open up the game included the 1958 instruction that it was no longer necessary to play the ball with the foot after a tackle had been made and, in 1964, the establishment of the ten-metre gap between the line-out and the backs. With scrummaging and line-out skills improving all the time, the conditions for a more expansive style of rugby were slowly being created.

1947–1952

1947 – England and Wales share championship
1948 – Ireland's GRAND SLAM
1949 – Ireland's Triple Crown and championship
1950 – Wales's GRAND SLAM
1951 – Ireland's championship
1952 – Wales's GRAND SLAM

The war had not meant the end of all rugby, and in between serving their countries many found some time to play their favourite game. Bleddyn Williams, a fine tactician and a talented runner, and one of the great Welsh backs of the post-war era, managed to participate in some revolutionary wartime matches which saw players from union and league unite as one to play union internationals – Wales raising a very good side that played mostly for charity. In 1947 Williams made his championship debut, for Wales against England at the Arms Park, at fly-half, though he had played at centre in the services and for his club, Cardiff. 'It was a strong Cardiff that was the basis for the Welsh team,' says Williams, who ran out with several club colleagues, including two other debutants, Billy Cleaver and

Jack Matthews, and also Haydn Tanner, whose career had spanned the war. 'He was one of the great scrum-halves of all time,' continues Williams – 'you could compare him with Gareth Edwards. It was reassuring to have him alongside me, but it didn't do us any good that day, mind, because we lost. Unfortunately, I pulled a hamstring in the first ten minutes – then, you just stayed on the field and became one of the numbers, but it didn't help my career as a fly-half! Nim Hall dropped a crucial goal for England. There wasn't much in it but we were at a disadvantage, mainly because of myself.'

Bleddyn Williams' fortunes changed when he returned to the centre and scored a try in Wales's highest total in Scotland since 1911. As in that year, so in 1947 the Scots lost all four matches. Meanwhile, France had started well, beating the Scots and then Ireland. Next it was Wales, and Williams' expectations of a tough match, having played for the Services team in 1945 against most of the French side, including the two giant second-row forwards Alban Moga and Robert Soro, were confirmed on the day. Wales won by a penalty-goal to nil: 'It was a hell of a hard game.'

The match is remembered most, however, for events off the field. Welsh forward George Parsons had arrived at Newport station and was ready to get on the train when he was sent for by the Secretary of the Welsh Rugby Union. On the strength of entirely hearsay allegations that he had been in discussions with a rugby league scout, Parsons was told he was not wanted, sent home and banned from playing rugby union. 'It really was a diabolical situation,' says Bleddyn Williams. 'The result was that we went to Paris with only fifteen players as there was only one reserve in those days – but there were 22 committee men! It was farcical, especially as the two codes had played alongside each other in the war. Let's be fair about it, we could all have been professional because we were all approached by rugby league scouts, but you didn't take too much notice of it. But there was some vindictive guy in the police force who might have split on George, and in order to play again he had to turn professional.'

Like many of the Welsh team at the time Parsons, a glassworker from Newport, was a working man. The players had a variety of backgrounds: 'Prop Cliff Davies was a miner and Haydn Tanner was a chemist, it was a fair old mixture,' says Williams. 'But above all, it was the working-class game, with the miners, the dockers and the steelworkers in the crowd, and this is where we would draw our strength from.' It was a very different social structure in English rugby, as Coventry prop Harry Walker, who also made his debut that season, testifies. 'I reckon I was the only working bloke in the blooming team!' says Walker, then a machine tool fitter. In England football was firmly established as the people's game and, in the north, rugby league had built a strong power base. 'It never bothered me at all, mind, and I never felt uncomfortable. As far as I was concerned, I looked at the people as they played on the park – and off the park there was no difference either.'

After his team's opening victory over Wales, Walker's task was to shore up the England scrum in Ireland, but his job was not made any easier by the selectors. As one of the few players from the north in the England team, Walker was travelling home from Wales in the train on his own. Some time into the journey the northern selectors and the Secretary of the RFU invited him into their carriage to tell him they had picked the team for the Irish match. 'Bugger me, the committee made two changes – I couldn't believe it! I said, "You can't do that – we bloody well won down in Wales, it's colossal." The Chairman, Bob Oakes, said, "What are you worried about? You're still in." I said I wanted to win the next one.'

The selection policy depressed Walker and his team-mates. 'The general talk amongst the players was, "If we have changes when we win, God help us if we ever lose!"' Ireland's stunning win over the English was a record: 22 points to nil, including five tries, two each for the wingers, Bertie O'Hanlon and Barney Mullan. 'It was a terrible day, very cold,' says Walker, 'but the attitude of the players wasn't conducive for a win. It felt bloody awful as we walked off the field. After the match I was changing right at the top of the long narrow dressing-room, and all the selectors came in at the bottom door and walked past everybody to where I was. They sat round me and asked what had gone on? I remember saying, "I told you what would happen." I wouldn't say we would have won, but I'm confident that if we had left the team as it was, no way would we have lost by that score.' The England administration was developing a habit of chopping and changing: it would be a constant problem for their teams over the coming years.

Austerity had not ended with the war. 'Clothes were on coupons,' Harry Walker explains, 'and at the end of that first season they wrote to players that we could either have a cap or a blazer badge, but if you wanted both you had to pay for one or the other. We weren't allowed to have taxis on expenses, and if you wanted a real egg and not powdered egg at the hotel you had to bring it yourself.' There were some compensations of playing championship rugby, however.

'At the Dublin dinner I didn't make the main course because I never got past the fish stage,' says Walker. 'Salmon was rare and I'd never tasted it before – that was enough for me, I just kept asking for it.'

For England's final two matches at home the icy winter took a firm grip. Never mind playing – it was enough of a problem getting to the games, especially for a young England back-row forward, Micky Steele-Bodger, then a student at Edinburgh University, when he was selected for the match against Scotland in London. 'I left Edinburgh at ten o'clock on the Thursday night, came down on the West Coast route and got into London at four o'clock on Saturday morning. The train was crowded, there were no sleeping carriages, and we had to dig ourselves out three times with shovels. All I had with me was a tin of Ovaltine tablets and an orange. When we got to Carlisle I sent a telegram to say I was on my way, and when I arrived at the team hotel I told my room-mate to wake me before the bus left. But he didn't. I took a taxi out to where the team used to have lunch and they weren't there, so I went on to Twickenham, put on my jersey and sat in the dressing-room waiting for them to arrive. I was slightly hungry, but as I'd gone through all that wretched business I thought that there was not much point coming if I didn't play. In my absence, Vic Roberts had been told he was to have my place – there was a bit of an altercation but I played. It was a funny game: three or four people went down with cramp from the cold – but it was quite comical. I remember one player was up-ended by an ambulance man, only for all his keys and money to fall out of his shorts' pockets onto the pitch!'

The match belonged to England, whose new captain, Waterloo centre Jack Heaton, first capped in 1935, converted all four tries in his team's big win. One of them was scored by his cousin and club colleague, winger Dicky Guest, who like Heaton had played for England before the war. The English also won against France in their final match of the season at the end of April after the weather had improved. Vic Roberts, the man denied his first appearance by Micky Steele-Bodger's dash from Edinburgh, finally got his cap and scored a try. With three victories each, England and Wales shared the first post-war championship but another team, Ireland, who after their famous defeat of England had lost to Wales, were soon to have their long-awaited day in the limelight.

'The state of English and Welsh rugby is sometimes serious but never hopeless,' the great Irish centre, Noel Henderson, once said; 'the state of Irish rugby is usually hopeless but never serious.'

Henderson would join a winning team on his debut in 1949, because in 1948 Ireland were far from hopeless – they were seriously good. It was Henderson's brother-in-law, Irish fly-half Jack Kyle, who of all the immediate post-war players made the greatest impact on the Five Nations. Here was a rugby genius, the like of which the championship had never seen before. He could box a team into the corner with his clever kicking and fearless cover tackling but, above all, if the defenders were not watching him for every second, he would come alive and dance his way to the line. Ireland's first Grand Slam season began in France, Kyle recalls. 'It kicked off in Paris on New Year's Day, not giving us any chance to celebrate New Year's Eve. But there was hardly such a thing as training in those days – I trotted out the afternoon before the match, checked my signals were OK with the scrum-half, and that was about it.' Ireland won with three tries, one to new cap and flanker Jim McCarthy, whose first experience of the French left him with lasting respect for them: 'France have been a force ever since. After the war they were a big team, but also had wonderful backs like winger Michel Pomathios. We were starting to realise that we must be a pretty good side to have beaten them.'

In their first match of the season, England and Wales shared the honours at Twickenham. The Welsh winger Ken Jones scored a try, followed by another in Wales's win over a Scotland side who had inflicted a second defeat of the season on France. Later that year, Jones would run for Great Britain in the London Games – Bleddyn Williams remembers an Olympic sprinter who was also a first-class rugby player, 'and he hadn't seen much of rugby during the war because he was based with the RAF out in India!'

For Ireland it was next stop Twickenham, where Des O'Brien, then of London Irish, was pleasantly surprised to gain his first cap at the age of 28, and ended up leading the pack. 'It was a very fast back-row,' he recalls; 'Jim McCarthy was exceptionally fit and trained every day of the year, and Bill McKay was a 400-yards champion. I played squash to international standard, and as a brewer in London I never used the lift – I was up and down seven storeys all day.' The game did not begin as he had imagined. 'We were pinned on our line for the first ten minutes and I couldn't even hear myself speak – it was like playing at the bottom of a well. At Twickenham, the noise came right down on top of you, it was a complete panic as far as I was concerned. Then we put a tight squeeze on a scrum – that wonderful move that we used to do as the whole pack swung round taking the ball up field – we got it up to the half-way line and things settled down.' After an early English score Ireland assumed control and scored three tries, from McKay, centre Dennis McKee and Jack Kyle. But Kyle had a heart-stopping moment as the end drew near. 'Thinking that we were running rampant, from the touch-line I ran across the field and threw a pass which was intercepted by Dicky Guest, who put it underneath our posts!' The kick was converted, leaving Ireland leading only by eleven points to ten. 'I've been glad to hear some final whistles in my day,' reflects Kyle, 'but I think that was the one.'

Kyle also scored in the win over Scotland, and now a win against Wales would secure Ireland their first Grand Slam. The Welsh had lost to France at home for the first time, conceding three tries, but they had always stopped the Irish from taking the top prize – could they do it again? 'I was even more nervous when I saw the Welsh team,' says Des O'Brien, 'because they seemed to be men and we seemed to be boys. In the first half, Barney Mullan got a tremendous try which he was never quite given credit for – he was on the 25, about a yard in from touch, and he went through three tacklers.' But at half-time the Irish did not feel they were doing well. They changed their line-out positions to prevent Wales's Rees Stephens dominating, and after the break started getting good line-out ball. Captain and hooker Karl Mullen's tight tactics of using the touch-line and the pack proved crucial in the critical score, when Haydn Tanner threw out a slightly slow pass. 'We hacked it down all the way to the line,' recalls Des O'Brien. 'It was Jimmy Nelson, myself and J.C. Daly. One forgets what an important part foot-control played in our type of rugby – we practised dribbling for hours on end to put it to good use at times like this. I tapped it over the line and Daly came under my elbow to beat three Welshmen. When he was running back he said to me, "Jesus, if Wales don't score again, I'll be canonised!"

When the final whistle went prop-forward Daly's shirt was ripped from his back and the stockings were pulled from his aching feet. 'He was an immensely strong character, and a great stimulation to the rest of us,' says O'Brien. 'He spent most of the war carrying a wireless operator's pack on his back right through North Africa, so he could hold the scrum, and as soon as the ball had gone he would be across the field almost as quick as the back row. At the end, there were incredible scenes. We didn't get off the field for about twenty minutes as we were all on the crowd's shoulders. I remember kissing Jimmy Nelson in the excitement – and looking at Jimmy ever after, I wonder how the hell I did!'

Daly, who had played his last game for Ireland before going to rugby league, was the hero of the hour, but captain Mullen also deserved the plaudits. 'He was a thoughtful guy who would never say much apart from, "Just play your own game," says Jack Kyle. 'I was a great believer in having a game plan and keeping it simple,' agrees Mullen modestly. 'I also preached the need to understand exactly what the gain line was, and funnily that hasn't changed much in the game today. I can recall my exact words before we went out onto the pitch: "We are good enough to win if every man does his best." And we were good enough to win. But I don't think we realised what we had done for our little nation, it was such a gigantic thing to do. We don't often get vintage sides in Ireland but then it was a good mixture – a front row and forwards to win us more possession than any of the other teams, we had a lot of pace, and we also had a match winner in Jack Kyle. He was just outstanding and without him we wouldn't have succeeded.' Mullen also emphasises the friendships that grew among the team during the year, recalling some wonderful parties at Jack Kyle's house. 'But in those days very few of us took drinks,' he adds – 'I think there were twelve teetotallers in the team.'

It seemed as if the whole of Ireland, though, woke up with a hangover the morning after that day before – but little did they know that it would be the only Irish Grand Slam ever in the Five Nations. 'The Irish are terrific sports followers for a small country,' says Jim McCarthy: 'the Gaelic football and hurling crowds are also the rugby and soccer supporters – everyone goes to everything – and if Ireland are doing well they will follow you anywhere, whatever the sport. They are passionate and demonstrative without taking it too seriously. The great thing about them is that when you're beaten, you're beaten, and that's it.' The 1948 side will always be known as a team of winners.

As Ireland celebrated, it was just a question of who would take the wooden spoon. After losing to Scotland and then to France by fifteen points to nil, England earned that dubious honour. Having moved from his normal role of flanker to cover at scrum-half for nearly the whole game against the Scots, in Paris Micky Steele-Bodger wondered if he had broken his wrist after colliding with the French full-back, André Alvarez. His subsequent adventure could only have happened during the amateur era. 'There was a huge queue at the only hospital that was open as it was Easter, but the liaison officer pulled a few strings and immediately took me to the radiologist. There we opened some champagne and, although the x-ray showed no break, three weeks later I found out it was broken after all. The champagne,' concludes Steele-Bodger, 'must have deadened the pain!' Steele-Bodger went on to become a selector, then President of the RFU, Chairman of the International Board and President of the Barbarians, but his most enduring contribution to the sport is the side that takes his name to play an annual fixture against Cambridge University. In his playing days, he says the committee men had many uses – not least on the practice pitch. 'The selectors would take their jackets off and shove against you in the pack. It was much more casual then – quite often people were smoking until the last minute before they went on the field.'

In France, Five Nations rugby was coming of age. Led by number eight Guy Basquet, alongside Jean Matheu and Jean Prat in the back row, the French had greatness in their ranks. In their first game in 1949 they met a Scotland team captained by another forward, Doug Keller, who had played for Australia against the Scots a season earlier. (More ammunition to fire at those who say it is only a modern trend to use so-called foreign players!) France lost that match but Prat in particular was emerging as a star, and in Dublin his four successful kicks at goal sent the Grand Slam holders crashing to defeat. 'He was as a good a back-row player as I came up against,' says opponent Des O'Brien – 'he was as much a back as a forward.' Although the French went on to lose narrowly at Twickenham they beat Wales in their final game: their results in the first three years of the post-war championship were proving France to be a real force.

Though Wales, including the experienced hooker 'Bunner' Travers, who had last played in the championship in 1939, beat England, Ireland were the Celtic nation of the moment and, after losing to Scotland, the Welsh were once more reduced to trying to prevent an Irish Triple Crown and championship title. Jim McCarthy followed up his two tries against the Scots with another in his team's defeat of Wales, and Ireland were partying again. 'I had my shirt ripped off, a year after Daly,' says McCarthy. 'We really couldn't imagine being beaten. We expected to win but not in a cocky way. All great sides have this, and it gives them real confidence. It was a great way to live, even though it was only for a short period.'

England's five-try demolition of Scotland in 1949 had hinted they might be ready to take over from Ireland, but a year later they struggled to find the right form and lost three matches – the only English win, ironically, was over Ireland, their first since the war. For Wales it was a different story. Nearly 76,000 gathered at Twickenham to see the Welsh in their opening game in 1950, and playing for the first time was an eighteen-year-old navy stores assistant, Benjamin Lewis Jones. Lewis Jones had been to Gowerton Grammar, the same school as the greats Haydn Tanner and Willie Davies, and he looked every inch a new legend in the making. 'Those fellows were like gods at school,' he says, 'and I remember the one incident that inspired people to say things like that about me. Full-backs usually caught the ball and belted it into touch, but when I caught the ball that day, I ran. Because of my tender age, I was precocious and I didn't have a care in the world – but I think I was sensible enough to know that if I started running, I had the option of kicking into touch at any time. The whole England side opened up for me, leaving these big gaps, and I went straight through, got to the 25 and thought, "Christ, what do I do next?" Fortunately, there was Cliff Davies, lovely man, big front-row forward with a wide neck that went right down into his shoulders as if there was no join. He just got the ball and went straight over.' Wales left Twickenham with victory and the new boy Lewis Jones a hero.

Another talented Welsh back in the spring of his international career, Malcolm Thomas, scored a try along with Ken Jones in the win over Scotland, and both men crossed the line again in their team's Triple Crown victory over Ireland. Lewis Jones had been moved to the centre and stayed there for the win over France, which sealed a second Grand Slam. It was their first for 39 years – Welsh rugby was back. For scrum-half Rex Willis, his debut year in the Welsh jersey was a remarkable one, leading on from the Grand Slam to finish with a British Lions tour. 'From Cardiff to Wales, the Barbarians and then the Lions,' he remembers: 'what a journey!'

France had never recovered from an opening-day defeat by Scotland. In between, however, was a win over England and draw at home against Ireland – perhaps especially creditable because, as Des O'Brien explains, the Irish had inadvertently employed a secret weapon. 'For some reason we were delayed in the tunnel, the French team behind us, while referee Tom Pearce checked the flags. We started to sing our only song: "The cow kicked Nellie in the belly in the barn but the kick didn't do our Nellie any harm" – we repeated this about six times. That night at the dinner Jean Prat said, "You know, we were quite scared before we went onto the field – your Irish folk songs really put the fright into us!"' Ireland's best performance that year was a 21-point thrashing of Scotland, but the season really belonged to Wales.

However, the French were now fully equipped to challenge for more than just the odd win and they started the 1951 season with an eventful game at home to Scotland. A great forward in the making, Lucien Miâs, made his debut that day, as did Scottish hooker Norman Mair, who went on to become his country's leading rugby writer. First Scotland kicked a penalty which the whole team thought had gone over – only to discover back on the half-way line that it had not been given. Then France missed a conversion which many people, including the official in charge of the scoreboard, thought was over! 'Someone was sent round to change it,' remembers Norman Mair, 'but either they didn't want to or they couldn't get through the crowd.' France were actually behind, therefore, while most of the crowd thought they were ahead. Reports later said the marker had locked the scoreboard door and could not hear the shouts! Eventually Jean Prat kicked a goal and France won by fourteen points to twelve – 'but if he hadn't scored,' says Mair, 'anything might have happened. As it was, several French newspapers still gave the score incorrectly.'

There were more surprises to come. Wales, who had beaten England with ease, went to Murrayfield as the hottest of favourites. 'They had eleven of the 1950 British Lions in their side; we had one, number-eight Peter Kininmonth,' explains Mair. The anticipation was such that the gates were torn down and some of the crowd ended up sitting on the grass. The estimated attendance of 80,000 – no-one succeeded in getting an official figure – was the biggest yet at a British international. Scotland took the lead with a penalty-goal from young full-back Ian Thomson, making his debut at the last minute for Tommy Gray, and in the second-half Peter Kininmonth dropped a magnificent goal from outside the 25 towards the touch-line. Tries came from new winger Bob Gordon, who crossed the line twice, and prop J.C. Dawson. Norman Mair picks out in Scotland's committed effort back-row forward Douglas Elliot – 'a big Border farmer, a raw-boned chap, who got in amongst their backs and was very much a big occasion player: he was the outstanding post-war Scot.' Scotland won by nineteen points to nil – arguably the biggest upset in the history of the championship. 'Theoretically, we should have beaten Scotland by forty-odd points,' says Benjamin Lewis Jones. 'It just goes to show that theory is nothing.'

After their stunning victory Scotland went on to lose seventeen consecutive internationals, and would have to wait until 1955 for their next win. But Norman Mair feels it could easily have been different. 'We scored 39 points to 25 conceded over the 1951 season, were never down on tries to anyone, and our try score over the four matches was seven scored to four against. England in 1991 scored five tries to four and won the Grand Slam! If the selectors had stayed with that young Scottish side – who knows? When changes were made and Scotland got belted by South Africa at the end of that year, it had the effect of an air-crash on Scottish rugby. The following year they capped 32 players, which was just ridiculous.'

In comparison, France were developing a winning habit and recorded their first-ever victory at Twickenham. Wales and Scotland were also beaten as France won three championship matches – something else they had never done before. Ireland, whose one-point victory denied the French a Grand Slam, followed this with close shaves against England and Scotland, but went to Wales unbeaten and looking for their second Grand Slam in four years.

Trying to counter this was a slip of a lad by the name of Cliff Morgan. Like Jack Kyle, Morgan was to make a huge impression on the championship. Some years later he had an equally significant influence on British broadcasting, becoming Head of Outside Broadcasts at the BBC and, behind the microphone, providing one of the most famous pieces of rugby commentary on the classic Barbarians game of 1973 against the All Blacks. Morgan will never forget the reaction to the news of his selection for his first international. 'They announced the Welsh team on the wireless and my mother was scrubbing the floor underneath the wash basin. She heard my name, jumped up with excitement and knocked herself out, and was lying on the floor when my father came in! And that night when I got home from Cardiff, there was bunting across the streets – it was like Coronation Day! – and there were dozens of people at the bus stop waiting for my bus. They were all there to say, "Wish you well."'

The actual confirmation of Morgan's selection came by 'invitation' the next day, in a manner which reflected the formalities of the period: he was politely asked whether he could let the Union know by return of post if he was able to attend. Morgan also received a telegram from his club colleague, Des O'Brien, who would line up against him for Ireland. It read, 'Congratulations, Cliff bach, I hope your life is insured!' Indeed, the stature of Wales's new stand-off was the subject of great debate, a point brought home to the man himself when he made his way to the ground on match day. 'I was standing on the bus and there were two blokes arguing, one saying, "He's only a tot, he's a shrimp – he's only about ten stone when he's soaking wet." The other said, "I don't know, I've known him for years and I reckon he's about eleven and a half stone." Then one turned to me and said, "What do you think he is?" I replied, "About twelve stone four or five." The man turned to his pal and said, "The trouble with these people who know bugger-all is that they always argue!"'

In the game, Ireland were hit by an early strike from an unlikely source – the Newport lock, Ben Edwards, who was playing his first game for Wales and landed a 45-yard penalty-goal. Ireland responded with a Jack Kyle try, a typically meandering run virtually under the posts, but the Irish were without a recognised kicker as full-back George Norton had damaged his shoulder in the previous game. The conversion was missed, one of many opportunities at goal which got away that afternoon to cost them dear. Kyle's try-saving tackle on Ken Jones at least gave the Irish a draw and the championship title, but the Grand Slam had gone. 'That match was a terrible disappointment,' says Jim McCarthy, who feels the result marked the end of a golden period – 'and this is not the memory playing tricks. We murdered Wales that day. Afterwards the team started fading. Bill McKay qualified as a doctor and went off to New Zealand, and one or two other guys got injured.'

For Wales, though, there were signs that the 1951 season had been just a temporary aberration, and with Cliff Morgan orchestrating affairs at fly-half success would return. Morgan himself was still getting used to the regimented world of international rugby. 'After my first game, we queued up for our expenses. Sitting at the top of the stairs at a card table was the Secretary of the Union, Eric Evans, who looked up at me and said, "Name?" I'd just played for Wales and I thought, he doesn't know our names! I replied, "Morgan, sir." Then he said, "Expenses?" and I said, "Two returns from Trebanog, five shillings." And he looked down at this black exercise book, flicked through the pages as if he was reading a bad novel, then slammed it shut and said to me, "You liar and cheat – it's 2s 4d return from Trebanog to Cardiff. That's 4s 8d, not five shillings!" The interesting thing for me was that I was telling my mother and father when I got home at midnight, and my father said, "What a stupid thing for him to do!" But my mother said, "Ah, but Mr Evans was right, wasn't he?"'

At the start of the 1952 season, the Welsh beat England at Twickenham. Once again many were locked out, and neighbours to the ground lucky enough to have television invited the disappointed supporters inside to watch. They saw the English backs, Albert Agar and Ted Woodward, score while Lewis Jones hobbled around the pitch with a pulled thigh muscle, still bravely making the extra man in one of Ken Jones's two tries as Wales came back for a famous 8–6 win. England, now captained by fly-half Nim Hall, and with J.M.K. Kendall-Carpenter in the pack, were emerging from a four-year slump and won their next three games, but it was Wales who were setting the pace and a victory over Scotland sent them to Dublin for the Triple Crown. Ireland had won against France and Scotland but this time their conductor, Jack Kyle, who had called the tune at the Arms Park in 1951, found himself on the receiving end. Cliff Morgan was showing how much he had learnt in a year. 'Cardiff was our first meeting and I saw greatness in Cliff at a very early age,' says Kyle. 'A year on, he made that wonderful try at Lansdowne Road when he cut inside me, ran from the half-way line and gave it to Ken Jones, who scored underneath our posts.' The Welsh forwards had killed the Irish passion with flanker Clem Thomas, in later years a much-loved and respected rugby journalist, scoring and also sending over Rees Stephens. Lock Roy John and the front-row of W.O. 'Billy' Williams, Dai Davies and Don Hayward were big men with big hearts.

Number-eight John Gwilliam's team went home to Swansea to meet France without the injured Cliff Morgan. His replacement, Alun Thomas, a versatile player, dropped a goal, but it was Lewis Jones's two penalty-goals which sealed the win to give Wales their second Grand Slam in three years. This turned out to be his last appearance for Wales, as later that year the man who had played just nine championship matches and won eight of them, including two Grand Slams, signed to play rugby league for Leeds. "I had a job driving lorries down at Carmarthen Bay power station,' says Lewis Jones. 'When the offer came, financially I thought, great – and that was it. I never regretted it and had a great time. People ask whether I'd like to be playing today and, yes, I'd probably be a millionaire and not broke,' he laughs, 'but the memories of the 1950s are fantastic and I wouldn't swap them for the world.'

1953–1958

1953 – England's championship
1954 – England's Triple Crown; England, France and
Wales share championship
1955 – France and Wales share championship
1956 – Wales's championship
1957 – England's GRAND SLAM
1958 – England's championship

At the start of the 1953 season, it was Rex Willis's turn to be injured. Willis and Cliff Morgan had established a great understanding at half-back, so the selectors decided that Morgan should not be left on his own for the game against England. In came the Newport pair of Roy Burnett and Billy Williams. Talented though they were, Wales lost, and the two never played for their country again. Willis and Morgan were re-united for the victory over Scotland, but the unfortunate Willis hurt his shoulder, and Morgan was forced to play his partner's role behind the scrum, one that he respected. 'He was my great protector,' says Morgan – 'my scrum-half and my better half, I called him. He was a most unlikely-looking rugby player – his hair was longish, he drove a fast car, his father was a very wealthy man – but he had shoulders which were so broad, he took all the bumps in the world and gave me the ball only when I could do something with it.' Willis missed the rest of the season but Wales went on to beat Ireland and France, making the defeat by the English all the more infuriating.

England had followed their opening win with a draw in Ireland and approached the match against France at Twickenham with confidence, as after beating Scotland the French had lost to the Irish. Making his debut for England that day was the sturdy Yorkshireman, Northampton centre Jeff Butterfield. Having pulled a hamstring in a club match against Waterloo two Saturdays earlier, his international season was also threatened by injury – but he was offered an unusual cure. 'We had a magician of a masseur,' Butterfield explains, 'and he said, "Right, there are three things you've got to do over the next fortnight and ultimately you will play for England." Firstly, as I'd torn the hamstring badly, I was not to run or take any exercise but, secondly, I should cycle to see him for physiotherapy every day after work. But number three was to get my landlady to buy a bottle of sherry and ask one of the farmers with whom I played to bring me some fresh eggs. Every morning I had to take two raw eggs with sherry. "Bloody hell, it isn't worth it!" I said. But he told me, "You do that and you'll be on the pitch." So every morning, having learnt how to take them – they were mixed up and gulped – I did it religiously. And when it came to match day my lunch, two hours before the game, was two raw eggs in sherry.'

The concoction certainly had the desired effect. 'Early on, Maurice Prat threw a rather loose ball into the middle,' continues Butterfield. 'I ran in, picked it up, shot down to the end of the field and passed to Ted Woodward who scored between the posts, and we had five points almost before the game had started. I had never felt fitter! After that, before every game I ever played, or any big occasion – even making a speech – I always had my two raw eggs and sherry. Let's face it, I was on drugs!' Butterfield also scored a try of his own and Eric Evans, the Sale front-row forward, got his second of the season. If England could beat Scotland at Twickenham, they would win the championship. The Scots had lost heavily to Ireland and England capitalised on their low morale, beating them by the same score as the Irish, 26 points to eight. The wooden spoon was conclusively Scotland's, whereas England could celebrate the championship title, their first since 1947 when they had shared with Wales.

Things did not improve for Scotland in 1954 as they earned the wooden spoon for the third year in a row. Their season took in the last championship game to be played in Belfast, but this was one of four defeats and they scored only six points in those matches, their lowest total since the Five Nations had begun. For England it was a rosier picture. Demand from spectators meant that the English victory over Wales was the first all-ticket game to be held at Twickenham, in front of a capacity crowd. Ireland were also beaten in London, with the Lancastrians, Martin Regan and Gordon Rimmer, forming a fine half-back combination. France, too, were well placed, Maurice Prat scoring two tries and his brother Jean converting one of them, in the win against Ireland – the championship was still wide open. It was a boom time for the tournament. 'It wasn't too long after the war, when everybody had been starved of sport,' says Bryn Meredith, the Newport hooker who was to become a cornerstone of the Welsh pack over the next few seasons. 'The gates were phenomenal, really, and the atmosphere was passionate.'

Meredith made his debut in the win over Ireland and Wales then went on to beat France. It was to be a tense final day of the championship: England had three wins and were going for the Grand Slam; their opponents, France, with two wins, and Wales, also with a couple of victories, both still had a chance to share the title. England had of course already won the Triple Crown but, in the end, the championship was divided three ways in a thrilling climax. Most matches had been close and home advantage was often the only deciding factor that season. For Wales, about to move to a permanent home in Cardiff, the victory over Scotland was the last Five Nations match to be played at St Helen's in Swansea.

France's win against England, giving them a share of the title for the first time, was a key point in their history, and they began the 1955 season with two more victories over the hapless Scots and Ireland. Scrum-half Gérard Dufau had now played over twenty championship games and knew that all around him were world-class players. Michel Vannier at full-back and forward Michel Celaya stood out, and their goal-kicking and try-scoring respectively set up a win at Twickenham. But nobody that day could surpass the skills of Jean Prat. Chic in appearance and approach, he brought a new style of play, as Jeff Butterfield, who was on the receiving end, recalls: 'Prat was not tall, but twice in that game he caught the ball at the back of the line-out, swivelled and dropped two goals. I've never ever seen anybody do that – just to casually pluck the ball down and score, it was great skill.'

Prat's final championship game was against Wales in Paris – could he end his illustrious career with a treasured first Grand Slam? The public sensed it was on and, for the first time, a French home game was made all-ticket. The record crowd of 57,000 were to be disappointed, though. Wales scored two tries to France's one and full-back Garfield Owen kicked two penalty goals, both from fifty yards. The decisive factor was the strength of the Welsh forwards, and Bryn Meredith feels this was where the game was won. 'The French had the skills, but their problem was that everybody wanted to run with the ball and nobody wanted to work for it. If you don't compete up-front, you've got no chance – that was why New Zealand were so good. In those days, it was ten-man rugby initially until you had worn the opposition down, and then you would spread it. France always seemed a yard faster but they didn't seem to have the temperament, and once you got your nose in front they were almost beaten.'

France had taken a leap forward but still had to overcome the final hurdle. That year, they had to settle for a share of the title with Wales, who had recorded wins over England and Ireland as well. A loss in Edinburgh, however, ended both Welsh Grand Slam hopes and Scotland's abysmal run – it had been four years since their last championship win, coincidentally on the same ground against the same opposition. A relieved Scottish side followed this with victory over Ireland, who had drawn with England, but a Calcutta Cup defeat prevented Scotland from ending their year with a Triple Crown.

The rejuvenated Scots began the 1956 season with victory over France at Murrayfield, with forward and Glasgow grain merchant Hamish Kemp, who would serve his country so well over the rest of the decade, scoring two tries. A week later, the Welsh descended on London for their great day out. The Five Nations experience was now an established part of the rugby calendar and, dressed in bowler hats and carrying giant imitation leeks, Wales's supporters would egg each other on to climb the goal-posts before the game – pre-match entertainment has certainly changed over the years. 'You were aware that the whole nation depended on you,' says Cliff Morgan, who recognised that his team's performance also had a much more serious significance. 'The pits, the steelworks – the production all depended on Wales winning and doing well on the Saturday.'

This was one occasion when the Welsh economy benefited, as the national side beat the English and scored the only two tries of the match. 'We never got the ball because Cliff kicked down the line all afternoon – they won by sheer control,' says Jeff Butterfield. However, he does admit to a little distraction in the build-up to the game, which exemplifies the gulf between the clinical match preparations of today and the more carefree attitudes of previous years. 'We always went to a show on the Friday night, and that time went to see Max Bygraves. We had one hell of a good evening, then went back for dinner and had a couple of nightcaps to stimulate the heart. But there had been a mix-up over the booking of the hotel, and I actually slept in the same bed as prop Ron Jacobs as he got ready for his first cap. Every time he rolled over I fell out, and he talked all night about me making a break down the middle of the pitch and giving him the inside pass for a score. By the time it came to the game, we had been through the move so many times, I think we were knackered!'

Ireland had picked a talented new scrum-half, Andy Mulligan, for their opening match in Paris, but they lost despite a try from the player who was really catching the eye, the flamboyant Tony O'Reilly. Matters then deteriorated further and they were heavily beaten at Twickenham. O'Reilly was an exceptionally gifted rugby

player, who would later go on to make millions as a newspaper pro-
prietor, and rise also to become president of the Heinz Corporation –
but in the 1950s the dashing back was sweeping the sport off its feet.
His versatility in the back line was matched by his sharp wit –
illustrated by the famous piece he wrote in the anthology *The Wit of
Rugby* that includes a description of the differences between the Irish
and English dressing-rooms. He begins with his own team-mates.

> Four of the forwards wearing headbands look like convales-
> cents from brain surgery. A fifth forward goes round sprinkling
> holy water on his team-mates. Three Northern brethren recip-
> ients of his thoughtfulness have religious doubts as to whether
> this is in the Lodge or not. The door opens – 'Ireland captain,
> will you toss?' Seven voices advocate heads and the remainder
> tails as he trots forth, calls wrongly. We face a strong sun and
> gale-force winds for both halves. The England dressing-room
> presents a different scene, as I once discovered. Being forgetful
> by nature, I turned up for an international without either
> shorts or laces. The kindness of the Rugby Union supplied the
> former, the latter apparently were no longer in stock. Ten min-
> utes before the off I entered enemy territory to find Eric Evans,
> the England captain, standing on a large table in the centre of
> the room, his face matching the red rose on his chest. For a
> moment, I was unseen. 'Remember Dunkirk!' he shouted. 'And
> Alamein! Discipline, that's where we can lick these b******
> Irish – all fire and fury, but irresponsible.' 'Excuse me,' I said
> politely. 'But has anyone got some hairy twine for my boots?'

Another O'Reilly try and his influence behind the scrum helped to
bring about victories over Scotland and Wales to ruin a Welsh Triple
Crown. Nevertheless, Wales were able to take the championship after
a tense win over France in which back-row forward Derek Williams
scored a disputed try. France's disappointment was assuaged by a
third consecutive win over an English side who had earlier beaten
Scotland.

It had been a terrible decade for the Scots, but in 1957, captained
by back-row forward Jim Greenwood, they discovered a full-back of
the highest quality with the most patriotic of names: Ken Scotland.
Scotland made his debut in Paris at the start of that season, scoring
all of his side's six points, and France could not reply. Despite the
win, the Scottish selectors could not settle on who they wanted to

play at fly-half – scrum-half Arthur Dorward had four different partners that season. Overcoming this disruption and with the pack staying the same, the Scots won against Wales. Scotland's right wing,
Arthur Smith, scored the try that helped to create the victory and,
three weeks later, he was appointed captain after the injured Jim
Greenwood was forced to pull out of the game against Ireland at
Murrayfield. Perhaps Greenwood had seen the weather forecast: the
match was played in a blizzard, and long before half-time the pitch
was almost completely white with snow. Ireland had earlier beaten
France and, driven on by their inspirational pack leader, Ronnie 'Kav'
Kavanagh, brought Scotland's winning run to an end.

Meanwhile, England had set off with a victory in Cardiff. Almost
a year to the day after his debut against Wales, scrum-half Dickie
Jeeps returned to the English team in an uneventful game that com-
menced a momentous season. 'The only score came after the Welsh
wing Keith Maddocks was off-side underneath the posts from a line-
out on the far side of the field!' says Jeeps. In Jeeps England had
unearthed a gem of a scrum-half whose name became a byword for
quality. In time he became a selector, then President of the RFU and
also Chairman of the Sports Council – as busy off the field as he had
been on it!

It had been four years since an English success in Wales, but a full
nineteen since a victory in Dublin. Playing for the majority of the
game with only seven forwards because of injury to winger Peter
Thompson, England finally won again on Irish soil, thanks to a try
from the other wing, Peter Jackson. Jackson went on to show how
crucial the wingers were to this England side by crossing the line
twice more in his team's victory over France at Twickenham. 'We had
one sole object in attack, and that was to pass the ball to Peter
Jackson or Peter Thompson,' says Jeff Butterfield, the man alongside
them both at centre – 'we hadn't any other tactic at all. Get it to either
of those two and if they got a bit of pace up, then cross-kick back into
the middle – that's all we knew. When Jackson had room to move he
could jink and side-step anything – when we played against him at
club level I used to say, "Whatever you do, don't tackle him, surround
him."'

Butterfield's centre partner was no longer the highly creative Lewis
Cannell, who had served England so well for nearly a decade, but Phil
Davies, who rejoined a team on the crest of a wave. One more win at
home to Scotland would give England the Grand Slam for the first
time since 1928. The English pack included David Marques and John

Currie, amassing a total of 22 consecutive internationals as second-row partners. The quality of players like these was too much for the Scots, and England ran out convincing winners by sixteen points to three. Captain Eric Evans's effervescent style of leadership had proved a hit with the players: 'Eric got a lot out of the word enthusiasm,' confirms Dickie Jeeps. 'He was the most enthusiastic guy you'd ever meet. Technically, he didn't know a lot about some parts of the game, but he certainly knew how to motivate the forwards.' These were the days when the selectors preserved an aloof distance from the players – 'they passed the time of day with you and you passed it back and that was about it,' is how Dickie Jeeps puts it – but Evans even managed to entice them to a communal lunch party at the Mayfair Hotel to celebrate the team's success.

The Welsh recovered in their last two matches, first by wallowing in the mud to beat Ireland in Cardiff. At one stage the conditions were so bad that the Scottish referee, Jack Taylor, ordered the players from the field to change their kit. Wales then defeated France in the Paris spring-time, a match which featured seven tries. But the Grand Slam winners were England, and this was the first year the achievement became known as such. The term had been coined in an article in *The Times*, and in the beginning, Jeff Butterfield remembers, was used rather self-consciously. 'I should think that was the beginning of modesty disappearing. If you had said you were "grand" you would have been regarded as a snob. When we scored then we didn't make a big fuss about it – we used to run back a little bit shy or stupid. We never jumped up and down. There was no feeling of greatness – it was just something you were very pleased to accept.'

The 1958 season started badly for England when Wales managed a draw at Twickenham and immediately ended any chance of repeating the Grand Slam, full-back Terry Davies saving the game with a long-range penalty-goal – his team's only points. Later some Welsh supporters were moved to return to the ground to saw-off the crossbar he had so dramatically cleared! On their way home, so the story goes, the guilty parties had the fortune to bump into their hero in a café in the Cotswolds. Davies autographed a section of the bar and, being a timber merchant, promised to help replace it. The disgruntled Twickenham authorities accepted a written apology from the fans and the incident was forgiven. The then-Secretary of the WRU, former winger Bill Clement, has another reason to remember that day. Wales had gone onto the field without a badge on their jerseys. 'They were packed and put away in the kit-bag to be taken to Twickenham,' says Clement, 'and when the parcel was opened, they did not have the three feathers crest. I was a bit shocked, but the players put the jerseys on and nobody knew anything until someone noticed it in a photograph in the newspaper. At least they were red – if they had been the white trial jerseys we would have run out in England colours!'

Wales, complete with crests, went on to beat Scotland and then Ireland as well. England also won against the Irish, then beat France and in their last match, at Murrayfield, the Gloucester prop George Hastings found himself with a late kick at goal to earn a draw that would maintain England's unbeaten record. 'He was a good prop, but he had a big belly,' Dickie Jeeps jokes, 'so it was sometimes hard to get the ball in under him – you had to keep him upright. But he was an excellent left-footed kicker. As the ball took on a lot of water in those days it was like a medicine ball by the time you finished – it was no surprise the forwards kicked.' Hastings' strength made sure he was successful, and England were left to wait and see who would win the title, knowing that Wales would finish top of the table should they beat France. Making his Five Nations debut for Wales that day was the Llanelli back, Carwyn James, a man who would become one of the game's great coaches, assuming legendary status after taking the British Lions to victory in Australia and New Zealand in 1971. It turned out to be a landmark day for the French: their first-ever victory in Cardiff. Like many other educated observers, James recognised what a significant moment this was for the championship.

France's losing start was now forgotten and after the Welsh, Ireland were beaten at the Stade Colombes in Maurice Prat's final championship match. That season the tournament also said goodbye to two other creative players who had shone like beacons at a time when defences were generally on top: Jack Kyle, who bowed out after the win over Scotland, and his great friend and rival, Cliff Morgan. Morgan has no doubt as to who was the best. 'Jack was the greatest outside-half in the world at the time. I remember his try on my debut back at the start of the decade: that day he taught me that I was a boy in a man's game – because you looked at him and he lulled you into a false sense of security. I thought, "You're not too good – I'll go out and chase the centre to show off a bit." But suddenly, as I went across, he pulled the ball back, side-stepped and scored a try under the posts. Jack was a great thinker.'

Equally, Kyle feels that Morgan was at the top of his trade. 'Of all the outside-halves that I played against, Cliff was the most difficult to mark. You just never knew what he was going to do, and of course he had that tremendous burst of speed to set him past you. Cliff was always wide awake. He was always probing, always on the go, challenging, trying a little tap ahead or something new. It was a full-time job keeping an eye on him.'

In short, both were phenomenal players, the likes of whom the championship has rarely seen, and for them the memories of the Five Nations are warm and everlasting. 'The difference was that then, we didn't have to win,' says Cliff Morgan, 'and if we did lose we'd be sad – we hated losing – but it didn't matter, it didn't affect us. For us it was easier in a sense. Now you have to be fitter, faster, stronger – everything – whereas we didn't have to bother.' 'The sense of honour of playing for your country as a young lad was something you probably never imagined even in your wildest dreams,' adds Jack Kyle, who emigrated to Zambia in the 1960s to continue his work as a surgeon. 'The old timers used to tell us, "The game's important, but it's the friends you'll make that will mean the most," and we used to laugh and say, "Listen to those old cods talking!" – but here we are fifty years later and when I go back to Ireland my team-mates are the friends that I see.'

1959–1963

1959 – France's championship
1960 – England's Triple Crown; England and France
share championship
1961 – France's championship
1962 – France's championship
1963 – England's championship

The reason for Cliff Morgan's retirement from the game at the age of only 28 was that the level of commitment required both in home internationals and on tours abroad was increasingly difficult to combine with a career. Like many others, he simply could not afford to play on. One of the great rugby league players, Welshman and Great Britain captain, Gus Risman, had been attracted away from Morgan's club Cardiff, and in 1959 his son Bev was already being tipped to follow in his father's footsteps. As a union player, though,

Action from the first Five Nations game – Wales v France at St Helen's, Swansea on 1 January 1910.

The Oxford University quartet of backs that helped Scotland to their first Grand Slam in 1925. From the left: Johnny Wallace, George Aitken, Phil Macpherson and Ian Smith, the 'Flying Scotsman'.

Wavell Wakefield, an inspirational forward, leader and tactician for England in the 1920s.

A flu-ridden Vivian Jenkins shakes hands in 1933 with HRH the Prince of Wales, who was about to witness the full-back play a major role in Wales's first win at Twickenham. The experienced Welsh captain Watcyn Thomas introduces his players and on Jenkins' left is fellow debutant Wilf Wooller.

The official attendance was 56,000, but many believe it was more like 70,000 who crammed into the Arms Park to witness Wales's meeting with Ireland in 1936.

The only Russian prince ever to play for England: Alexander Obolensky strides away to score a typical try in the 1930s.

Ireland's only Grand Slam-winning team to date – 1948 the year. Captain Karl Mullen is holding the ball, the great fly-half Jack Kyle is seated on the ground second from right, while prop forward and try-scoring hero J.C. Daly is standing fourth from left.

Scotland v Wales at Murrayfield in 1963 featured an incredible 111 line-outs – ultimately forcing the lawmakers to respond.

Two more fly-half greats, this time from Wales. Cliff Morgan goes through the English defence in his penultimate season in 1957. And Barry John takes on Ireland in 1971 – a year later he would retire from the game.

(Opposite) Welsh wizard Gerald Davies had a spiritual quality to his play, and once again he lights up the Arms Park.

'My mother says she thought I was cut wide open.' Gareth Edwards after his classic score against Scotland in the Cardiff mud in 1972.

he was faced with a different choice – to play for England or Wales? 'There was a lot of soul-searching,' he explains, 'especially as I would have been following Cliff Morgan. I was living in Manchester at the time, born and bred there, and my father said that, as my mother was English, I was more English than Welsh. But it took me quite a while to decide.'

Risman joined an England side in transition after the championship-winning era – Eric Evans had retired and half the team members were new. Cardiff had a special welcome for the fresh fly-half: 'The pitch was under about two feet of water – it was a complete quagmire. Believe it or not, I actually scored a try in the first twenty minutes, but the line was completely obliterated and the referee disallowed it because he couldn't see whether we were over or not. I was totally distraught – I knew there was no doubt about it! Then their winger, Dewi Bebb, got the decisive try and they won five–nil.'

In Dublin, Bev Risman learnt an important lesson about the international game. 'I was used to running rugby when playing with the university,' he says, 'and I was all for throwing the ball about. We were just outside our 25, it came beautifully to me and I thought, "This is a good chance." I gave it to Jeff Butterfield and he immediately smashed the ball straight into touch. "What the hell are you doing?" he said – "passing me the ball inside our own half?" "I was just playing my normal game," was my reply, and he came back, "Well, don't play it here, son – this is an international!"' England had built a reputation for attacking play, but even Jeff Butterfield, the newly appointed captain, and as fine a player going forward as any at the time, would often err on the side of caution in defensive positions. At least Risman's penalty-goal gave England the victory.

Despite the presence of other talented backs like Malcolm Phillips and André Boniface, there were no tries when England met France at Twickenham. The match was drawn with a penalty-goal apiece, and England's low-scoring season was concluded with another three-all draw against Scotland – for the first time ever in a Five Nations season they had failed to score a try. The Scots won only one match that year against Wales, thanks to a 'foot-rush' try which was finished by hooker Norman Bruce. Ireland, still exponents of this 'helter-skelter' style of play, too, gained victory over Scotland but then went down to Wales. That year France scored only four tries – pack member François Moncla getting one in the win over Scotland and two more against Wales – but they were enough to give the French their first outright championship title. At last they had their prize.

France had been threatening success ever since their return to the competition in 1947, but in 1959 their guiding hand was Lucien Miâs. In effect he was the architect of the final phase in the modernization of French rugby, which began, he believes, with their heavy defeat by South Africa seven years earlier. It taught Miâs the effectiveness of the team game, and he realised the direction that France must follow. After taking time away from the sport to concentrate on his medical studies, he returned to pit his skills against the Springboks again in 1958, in a two-test series in South Africa. France's captain, Michel Celaya, withdrew because of injury and Miâs took over the reins, to great effect. 'When I first started playing for France,' he said later, 'we had no sense of belonging to each other. Now the team began playing for each other and we found the secret for harnessing the real strength of a team.' France became the first nation to win a series on Springbok soil for sixty years: the foundations had been laid for the first truly great period in French rugby.

France were also starting to lead the way with new innovations. Their forwards were carrying the ball more effectively than their Celtic or English counterparts. 'They produced a lot of what I call clever, big second-row forwards,' acknowledges Dickie Jeeps – 'Miâs, Celaya and people like that, and I remember on one occasion after a wing three-quarter got injured they moved a prop out there to take his position!' For once that season, though, the newly-elected champions met their match as Ireland, captained by hooker Ronnie Dawson, won the final game, winger Niall Brophy scoring as he had done two years previously against the French. Despite the victory, pack member Noel Murphy recalls an important change in the opposition's approach: 'Before this period they got easily flustered, arguing amongst themselves, but they found a discipline – I don't mean in the context of having been a dirty team, I mean that their decision-making was now good. They were efficient, didn't get ruffled.' Lucien Miâs retired after that loss in Dublin, but had the satisfaction of knowing he had helped to change the French game forever.

Confidence in France was now high: in 1960 they scored eleven tries. They were too much for Scotland at the start of the season, and also for Wales and Ireland at the end. All three were beaten by a team of increasing flair, with fly-half Pierre Albaladéjo showing they could kick, too: against the Irish he landed three drop-goals – still a world record today. Only England seemed to have the necessary power to counter this French surge, but first they would have to beat Wales and Ireland.

The Welsh arrived at Twickenham led by lock Rhys Williams in his final international. England winger Jim Roberts celebrated his first championship game by scoring two tries in their victory, with another newcomer, full-back Don Rutherford, kicking a conversion and a couple of penalties. Rutherford would go on to serve the RFU as Technical Director, but back in the 1960s he was still a little wet behind the ears. 'The first thing I remember was Dickie Jeeps coming up to me after we had won a penalty. When you're on the field you can't hear anything, and I sort of lip-read him saying, "Do you want to kick at goal?" I glanced at the white line where he was standing, looked at the posts and said, "Yes." I came up and made my mark, and when I looked again at the line below my boot I thought, "Christ, this is not the 25 – I'm actually inside my own half!" Needless to say, it just missed! But it was a fantastic lesson – I discovered that with a big crowd the pitch suddenly looks much smaller. I never made that mistake again and have often relayed my experience to players in their first international.'

Wales bounced back to win at home to Scotland, but England found the Irish tougher opponents, in a match that marked the Five Nations debut of a 21-year-old Irish full-back, Tom Kiernan, who one day would lead his country with distinction. A late second-half try from David Marques was successfully converted by Don Rutherford to seal the match for England and, although the Irish would not challenge for the title, going on to lose narrowly to both Scotland and Wales, the English full-back is in no doubt about the challenge Ireland always presented. 'The illusion was that you were playing against thirty people,' says Rutherford. 'They were the only country that, if the ball was on the ground, never picked it up – they would kick it. Believe me, that was very disturbing: you lost your shape, as people were not where they should have been – they would just gobble you up. They are still the best at it, and now when I watch Keith Wood kicking the ball and chasing, it takes me back donkey's years – because of course Keith's father Gordon was playing in the Ireland front row in my day.'

So France and England, the two teams of the moment, met in Paris – a game that ended in stalemate. England scored the only try through centre Mike Weston and, in accordance with their new captain's tactics, neutralised the French game-plan. 'Once you'd let a Frenchman run round the end of the line-out and get across the gain line, there were swarms of them,' says skipper Dickie Jeeps. 'We were still doing old-fashioned things – we'd pick a blind-side and open-side. They'd just pick two runners and always a big number-eight. If you didn't tackle them on the gain line you had problems, because they ran at your midfield. Their use of the back row was also different from everybody else's in that they would run off the scrum, linking with the scrum-half. They didn't worry too much about the set scrum.' France's enterprise was enhanced by their ability to retain possession. 'The thing about the French at that stage was that they would turn before making contact,' explains Don Rutherford, 'so you got presented with a Frenchman's back and the ball was rolled on to their next man. It was quite a new technique and difficult to stop.' But this time France had to rely on a more traditional three-point penalty-goal scored by Michel Vannier to ensure a draw against a resilient England team.

For a young man in Paris for the first time, there were other attractions, Don Rutherford admits. 'I was 22 and I couldn't believe it – I went around the Pigalle district and was introduced to some "interesting" sights I'd not seen before! It was a great tradition to take England players out to various shows and, on the Friday evening, Sophia Loren was in the audience. I remember her coming down the central aisle – it stopped the show for me. She was at her peak then, fantastic, stunning – the previous entertainment just passed into history. It was also very unusual to see the Chairman of Selectors, Mr Carston Catcheside, do a striptease accompanied by a lady playing the piano at the official dinner. He got up onto the stage having borrowed the waiter's towel, took a few things off, used the towel skilfully and brought the house down!' England returned home to win the Triple Crown by scoring three tries in their best-ever victory over Scotland. Rutherford's kicking proved vital again and the influential back-row forward, Peter Robbins, had a particularly effective game. A late try from scrum-half Onllwyn Brace in Dublin helped to snatch third place for Wales, but France shared the title with England.

It had taken France fifty years to exert such influence on the Five Nations and, although they were still not part of the sport's governing body, the International Board, there was no stopping them on the pitch. In 1961 they won the title outright by beating Scotland, Wales and Ireland. As in the previous season, only a draw against England prevented them from taking a first Grand Slam. Though Lucien Miâs had now gone, a forward of similar stature was now established in the national side. Those who saw Michel Crauste in action assert that he too was one of the greatest, and his nickname of 'Attila' gives away the manner in which he played the game. 'I was in a café in

Toulouse recently,' says Ireland's Noel Murphy: 'I mentioned his name, and automatically the eyes shone.' It was a relatively poor season for the English, their only other championship points coming from a victory over Scotland, to deny them the Triple Crown. Defeat by Wales left bottom place to Ireland.

1962 was another championship-winning year for a French team that recorded victories over Scotland, England (Michel Crauste becoming the first forward to score a hat-trick of tries in a Five Nations game, a quite remarkable feat) and Ireland – when he scored again. It was a marvellous French side that included terrific players like the backs Jean Dupuy and Jacques Bouquet, and the hardened forwards Alfred Roques and his front-row colleague Amédée Domenech. Only defeat to a Kelvin Coslett penalty-goal in Cardiff prevented that elusive Grand Slam.

The team that finished second to France that year was Scotland. After losing to the French, the Scots went to Cardiff to play a Welsh side that had drawn nil-nil with England. The odds were not in Scotland's favour – they had not won at the Arms Park since 1927 and, in the build-up to the game, their first-choice scrum-half, Tremayne Rodd, had to pull out with an injured hamstring. But the weather in Cardiff turned, and so did Scotland's luck, because the player who took over Rodd's jersey was Stan Coughtrie, in wet conditions the ideal man for the job. 'Stan could have been a forward – the largest scrum-half I've ever witnessed in my life – and he had a wizard pass,' says Scotland lock Mike Campbell-Lamerton. With Campbell-Lamerton alongside Frans ten Bos, a Dutchman who had learned the game at Fettes College and Oxford University, 18 stone and $17\frac{1}{2}$ stone respectively, it was the first time Scotland had the presence of two such big men in the second row, and it made all the difference.

Tries from ten Bos and flanker Ron Glasgow gave Scotland victory, and after many barren years it was a jubilant but tired Scottish team who made the journey home from Wales. Even forward Hughie McLeod, normally a strict teetotaller, allowed himself the luxury of a couple of sherries. One of the best post-war props, McLeod had played 34 times for his country in the championship and, together with hooker Norman Bruce – 'a man of many words,' comments his team-mate Mike Campbell-Lamerton, 'as all hookers are' – and prop forward David Rollo, it made a formidable trio.

'And on the wing there was dear Arthur,' adds Mike Campbell-Lamerton. It was the skipper, Arthur Smith, who perhaps merited most praise. 'Speed of thought and acceleration and a really strong determination made him into a great player,' says Campbell-Lamerton. 'He was also a bright and able person with an immense general knowledge. He led by example on the field and explained things off it – I remember Arthur once gave us a lecture on the theory of black holes and had us enthralled.' His two tries against Ireland helped Scotland to their biggest score there and set up a Triple Crown attempt against England. 1962 was his final season in the championship; tragically he died at the age of only 42.

The English had also beaten Ireland, and at Murrayfield they frustrated the Scots' ambitions: for the third time in five years the Calcutta Cup ended as a three-all draw. Scotland remained a team of nearly-men, but second was their best placing in the championship table for twelve years and nobody was lamenting the loss of a 'greater prize'. 'The great secret was that the Scotland team was like a club side,' stresses centre Ian Laughland. 'People would look forward to coming together on a Thursday because we'd meet our friends – and then decide we had an important game to play on the Saturday.' 'They would die for one another,' adds Mike Campbell-Lamerton. 'It was a magical side to be part of. I think we did deserve a Triple Crown, but then, that's life.'

There was, however, some unfinished business that season, as the game between Ireland and Wales had to be postponed owing to a smallpox outbreak in the Rhondda. The match was eventually played in the November of the 1962–1963 season, Welsh skipper Bryn Meredith winning one final cap. 'I thought Wales should have been looking to the future,' he says, 'but I agreed to play. It was a fearsome day, so I said to our outside-half, "You know what to do with it – kick it out." And what did he do? – he ran it all day long.' The game was there for Wales's taking, but they had not used the elements and ended up with a draw. Meredith came off the field and gave his last Welsh jersey, covered in mud, to a friend: 'On reflection, I'm not sure how pleased he was to receive it in that state!'

Scotland's improving record continued into the 1963 championship with a win over France. It was a particularly severe winter – and some of the unions' attempts to deal with the weather, as Ken Scotland recalls, were more sophisticated than others. His team had arrived in Paris to find snow on the ground, and the covering of straw the French had put down insufficient to keep the pitch from freezing. 'Their answer was to set the straw alight, and the game was played on a virtually brick-hard and black pitch. It looked as if we were playing on a farmer's field – the ball was bouncing around all over the place!' For France, the Boniface brothers, Guy and André, played together as centres in the championship for the first time. Their scrum-half and captain, Pierre Lacroix, tried to release his fraternal combination, but Scotland held on to record a dramatic late victory, brought about by a mistake from Ian Laughland: 'We were into the last five minutes, I took a drop-goal and missed the posts by about a hundred yards! – then winger Ronnie Thomson came in and scored under the posts.'

A fortnight later, in the final game for the great Irish back Cecil Pedlow, Ireland were unable to stop France as winger Christian Darrouy stamped his mark on the match with a hat-trick of tries. Meanwhile, Wales's opener against England saw fly-half David Watkins as one of a number of players setting out on their championship careers. Calamity almost struck, however. Flanker David Hayward, another newcomer, was due to pick up Watkins on the day from his home – some thirty miles from Cardiff – so they could join the team at the Royal Hotel for a light lunch, before meandering over to the ground for the three o'clock kick-off. 'I went down into the village,' says Watkins, 'and hundreds of people were moving off to the match early, saying, "All the best, Dai, have a good game – we'll be thinking of you." I'm waiting with my kit bag on my shoulder – and Dai Hayward forgot to pick me up! I was waiting, waiting and waiting – and I thought, "My Godfathers, I'm going to be the first international in the history of the game not to turn up!" Eventually, some supporters suggested they give me a lift – but once I got there, Dai had gone. He had, of course, suddenly remembered and gone to fetch me, only to find that I wasn't there – so he then had to rush down and also nearly missed the game. It could have been a thirteen-man team!'

Another man winning his first cap that day was Watkins' half-back partner, Clive Rowlands, who, unusually for a debutant, was given the added responsibility of captaincy. 'People often say it must have been marvellous to play for Wales fourteen times and be captain on all of those occasions,' reflects Rowlands – 'but I wish I had played for Wales once or twice without being captain. Then I would have been allowed to play the way somebody else wanted me to, instead of the way I thought I had to for the team.' On that Cardiff day the 1963 winter was continuing to bite. 'It was so cold, we didn't even have the anthems on the field,' Rowlands remembers – 'we were underneath the stand waiting to come out. England played very well and we had few chances, and for the next 28 years I was known as the last captain who lost to England at the Cardiff Arms Park!'

Wales had not beaten Scotland in Edinburgh for ten years, and for his next game in charge, Rowlands would famously put a result for his team above all other considerations. Again, the weather was awful, but the pitch had survived the cold because of the undersoil 'electric blanket' now installed at Murrayfield, and Rowlands devised his game plan in response to the conditions. The ball was kicked into touch all afternoon, resulting in an amazing 111 line-outs. 'It's a heck of a lot isn't it,' agrees Rowlands. 'It all began when Dai Watkins started slipping on the surface, and we decided to play it tight and it worked. But Scotland put it there as much as I did – they threw in as many balls as us. It takes two sides to play a good game.' Wales won, but unsurprisingly there were no tries. It proved that something had to be done about the laws of the game – constantly kicking the ball out of play was no longer an acceptable way to spend an afternoon, for the backs or the crowd. 'The law change came some years later, but this was the game that prompted it,' confirms Rowlands. 'I'm glad to say that the people who followed benefited from the introduction of no direct kicking to touch outside your own twenty-five.'

The flight up to Edinburgh had also been instructive for David Watkins, who discovered that selection for the team could be governed by factors unrelated to players' form. 'Because of the numbers who were going up to Scotland, we just sat down as we walked onto the plane,' he recalls. 'A rather large gentleman in a trilby hat and big overcoat sat next to me, and asked whether I would like to play against Ireland, which was still five weeks away. I replied that I hadn't played against Scotland yet – what a silly thing to ask me – and he said, "Well, if you give me your jersey after the game, there will be no doubt you'll be playing against Ireland."' On arrival at the airport Watkins enquired of his team-mate, forward Alun Pask, as to the gentleman's identity, to be told it was one of the senior Welsh selectors. Changes to the Welsh team did not seem necessary for the Ireland game in Cardiff, but the Irish won the match, their only victory of the year, and Wales's poor season finally came to an end with defeat in France, to finish bottom of the championship.

Scores in the other games were few and far between – England drew nil-nil with Ireland and beat France by six points to five, while a solitary penalty-goal from Scotland was the only score in their game against the Irish. Some sparkle was urgently required to prevent the backs from handing in their notices, and it was supplied by the English fly-half, Richard Sharp, in the Calcutta Cup game at

Twickenham. England's win gave them the championship and the magic of Sharp's try will live forever. Following a neat scissors move with fellow back Mike Weston, his memorable diagonal surge to the line caused panic in the Scottish defence. But the would-be tacklers had no time to address the problem. Sharp twice straightened the line of attack, dummied the pass and sped over to provide an elegant climax to a previously barren season.

1964–1969

1964 – Scotland and Wales share championship
1965 – Wales's Triple Crown and championship
1966 – Wales's championship
1967 – France's championship
1968 – France's GRAND SLAM
1969 – Wales's Triple Crown and championship

In Wales, a turnaround in rugby organisation and style was being initiated under the direction of Clive Rowlands. The shock of a crushing defeat in South Africa later in 1964 would prompt the change in thinking. 'It was the first time that the Welsh national side had travelled abroad and we got a hiding,' says Rowlands. 'I think, though, it was the start of what was to come in the 1970s as, after that defeat, we formed a coaching committee and coaching began within the clubs themselves. It was another three years before a national coach was appointed, but there can be no doubting the impact of that loss to the Springboks.'

In that most conservative of victories over Scotland in 1963 Rowlands had played to the team's strength, a strong pack backed up by his meticulous use of the boot, as the way to ensure success. This was generally the way Wales started the 1964 season at Twickenham, though their winger Dewi Bebb did cross for two tries, as many as his team had scored in their previous two championships. But as David Watkins explains, one of the scores was a little fortuitous. 'We were six-nil down, I had the ball and aborted a drop-goal, slicing it completely. But it went over the top of the English three-quarter line to Dewi Bebb who picked it up on the first bounce and dived over in the corner. I always remember Vivian Jenkins writing in *The Times* something like, "A deft kick by the young stand-off half, Watkins, enabled Wales to capture a draw"!'

The draw gave Wales the confidence to expand further against Scotland and that year they became the only side to beat the Scots. Rowlands, still calling the shots from scrum-half, worked a score for centre Keith Bradshaw, one of two more tries for the Welsh. Ireland in Dublin were their next task. It was an Irish side which had won impressively by eighteen points to five at Twickenham, a day when Cambridge University student and future solicitor Mike Gibson had made his Irish debut at fly-half already looking every bit the rugby star. Gibson would play 56 Five Nations games between 1964 and 1979 – a championship record that still stands. Although Ireland had then lost to Scotland, they were led by the experienced lock, Bill 'Wigs' Mulcahy, and were planning a spiky reception for the Welsh. In the game, though, Mike Gibson was continually hunted down by David Hayward and, after the Irish had managed to resist for almost the length of the match, it was the new Welsh centre, John Dawes, selected at the eleventh hour as an injury-replacement, who made the biggest impression by scoring the crucial try. 'There wasn't time to get nervous,' remembers Dawes. 'I touched the ball twice, because we still had a predominantly kicking game. But the second time I touched it, I got a return pass from winger Peter Rees and, after a mad sprint from five yards, fell over the line.'

Dawes retained his place for the France game – 'If a Welsh team won in those days it was hard to get out of.'· Winger Stuart Watkins, like Dawes in his first season, scored a late try as Wales drew and managed to go through the championship unbeaten. Perhaps more importantly, with all fifteen men being brought more into play, their style of rugby was finding wider appeal. 'That was definitely the way I played,' says John Dawes. 'There was still a certain reluctance in the Welsh camp to be as adventurous as we would be in the 1970s, but the seeds were sown. We began to realise the enormous potential we had on the wing – initially it was Stuart Watkins and Dewi Bebb, and then Gerald Davies and Maurice Richards, they were all great wingers and British Lions class. Of course, in Wales much was lacking in the way of pitches in those days – they were quagmires more often than not, which didn't suit the running game. But with the improvement in playing surfaces and a slight change in attitude we began to develop a pattern of play in the best interests of Welsh rugby.'

The 1964 championship, though, did not solely belong to Wales.

Despite having beaten the Scots, the Welsh saw their main rivals win their other three games. Three big names of Scottish rugby, the forwards Peter Brown and Jim Telfer, plus the full-back Stewart Wilson, all made their debuts that season in a team with plenty of talent. At half-back, for example, Scotland were able to call on the Melrose combination of David Chisholm and Alex Hastie, and for them all the win at Twickenham, their first against England in thirteen matches, was particularly satisfying because it meant they shared the title with Wales. For the French 1964 had been a mixed year: they lost their first two games before coming back to earn the draw against Wales and a victory over Ireland that included six tries, two from winger Christian Darrouy.

The following season saw France and Darrouy start where they had left off with two more tries against Scotland. He scored again in the draw with Ireland and once more in the defeat by England. Wales's Stuart Watkins, like Darrouy, could not stop scoring tries – two in the win over England and one in the victory over Scotland, a match which contrasted greatly to the line-out ridden farce of two years earlier. With the Irish also having beaten England and Scotland, both Wales and Ireland were going for the Triple Crown in the same match for the first time since 1911. The Welsh crowd watched anxiously when John Dawes was carried off unconscious, to be attended by the medical officer, the former Welsh centre Jack Matthews: 'He took me into the old north stand,' recalls Dawes, 'gave me a cup of tea and asked me to open the rear window overlooking the cricket pitch. He wondered whether I could see the scoreboard on the far side? My first reaction was that I couldn't see anything, but my second was, "Yes, of course I can see it," so he told me to go back out again. These days I would have been out for at least three weeks – I'm just glad there wasn't any cricket being played, because he might have asked me to tell him the score!' Dawes returned to help Wales secure their tenth Triple Crown, and Ireland bade farewell to David Hewitt, a wing and centre and the latest member of the Hewitt family to play for his country, who had been part of the side for eight years. The son of Tom and nephew of Frank and V.A., who all played in the interwar period, his cousins W.J. Hewitt and F.G. Gilpin were also Ireland internationals. There are many instances of 'Five Nations families', but few can match the Hewitt lineage.

But with the Triple Crown in the bag, Wales met a French side in the mood to inflict damage. 'I realised then and I am still of the opinion that the best side in the championship is France,' says David

Watkins. 'They can play a brand of rugby that nobody else is capable of. We went to Paris with a side that had been good enough to win against all our opponents, but on a hard surface in the spring France were absolutely brilliant. We were twenty-two points to nil down at half-time and it looked as if it could be the biggest-ever defeat in the history of Welsh rugby. We did salvage something from it but finally lost by twenty-two points to thirteen, and mainly because the French made mistakes trying to play too flamboyantly.' The defeat served as a further reminder that running the ball at the opposition was not only the most entertaining, but could also be the most effective, route to victory.

Wales still won the championship, but the greatest impression of all the rugby played in that season was made by an extraordinary try. The scorer was Andy Hancock of England. Hancock was a solid club player who appeared in only three Five Nations matches, but 'Hancock's half minute' was as memorable as any spark of inspiration in the tournament's history. When England and Scotland met at Twickenham for their final match they could muster only one win between them. Trailing by a drop-goal to nil and with time running out, England's Mike Weston passed to Hancock deep inside their own half. Hancock describes what followed. 'It had been a wet, muddy afternoon and I think I'd had just one pass in the first half – which I dropped. When Mike passed it out, he didn't need to say anything: the look in his eyes said, "Run!" – so I did.' Hancock went outside the Scottish players nearest to him, was nearly caught by another coming across, and now he had reached the full-back, Stewart Wilson. 'I tried to run in-field and then went outside him. Had it been dry, he would have put me in the stand, I think, but he lost his footing.' Now, conscious of more covering defence coming across, Hancock looked inside, saw team-mate Budge Rogers, the back-row forward and, though he could not pass because a Scot was right on Rogers' back, it was enough to hold up the cover. 'And then it was head back to the line, tiring all the way. Ian Laughland caught me from behind and tapped my ankles as I went over. Had I been clever enough or fit enough I should have gone under the posts!'

The conversion was missed but England had managed to salvage a draw, and Hancock was the hero of Twickenham. 'It was just like being in some kind of dream. Believe it or not, I never noticed the crowd noise. One minute you're on the field, the next minute it was all over and you think, "What the hell's happened?" Remarkably, Hancock has never watched a re-run of the BBC film of the try with

Peter West's famous commentary, even though Cliff Morgan subsequently gave him a copy – 'It has been in the attic for years because we've never had anything to play it on! People keep saying, "I saw it on the telly the other day"– all I know is that it must be in black and white!' Ian Laughland, the man who so nearly prevented the famous try, had to endure Hancock's company at the after-match dinner. 'If one person came up to say, "Well done," to him, fifty did. So I told Andy, "Every time somebody comes to congratulate you, buy me another whisky" – it felt better after that!'

The Scots' failure to beat England had consigned them to the wooden spoon, but a year later it was the turn of the English. In 1966 they lost three matches and drew the other against Ireland. The Irish themselves were struggling to mount a serious challenge but were as ever determined to enjoy themselves. 'I think the players mixed a lot more than they do now,' testifies Noel Murphy, the most capped member of the 1966 side. 'We used to have parties in each other's rooms, and there was always a dance or social occasion. People like Richard Harris, Lord Longford and Spike Milligan would turn up at our games on a regular basis. Once Montgomery of Alamein came in and wished us well at Twickenham.'

With Murphy in the Irish back row in 1966 was Cambridge University student Mick Doyle, a man who certainly enjoyed the 'craic'. In Paris they met a French side that had previously drawn with Scotland, and with two more tries in France's win Christian Darrouy took his tally against the Irish to eight in four matches. Of all the Five Nations cities Paris had always had the reputation for a volatile crowd, but on this day matters off the ball took a threatening turn. 'All of a sudden, two things happened,' Doyle remembers. 'First, a flick knife from the crowd landed at the back of the line-out and nearly hit Murphy and myself. That was closely followed by a full can of beer. At the end of the match, the fear factor was very high. The police were waiting to escort the referee, Peter Brook, and his touch judges off the field, so Murphy and I linked our arms around them and helped them off.' Then a spectator spat at the referee. 'Murphy reached over, grabbed the touch-judge's flag and hit the offending fan on the head. The guy was tottering around all over the place and didn't know where he was – but he wouldn't do it again!'

Despite their defeat, the Irish decided to extend their 'commiserating' long into the night. Mick Doyle, still a renowned raconteur, remembers that the squad ended up at a typical Parisian night-club. 'We were all at varying stages of inebriation. The MC called for an idiot or recruit to come up on the stage and be tied up to a totem-pole. This was covered in silk and various nymphets would strip in front of him. Up went one of our gentlemen but, on the way, he grabbed a pot plant of some sort, tore the top off it and stuffed it down his trousers. He allowed himself to be tied onto the pole and, as the girls were doing their bit, he got one hand free, unzipped his fly and produced this bulbous root. With that, the whole place went bananas. Seasoned professionals at clubs like this were sent running for the door – and I must say a legal friend of mine got up and left!'

Ireland's next home match and night out was in Dublin, but two tries from Scotland's winger, Sandy Hinshelwood, helped to see the Scots home. The Irish went into the game against Wales still without a win, their opponents just one victory from a second consecutive Triple Crown. Few were predicting a Welsh defeat, but with Tom Kiernan now in charge and a try from centre Barrie Bresnihan, Ireland ended their season with a big upset.

Nevertheless, Wales knew that victory over France would retain the title. The French scored two tries but it was a single score from Wales's Stuart Watkins which proved decisive. 'Stuart was a big guy, just over six feet tall and about fourteen stone, which was heavy for a three-quarter at that time,' says David Watkins, recalling one of the most thrilling sprints to the line ever seen at the Arms Park. 'He was always a player capable of doing an awful lot in games and, on this occasion, he intercepted from the little French back, Jean Gachassin, and streaked the length of the field. He didn't have the confidence to go all the way on his own and sort of hesitated to pass to Haydn Morgan for what seemed agonisingly like minutes. Full-back Claude Lacaze, between the two of them, was looking at Haydn wondering whether he was going to have it or was Stuart going to continue his run, until in the end Stuart ran out of ground, crashed over and scored what was a brilliant try.'

Wales won the 1966 championship, though the omission of John Dawes had not helped the development of the fluent style that would characterise the team in later years. 'If anyone is starting a fund to get John back in the side, the first £1 comes from me,' David Watkins said at the time. 'The next £50 comes from the fifty wingers in Wales.' Watkins himself was suffering from the whims of the selectors, returning home after captaining the British Lions to lose his place. His replacement had potential, however: it was a youthful Barry John who played in the defeat by Australia in December 1966 and kept his place to start Wales's Five Nations campaign in 1967. Scotland, inspired by the performance of their captain and back-row forward Pringle Fisher, had already beaten France, and now they were too strong for the Welsh. David Watkins was recalled to lead Wales against Ireland, and their three-nil defeat led to more changes for the game against France, including the selection of a new young scrum-half, Gareth Edwards. Watkins' account of their first encounter illustrates the difficulties international rugby players still had in those days preparing properly for a big match. 'I went across to Cardiff to meet this young man and we decided to have a run out at the Arms Park. When we got there, they wouldn't allow us to have a ball to practise with because they did not want us to go on the pitch. The groundsman helped out, though, and tied up two jerseys with a bandage so we could pass that between ourselves for an hour and a half.'

The Welsh played well, but still ran out losers again in Paris, and now England were due in Cardiff on the back of victories over Ireland and Scotland, winger Colin McFadyean scoring in both games. Welsh heroism came from an unlikely source. 'They named Keith Jarrett as the full-back,' David Watkins explains. 'He had played there at the request of the selectors for Newport the previous Saturday when I was captain. He was so bad that for the second-half we shoved him back into the centre. But he was then drafted into the Welsh team for his first cap, and I thought, "My God, what's going to happen against England?"'

The answer was that the eighteen-year-old Jarrett, who had only left Monmouth School earlier that year, equalled Jack Bancroft's record of nineteen points in a Welsh international, that had stood since the first year of the Five Nations. He also became only the second Welsh full-back ever to score a try, following Vivian Jenkins in 1934. On top of this, 34 points against England was a record for the Welsh team and Jarrett had reserved a place in rugby history. Understandably, that night was just as noteworthy. 'The dinner was called to a halt at about half past eleven,' continues David Watkins, 'and of course there was no stopping over in those days – we all had to make our own way home, regardless of where we lived. At midnight Jarrett was seen in his cap wandering in St Mary's Street in Cardiff. A driver of a single-decker bus pulled up alongside him, wound the window down and said, "Keith Jarrett – nineteen points against England this afternoon, what a performance! What are you doing walking the streets of Cardiff at this time?" Jarrett replied, "Well, to tell you the truth, I haven't a lift home." "Get in," the driver said. "I'll take you – where do you live?" Jarrett tentatively suggested,

"Newport," and the driver told him he'd have to clear it with the inspector at the depot. When he tried to explain to his boss that he wanted to take the bus to Newport, the inspector would have none of it – the bus had to remain in the depot after midnight and that was it, full stop. "But guv," said the driver, "the guy in the bus is Keith Jarrett who helped us to beat the old enemy at the Arms Park this afternoon." "Put that bus away!" the inspector immediately responded. "Get a double-decker – he might want a smoke!"'

On the same day as Jarrett's golden debut, France secured the championship title by beating Ireland. Their star that season had been fly-half Guy Camberabero, playing in a half-back pairing alongside brother Lilian, and he had scored ten points in his first appearance in the win over England. There was more kicking success against Wales, and a try as well, and eight points in the final-day victory over the Irish took Camberabero's tally for the season to 32. Though Ireland's win over Scotland brought only eight points, the days of the dominant defence seemed to be on their way out. This championship had been packed full of tries – thirty in all.

At the end of the 1967 championship, though, rugby league made David Watkins, arguably the most gifted player of the decade, an offer he could not refuse. 'Salford offered £8,000, then £10,000 and then they went up to £16,000. It was a huge sum of money – you could buy four houses for that in those days. I thought that at twenty-five years of age, with twenty-one caps for Wales and having been captain of Wales and the Lions, I had done it all. This was the opportunity to secure my life, especially as I was getting married.' It was a record fee paid by a rugby league club, but Watkins was also influenced by rugby union's draconian attitudes to all matters financial. 'I remember after victory at Twickenham the year before, we decided to have a few drinks on the way back to celebrate a fine win. The Secretary of the Welsh Union said we had overstepped the mark, and on the Tuesday after we had come home we were all invoiced as individuals for the drinks we had taken above our allowance. There was an accompanying letter saying that if the deficit wasn't paid before the next selectors' meeting then none of us would be chosen to play for Wales.'

Wales had taken 'professional' steps of their own by appointing David Nash as the first coach of the national training squad. The days of turning up to meet their fellow team-mates just before an international were past. Over the next few years, weekend training sessions would become commonplace, and the clubs were asked not to choose their national squad members for more than one match a week. The other nations soon followed.

In 1968 coach Nash started well, earning a draw at Twickenham and a win over Scotland while Ireland, after an initial loss to France, went to Twickenham to face England's new kicking machine, Bob Hiller. The tall Harlequins full-back had shown himself to be an able cricketer in his days at Oxford University, and had now taken over from Roger Hosen, whose 38 points the previous season had been an English championship record. Ireland were in front by nine points to six when, after a controversial incident, Hiller was presented with a chance to square the game. 'The ball was thrown into touch,' explains Irish forward Mick Doyle – 'or should I say it left our scrum-half Brendan Sherry's hand? He claimed that he was trying to pass to somebody else, but the referee received that explanation with the usual disdain and awarded the penalty. To everybody's chagrin, Bob Hiller kicked it. That evening, Mike Gibson and myself were sitting in our hotel room listening to the BBC News and the announcer said, "This afternoon, Ireland drew with England." Both our boots hit the radio together – because England had just managed to draw with Ireland!'

Hiller scored two more penalty-goals in England's defeat by France, and his boot contributed to victory against Scotland. Despite an increase in attacking broken play, the value of kicking at goal was as great as at any other time in the championship's history. 'Although now the goal-kicker helps amass loads of points and is often the one who wins the game,' says Hiller, 'in those days, if they scored a couple of three-point tries and you scored three penalties you won the game.' Refereeing tended to be more forgiving, so fewer penalties were conceded, and the kicker had less margin for error. 'Those kicks at goal were vital but you didn't actually get many,' confirms Hiller. 'If there were six in a game that was a lot.' Hiller employed the most popular kicking technique up to that time, the 'head-on' kick or 'toe-punt'. 'The late 1960s was when round-the-corner kicking took off,' he explains – 'until then, it had been virtually all straight-on kicking. I had my style and I couldn't change it, really, and the advantage of the straight-on method is that you are not affected by which side of the pitch you are kicking from. The disadvantage is that you've got to be a bigger bloke with much more strength of leg, because you don't get quite such a long swing at it. That's why so many kickers in the early days were forwards.'

After the disappointment of Hiller's late equalising kick, Ireland bounced back to beat Scotland at home, with winger Alan Duggan scoring twice. The game was the great Scotland prop David Rollo's final championship appearance, but his opponent Syd Millar remembers the day for an interesting exchange between the two other props, Sandy Carmichael of Scotland and Phil O'Callaghan of Ireland, 'a character who could get a bit over-excited,' recalls Millar. 'I explained to him that what he needed to do was put some physical pressure on Carmichael. The referee soon blew his whistle and said, "Penalty, Scotland." O'Callaghan looked at him and enquired, "What's that for?" The referee said, "You're boring him, O'Callaghan, you're boring him," and Phil hit back, "You're not so bloody entertaining yourself, man!"'

The referee featured strongly in Ireland's next game against Wales in Dublin. Gareth Edwards' drop-goal attempt was judged by Mike Titcomb to have gone over the posts – but the majority of those present thought otherwise, and play had to be suspended for five minutes after spectators ran onto the field in protest. 'I could have sworn it went over,' says Mick Doyle, 'but Tommy Kiernan was playing at full-back, and when he got the ball and approached the twenty-five to drop it out, I thought, "What's he done that for? He should be kicking off!" Sure enough, the referee came back to the half-way line and the controversy started.'

No sooner had the irate spectators been cleared than there was another contentious drop-goal, this time from Ireland's Mike Gibson – Wales's John Taylor getting his hands on the ball as it was on its way over to create an 'in-off', and therefore no goal. 'The referee never saw or heard it,' says Mick Doyle – 'nobody else was near enough to know. But the crowd continued to boo Mike Titcomb for his earlier error, so a couple of us went over to the touch-line to say, "For Christ's sake, cool it down – we're not going mad about it, why are you?" They were baying for blood and the referee was shaking in his boots, worrying about his marriage prospects and everything else! I think he played eight minutes of injury time to make sure that play finished where he could easily get off the pitch!'

Ireland eventually won as the match finished with more controversy, for during this extra time Doyle himself managed to score. 'We had a move called Africa – scrum-half Roger Young put in, we swung to the left on the call and went all the way round so that Ken Goodall stood up and blocked the Welsh back row. Willie John McBride pushed the ball out to me, I picked it up, beat a couple of guys and scored on the line and I have the photographs to prove it. The referee took plenty of time but decided to "give it or I'm going to be killed here." He blew his whistle in the corner that was the nearest to the Lansdowne Pavilion and a police escort!' jokes Doyle.

Ireland took second place in the table, their best performance since 1959 – the year when France had won the title outright for the first time. Nine years on, could the work begun by Lucien Miâs and continued by Michel Crauste give Christian Carrère's transitional side a first Grand Slam in 1968? The season started well for France with three wins in which they scored five tries and conceded only one. But they went to Cardiff for the decider as the underdogs, with experienced players like Benoit Dauga left out of the team. 'But we knew luck was on our side,' says Jo Maso, their creative genius who played alongside Claude Dourthe in the centre. 'In the days before the match, it rained and the pitch turned into a mud bath. The famous Welsh back division would not be effective, and the match turned into a contest between the forwards.' Wales went into a 9–3 lead, but then Guy Camberabero kicked with deadly accuracy in difficult conditions and his brother Lilian crossed for a try, as did their captain, Christian Carrère.

When the final whistle sounded, and after 58 years of trying, France had eventually become Grand Slam winners. 'The team had been assembled in two parts,' explains the proud Carrère: 'a side for the first two games made up of essentially the old, established players, and then many other players for the final two matches. The Arms Park was a ground only for forwards – the mud was everywhere – and we had a very good pack. There was of course Walter Spanghero, plus Elie Cester and Alain Plantefol at lock, and Jean-Claude Noble, Michel Yachvili and Michel Lasserre in the front row. And there was a truly great player who played only four or five games for France, Michel Greffe, a number-eight, a very technical player and a great warrior.' The French won the title by playing a mix of fluent and pragmatic rugby, balancing the cautious and progressive. Certainly in the Camberabero brothers France had a huge asset – 'the best of all time in France,' says Carrère. 'If the ground was dry, they were good, but if the weather was bad like in Cardiff they were good too – they could adapt to the situation. To beat all the British teams was legendary for France.'

As the 1960s, a decade that had transformed the style of the game, drew to a close, a Welsh/French power base was emerging in the Five Nations. But by 1969 the Camberabero brothers had decided to end their international careers, new players like the cerebral Pierre

Villepreux appeared, and France were starting from scratch. History was made in the championship when Scotland began the season by visiting Paris, with the first replacement brought on to cover for an injured player, when Scotland's Ian McCrae came on for scrum-half Gordon Connell, and later had a hand in the only and winning try. McCrae dispossessed the French scrum-half and the ball found its way to back-row forward Jim Telfer, who had to beat Pierre Villepreux to score – 'I didn't try to side-step him,' says Telfer: 'I just ran at him and I got in the corner. I only remember it because I've seen it on video recently – the memories are in black and white like the pictures!' Scotland held on for the rest of the match to record their third victory in four visits to Paris. 'At the dinner,' says Telfer, 'one of the speakers said that Scotland didn't need to fly home the next day, as we could walk across the Channel!'

It would be 26 years before Scotland would win again in France's capital, long after the French had left their ageing home at the Stade Colombes, the old Olympic stadium where Telfer remembers water was dripping down from the ceiling as his side walked under the stand out onto the pitch. 'At the time, it felt like just another game against the French,' adds the modest Telfer, 'but today it stands out because of the historical aspect. Thankfully Gavin Hastings' try in 1995 now supersedes mine.' The Scots failed to capitalise on their French success and returned home to lose to a Welsh side featuring two new caps setting out on illustrious international careers, full-back JPR Williams and number-eight Mervyn Davies.

Meanwhile, the French were looking a pale imitation of their Grand Slam team and had lost again, first to the Irish and then to England. Ireland, however, were gathering momentum and, after scoring four tries and not conceding a single point in another win against Scotland at Murrayfield, went to Cardiff for the Grand Slam. In a fiery and forward-dominated game, during which captain Brian Price was lucky not to be the first Welsh international to be sent off when he punched Noel Murphy to the floor, Price's team were easy winners.

The Welsh would now have to beat France in Paris and then England, who had previously defeated Scotland, for the Grand Slam. At the Stade Colombes, Wales met a French side desperate to avoid a whitewash of defeats after their great triumph, and although they led by eight points to nil, France had the grit to pull the game back to finish all square, extinguishing the Welsh Grand Slam dream. Towards full-time, Wales made their first use of the new replacement rule to bring on the young Llanelli back, Phil Bennett, to make his debut.

In time Bennett would become the latest in a long line of greats to play at fly-half for Wales. His impish cheek and dancer's feet would frequently throw the opposition out of step, but it was an overawed youngster who entered the side. 'I was coming in with the great hard men of Welsh rugby,' says Bennett – 'forwards such as Brian Price, Denzil Williams, Norman Gale and Brian Thomas. As a replacement, I walked out in my tracksuit behind the teams and I looked at the French players and thought, "Oh, my Godfathers, are they gangsters or rugby players?" I thanked God I wasn't playing against that lot. But with about four minutes to go, Gerald Davies went down in absolute agony and was brought off holding his arm and it was clear he wouldn't go back on. I started to take off my tracksuit but I couldn't get the zip to the bottoms unfastened – my togs had tied and I was in a panic! Thankfully big Norman Gale was sitting next to me. He was seventeen stone, hard as nails and he grabbed each leg of the tracksuit, gave it a rip and pulled it in two pieces. My initial reaction – I was half-shaken that he'd ruined my Welsh tracksuit!'

When Bennett ran on to take over at centre, he says, 'I realised how small I must have seemed – I was about ten stone ten in those days, pale as a ghost, white legs, brand new shorts. Barry John took one look at me and didn't pass the ball for all the four minutes left in the game. But that time went in a flash and, on the final whistle, these giant Frenchmen shook my hand. I felt that I hadn't done anything yet but, at the dinner in the evening, I drank enough red wine to fill the valleys alongside these great old stalwarts. They made me feel at home, and I couldn't wait to play a full game and to earn the honour of winning another Welsh cap.'

The Grand Slam had gone but the Triple Crown was still available, though Bennett had to wait his turn and sit out Wales's final match at home to England. Cardiff Arms Park was being reconstructed, and at a building site masquerading as a rugby ground, the pitch hard and strewn with straw, Cardiff winger Maurice Richards scored four tries in a crushing win. 'You think of a valley boy who has one ambition which he never thinks will ever happen,' says Richards: 'he manages to get into the Welsh team and wear the jersey. Then those four tries – there's nothing you could replace it with, other than perhaps six tries. With these memories, if you asked, "Would you like a million pounds or that?" – no contest really!'

Nobody could say now that Wales were failing to make use of their talented backs. 'I think that performance against England was confirmation of the type of game that we wanted to play,' confirms John Dawes. The coaching system was firmly in place, and in years to come he would contribute off the field with his tactical expertise. There was a growing confidence in Welsh rugby which would ripen as the 1960s turned into the 1970s.

An unsuccessful tour of New Zealand and Australia followed, however, which exposed Wales's lack of forward power to match the brilliant running game of their backs. Afterwards, Maurice Richards departed for rugby league, but though his decision was yet another shock to Welsh rugby, this was a time when such blows could be better absorbed. England had lost some top-class fly-half playmakers to professionalism – Martin Regan from the 1950s, and Bev Risman and Tom Brophy of the 1960s, had gone to league, and the strain was beginning to tell on English resources. In Wales, however, John Bevan emerged to soften the loss of an outstanding winger like Richards. 'It's too harsh to say that we didn't miss the defectors,' says John Dawes, 'but it was minimised by the arrival on the scene of equally good players. For example, if Terry Price had not gone north, then I don't think we would have seen JPR Williams on the international scene for a few years more. Terry could do everything that JPR could – and perhaps a little bit more.' And that is saying something!

Throughout the 1960s a more open and flowing game had evolved, catalysed by the changes to the laws encouraging the gifted player to express himself on the field. But the major liberating factor was still to come. At the end of the 1960s, explains Tom Kiernan, then the Irish captain, who finished the century as a leading Five Nations administrator, the single most important innovation was the adoption of the Australian rule allowing direct kicking to touch only from inside a team's 25. 'Until then, the type of rugby you played depended on your team,' says Kiernan. 'But after the introduction of the Australian dispensation, rugby opened up and, quite apart from the practical side, I think the attitude of the players became more positive. When I say players, I mean right down to the grass roots – people playing rugby were no longer prepared to stand on a touch-line for an hour and a half and get just one pass. The ordinary player was running and challenging more with the ball. The Lions reflected this in 1971 and especially in 1974. And you had the emergence in 1969 of the great Welsh team, which went on to play superb rugby for another decade.'

PART THREE
1970–1979

In the 1970s Wales and France would rule the roost. Wales, above all, were entering a golden age, illuminating the period with their dazzling play and producing one of the greatest teams ever to grace a rugby field. Between 1971 and 1979 the Welsh won three Grand Slams and five Triple Crowns – in only two years did they not at least share the title. France repeated their success of the end of the 1960s by winning a second Grand Slam in 1977 and, though Ireland won the championship in 1974, otherwise they, along with England and Scotland, had to content themselves with a supporting role.

This was a romantic spell for the sport, when the circumstances were perfect for the blossoming of the Five Nations. The simplicity of the tournament's concept of pitting local rivals against each other at the same time of year, its ever-growing historical significance and its position as the annual highlight of the rugby calendar made for one of the great sporting experiences. The players knew that, apart from the odd British Lions tour or rare test match against New Zealand, Australia or the increasingly politically isolated South Africa, the Five Nations was the pinnacle of their career. They were taking part for the love of the game, expecting no financial reward, and whereas the desire to win was as strong as always, the mortgage did not depend on the performance on the pitch. Coaches and tacticians had arrived and were making an impact, but their influence was limited by the time their charges could give to the sport. In 1972, the number of points awarded for scoring a try was increased to four, placing the emphasis more on skills than on power. It was all less scientific and less muscle-bound than its modern counterpart, a game for all sizes – not a better game, but undoubtedly different.

1970 – France and Wales share championship

Having denied Wales the Grand Slam in 1969, France then set about winning it themselves at the start of the new decade, and early victories over Scotland and Ireland sent them to the top of the championship table. Wales would have to play catch-up, as their opening match soon underlined. Scotland raced into a first-half lead, and for once the fly-half in the spotlight was not Barry John of Wales but a Scot, Ian Robertson, later to become the rugby correspondent for BBC Radio. Even the Arms Park had an unexpected atmosphere, remembers Robertson, the old grandstand having been knocked down while the ground was being rebuilt: 'We had to change in a hut outside on the back pitch – it was all very junior club.' Scotland took the advantage playing with the wind – Robertson dropping a goal and scoring a try: 'It was my half-back partner at Watsonians, Graham Young, winning his only cap that day, who linked for the try down the blindside after JPR Williams had missed touch. It was rare that JPR made a mistake, but the wind was swirling and it was just impossible.'

Just before half-time, however, Wales broke and Laurie Daniel on the wing – like Young, winning his only cap – finished off a length-of-the-field move to score. Then Daniel converted his own try from the touch-line. In the second half Robertson's luck changed as he had a kick charged down by John Dawes to lead to another score and Wales, with Barry John and Gareth Edwards now established at half-back, came back to win comfortably in the end, with four tries in all. 'When Barry and Gareth first came together,' says Ian Robertson, 'they had a pretty poor run – had they been English they would have been dropped and never heard of again. Nineteen-seventy was the year they arrived.' With a growing greatness in the back division, Welsh rugby was building a strong power base.

England started their season with victory over Ireland at Twickenham. On the wing the Irish had brought back Tony O'Reilly, fifteen years after his debut and following a seven-year absence from international rugby. O'Reilly had actually written a piece for the match programme, but received the call because of a late training injury to Bill Brown. By now a highly successful businessman, he arrived in style: in a Rolls Royce. In the game, however, he barely touched the ball, and one Twickenham wag was heard to shout, 'They might as well have played the bloody chauffeur!'

On the same ground two weeks later, England faced Wales with new confidence and made a storming start, rocking them with two tries, including one superb team effort finished off by back David Duckham. Despite his large frame, the Coventry man was always full of grace and poise. His blond hair flying, he could leave defenders behind with his characteristic swivel of the hips. Duckham's try had helped to establish a 13–3 half-time lead. When mid-way through the second half Welsh captain Gareth Edwards had to be taken off injured, his team's hopes seemed to be in tatters. Enter Edwards' replacement from Maesteg, Raymond 'Chico' Hopkins, to become a one-cap wonder.

In the little time available, Hopkins made an indelible impact on the Five Nations. 'The other day I was watching the video of the game,' he recalls, 'and I looked at the clock: I came on at about ten past four, and the game was over at twenty-five to five. I'd already been subbing eighteen times for Wales – me and Phil Bennett were used to sitting in the stand. Gareth was worse than Barry John, though – he would never leave the field. On the 1969 Welsh tour, he was strapped from his knee to the top of his thigh with a hamstring problem – but would he come off? But that day at Twickenham, I remember saying to Phil I had a funny feeling I was going on. I wasn't particularly nervous – a feeling of real calm.'

Wales desperately needed some inspiration, and when Hopkins sprang to his feet he received his orders. 'The selectors said, "Look, we've got to get the ball down in their half. Bang it up and chase it!" I was out of condition, a stone overweight because I hadn't played for eight months due to injury and, believe me, it was nerve-wracking when I got out there. But it was as if I was playing in a dream and everything was going right. The first time that I had the ball, funnily enough it was a good kick, up high it went on the half-way line. We caught them in possession, steamrollered them and scored in the corner – like it was meant to be.'

Hopkins was sparking a revival which Welsh supporters had feared impossible only minutes earlier. The turnaround was nearly complete when a Welsh line-out did not go according to plan. 'The ball should have been thrown to the front two,' says Hopkins. 'In those days you didn't have lifting – Christ, you could lift a dwarf up now and he'd win the ball! – but this was a bad throw and it went over the second-row's head. The ball was knocked at an angle, Dai Morris missed it by inches and it dropped into my hands. I just had to duck and dive over.' The man himself had scored a try.

JPR Williams converted, Barry John dropped a goal and, dramatically, Wales had won.

Subsequently a fit Gareth Edwards returned to occupy the scrum-half position for the best part of a decade. Hopkins left to go north for rugby league, and never played for Wales again. But the perennial benchman deserved his day of glory: 'I played a lot of rugby before and after, but I have never seen established players coming off the field crying like they were at Twickenham that day. I couldn't believe it had happened, and I was so exhausted. That night, my uncle was staying in the team hotel – at about nine o'clock he was coming down in the lift as I was getting in to go up. "Where are you going, boy?" he said. I replied, "To bed!"'

Ireland, meanwhile, had been boosted by a victory over Scotland. Now, after their narrow escape, Wales crossed the Irish Sea in search of the Triple Crown. The match marked the final appearances of three Irish stars – back-row forwards Ken Goodall and Ronnie Lamont, and the great prop Syd Millar. First capped in 1958, Millar was approaching his 36th birthday but felt ready for one last go at Wales, especially after their controversial victory the year before when Ireland had been going for the Grand Slam. 'I had the opportunity to bring my two young sons to Lansdowne Road and I thought, "Well, if I never play in another game, then so be it." There was a score to settle, certainly an intention to make the game very physical and very hard. I don't think Wales were looking forward to it.'

Ireland's game plan was to get at the Welsh half-backs. 'We worried about them moving the ball,' explains Millar, 'so Ronnie Lamont and Fergus Slattery were key. Lamont broke through on Gareth and Slattery's job was to run at Barry all day. Slattery was as quick in the last minute as he was in the first – in fact, Edwards and John gave so many bad balls that if they had been lesser players I'm sure their careers would have been terminated there and then.'

Wales were gradually worn down, and their Triple Crown hopes torn to shreds. It just needed the finale that the delirious Dublin crowd demanded. Appropriate, then, that Ken Goodall should end his distinguished, if short, Five Nations career by scoring his team's second and clinching try. Collecting a Barry John kick near the half-way line, Goodall kicked the ball over a defender's head and caught it, to be confronted by JPR Williams. 'As it had worked once,' explains Goodall, 'I thought it would work twice, so I did the same again. He had to turn to chase and I beat him to the touchdown. We hadn't just won, we had hammered them.' It was the first time his mother-in-law had come to see him play, and before the match she had asked him to score a try for her. 'When I did,' says Goodall, 'she bent the ear of the people beside her. It is every bloke's dream to impress the mother-in-law like that!'

After their Irish mauling, Wales made seven changes to their team and recovered to beat the French in Cardiff in what was their only defeat that season. Scotland recorded their sole win by beating England at Murrayfield, despite a spectacular race-away try from English three-quarter John Spencer. The further try Spencer scored in the final match of the season in Paris was scant consolation to set against the six France ran in. The English full-back, remembers the Northampton back-row man, Bob Taylor, who was captaining England for the one and only time, 'was like a traffic policeman on patrol as they went past him.' The French had made sure of a share in the first championship of the 1970s by sending England to their heaviest-ever defeat. Wales joined them at the top of the table – an outcome that would become familiar during the decade.

1971 – Wales's GRAND SLAM

Only one of the Five Nations can claim that rugby union is its national sport, and that country is Wales. In 1971 it was apparent that the Welsh team was blessed with an almost embarrassing array of talent. Surely one of the richest nuggets ever mined in the valleys was at fly-half, where Barry John had matured into one of the greatest-ever tacticians. His ability to control games with an almost spiritual quality was central to Wales's success, while his rapier-like runs and bludgeoning kicks had made him into the supreme rugby player of his time.

John feels that this was his finest year in a Welsh jersey. 'It was a cracking side, and of course a few months later we formed the backbone of the great Lions squad which went to New Zealand. During the last twenty-eight years, I have been asked so many times why it all came together for Wales then. But my response is, "Why look for reasons? Why not accept that the cards were dealt?" Having said that, not enough praise is given to our coach, Clive Rowlands. He must have seen that he had these boys in his side, but even though we were kids he decided to leave us alone. When you've so much raw natural talent, backs like JPR Williams, Gerald Davies, John Dawes,

Arthur Lewis, John Bevan and Gareth Edwards, it must have been tempting for Clive to tell us what to do, but I can never remember him doing that. As fly-half I was left to conduct the orchestra, and that's the way I liked it.'

Wales certainly had England dancing to their tune on the opening day of the championship. It was the English RFU's centenary year, but the Welsh were also celebrating their first Five Nations game at the revamped Arms Park. The National Stadium, adjacent to the Cardiff club ground, had evolved into a rugby arena to match all others, and perhaps surpassing them in atmosphere. Wales scored three tries in a comfortable win, two of them by Gerald Davies. Next it was Scotland, who had lost in Paris but would as always be passionately supported at Murrayfield. Scotland captain Peter Brown told his team to excite the crowd, to attack Wales from the first whistle and never let up. Their aim was to keep the ball away from the talented Welsh backs for as long as possible, and at half-time, Wales leading by only eight points to six, the plan seemed to be working.

The crowd were now at fever pitch expecting a classic second half, and it came. Scotland went into the lead, but then a brilliant tackle by the Scottish winger Billy Steele just failed to prevent Barry John scoring Wales's third try. 'The only way he could save the score was to challenge me with such force that I would drop the ball,' recalls John. 'I just managed to hang on, but in doing so I whiplashed my neck and smacked my head on the ground. Then one excited idiot from Wales came out of the crowd, picked me up and shook me like a rag doll – it was not what I needed!'

Scotland, however, refused to lie down and, after a determined late try from centre Chris Rea, they were well placed. But dramatically, Peter Brown hit the post with his conversion kick and Wales went inside Scotland's half from the re-start. In the gathering gloom and mounting tension, the noise of the crowd drowned out Scotland's calls at a line-out. Directly from the mistake and Delme Thomas's unchallenged palm-down Wales produced another outstanding move for Gerald Davies to slip through to score in the corner. Now John Taylor, the fuzzy-haired flanker from London Welsh, and one of the most natural goal-kickers in the world, was faced with the kick to win the game. It was a moment of high tension, the likes of which he nowadays describes in his role as ITV's rugby commentator. Back in 1971 Taylor had to keep his nerve. The Scottish second-row forward Gordon Brown was still fuming at the 'total cock-up' of the line-out, and for a moment he dallied with the idea of running out early to try and put Taylor off. 'But, despite all the anger that was going through my brain, I thought, "That's not rugby."' So, Brown stood and watched Taylor stroke the ball through the posts. 'To this day,' he reflects, 'I've charged down that kick so often.' With a casual sweet clip of his boot, Taylor had ended Scotland's premature celebrations and kept Wales on course for the Grand Slam.

By the time Wales met Ireland in Cardiff for the Triple Crown, the Irish had amassed a mixed bag of results – a draw against France, a loss to England and a victory over Scotland, the Melrose hooker Frank Laidlaw's final championship game. Although Ireland had prevented a Wales Grand Slam the previous year, in 1971 they could not counter the Welsh blitz of fourteen points in almost as many minutes which secured the win. There were two more tries for Gerald Davies, who was having a magnificent season, and two for the equally impressive Gareth Edwards. The French were also unbeaten, having drawn for the second time that year, on this occasion with England: once again, Wales's Grand Slam decider would be against France.

Meanwhile, Scotland tried to gain their first victory of the championship in their final match at Twickenham. England had not lost to Scotland at home for 33 long years. With the English in front towards the end of the game by fifteen points to eight this record did not look set to change. It was then that Scotland received their rallying call from Peter Brown. Gordon Brown sets the scene: 'Standing behind the goal-posts, Peter was screaming at every single one of us, saying that we had ten minutes to put it straight. He was looking at a team full of Ayrshiremen, five mates from his club Gala, plus his brother – if he couldn't get a response out of us, he was never going to get a response out of any team! We went up the park, there was a ferocious ruck, the boots were flying, and the ball came back to scrum-half Duncy Patterson, who scored a try.' Scotland now needed just a converted try to win the game. From another ruck, with England reeling amidst the mayhem, the ball came to Peter Brown himself who 'in his eccentric way,' as his brother puts it, 'threw an overhead torpedo pass to Chris Rea.' Rea scored the try, which left Peter Brown the conversion for the match.

The kick, however, was from an awkward angle and Gordon could hardly bear to watch. 'You see, our father was an international footballer and we were soccer fanatics, and when he was a wee boy my brother dreamt that one day he would kick a penalty in the last minute to win the game against England at Wembley! As Peter plonked the ball down, turned his back and walked away, he thought,

"Right scenario, wrong game, wrong venue." On the half-way line I was thinking, "Come on, Peter, none of your messing about and bloody circus act," but he did what he normally did – dug his heel in the ground, blew his nose all over the place, had a quick look at the posts, shuffled up to the ball and hit it. The thing blew like a ballistic miracle, tumbling and falling but landing between the posts. We all erupted and I thought, "My brother has just done this, my hero!" so I started sprinting towards him with arms outstretched shouting, "I love ya! I love ya!" He looked in horror and waved his arm yelling, "No, no, we've still got a minute to play!"' Scotland hung on, and the Brown brothers had been part of the team that ended the horrific Twickenham sequence.

At the other end of the table, could France deny Wales in Paris for the second time in three years? 'It was probably the greatest game I've ever been involved in,' declares Barry John. 'Both sides were outrageous in attack and defence, and from hooker to full-back all the players seemed to produce their best.' Wales scored two tries, one from Gareth Edwards following JPR Williams' interception and almost length-of-the-field charge, and the other from John. Injury made the match a memorable experience for him once again – this time the result of tangling with the giant Frenchman Benoit Dauga. 'I grabbed him by the throat but he shrugged me off and I went flying. I was on my back and then he landed on top of me and the lights went out. His elbow went right into my nose. But there's a joy in being ignorant sometimes, and I can prove it. My understanding of the French language was virtually nil, and as they looked at me on the touch-line the French doctor said something and I replied, "Oui, oui." I thought he'd said, "You've bloody well had it, mate," so I signalled to Phil Bennett in the stand to come down. But what the doctor really said was, "Shall I put your nose back now?" It was too late. I remember *crick – crick – crick*. I shouted out in pain, there was blood everywhere, and my tear ducts were broken so I couldn't stop crying. I was a terrible sight.' But John had helped to take Wales to their first Grand Slam since 1952, and what nobody knew was that the good times had only just begun.

1972 – Wales's championship

The public adoration that Barry John was receiving was a sign of changing times. Rugby players were assuming a much higher profile.

The big names had always been held in great esteem within the rugby community, but the increase in television coverage and the wider awareness of their skills were fanning the flames of publicity. John was considering getting out of the fire. 'People forget that in the early seventies I had to go to work on a Monday. There were dinners and functions, from the local British Legion to Downing Street, and you still had to be fit enough to play top class rugby and find time for your family. Nowadays I would be a professional rugby player. Of course, it was going to be difficult to walk away from the game, but something had to give, and I said before the first game against England in 1972 that unless things cooled I would seriously consider giving the game up. I couldn't sleep, and my body couldn't take it. I was living three different lives. There was no hope.'

Wales's opening game at Twickenham only confirmed Barry John's sense of falling between two stools. The men in red were victorious – it was now twelve years since England had won on their home ground against them. Down in the tunnel, however, as he left the field, John had an unusual surprise. In the dark he was grabbed by Eamonn Andrews, told, 'This is Your Life,' and whisked away for the television programme. But at the end of this remarkable experience, all his family and friends having come up to London for it, and wanting to stay with them, John had to go to the international rugby dinner.

The pressure of that Five Nations season proved too much. 'I felt totally alienated,' says John. 'Even in a crowded room, there would be a yard between myself and others. People kept putting me on a pedestal and I couldn't do any wrong. You felt like doing something daft and saying, "Look – I do these things!" It finally came to a head when I went to open an extension to a bank in North Wales, and a young girl bank worker curtsied. Everybody thought it was hilarious, but I said, that was it, I had to get out. I had a long chat with my wife and my father and I signed with the *Sunday Mirror* to give them the story. Even then the sports editor, who was a rugby fanatic, told me that, despite the fact he was sitting on a scoop, he wouldn't date the story because he wanted me to carry on playing. But I had made my decision, and I filled in the date.'

That date was to be the end of the season, when John would terminate one of the great half-back partnerships of all time. The story goes that, in his first training session with Gareth Edwards, the scrum-half asked John how he wanted the pass. 'You just throw it and I'll catch it,' came the reply. By the time of John's retirement the relationship was almost telepathic. But if anybody thought Edwards would be lost without his partner they were going to be badly mistaken, for he embarked on an unbroken run of 53 caps for his country. His solo effort against Scotland at the Arms Park in that 1972 season – arguably his best try ever – was the perfect example of his dynamic game.

Wales had had a difficult first half against a spirited Scottish side who had already beaten the French at Murrayfield, where fly-half Colin Telfer had scored the first four-point try in a Five Nations match, and went into the interval knowing they had to raise their game. The second half started well with Edwards himself scoring a try from close range that roused the crowd. Then Mervyn Davies won the ball at a line-out deep inside Wales's own half. 'There was a buzz now,' recalls Edwards, 'and the adrenalin was flowing, so I thought I'd have a crack on the blind-side to test them.' At first, assuming that flanker Dai Morris, "the Shadow", would, as always, be in support, Edwards was thinking of just 'a five-yard dart.' He passed the Scottish forward Rodger Arneil and was away.

'What happened over the next few seconds seemed to unfold in slow motion. I was looking all around and, for the first time ever, Dai wasn't on my shoulder. The crowd started to respond and I looked downfield to see that their full-back, Arthur Brown, was the only man in front of me. I wasn't thinking about scoring but I knew if I kicked ahead it would at least keep the move going. When I chipped over him Arthur could have taken me out, but he didn't, and that speaks volumes for him. Then I just kicked it along the floor through the mud and the crowd were going berserk, it was like a tidal wave pushing me along.' The Scottish centre Jim Renwick was coming in from Edwards' left, but the ball was curving towards the corner flag – 'contrary to what some people have since said, it wasn't me being crafty and going for the corner,' explains Edwards: 'I actually felt, "Oh, God alive, it's going to go dead – all that distance and nobody is going to remember it!" But I got down in the mud, and my momentum threw me there.'

Edwards, the complete rugby athlete, had scored a try to rank alongside the best of all time. Winded by his fall and covered in dirt from head to toe, he was congratulated by his team-mates. 'The first thing I remember amidst the tremendous noise is Gerald Davies' grin as he stood over me. I didn't realise what I looked like, but I was covered in the red shale of the race track around the Arms Park, and my mother says she thought I was cut wide open.' Edwards walked back to the half-way line, cheered by the supporters, his barrel chest heaving up and down, looking every inch the gladiator. With him in their side, Wales had to end up as winners.

Ireland's dismal record in Paris – no victory for twenty years – was ended in 1972 in their first game, scrum-half John Moloney and prop Ray McLoughlin scoring the tries in what remains to this day the last time the Irish won in the French capital. At lock was the imposing figure of Willie John McBride, who went on two years later to lead the Lions with such distinction. 'I consider winning in Paris to be the toughest of the lot,' he states. 'Away matches against France are always fast and furious, but back in the seventies there were no interfering touch judges or cameras poking into the rucks and mauls and it was really a case of the survival of the bravest. We were the underdogs – aren't Ireland always the underdogs? – and that victory was certainly one of the highlights of my Irish playing career. Con Feighery of Lansdowne was in the second row with me, and after the game I remember saying to him, "You lucky b****** – I've been trying to win in Paris for the last ten years and you come along and do it first time!"' The celebrations started almost straight away, and McBride's recollection of that night is hazy, but he does remember that a couple of the side did not even make it to the after-match banquet!

Ireland's next game brought victory at Twickenham, only their third on that ground since World War II. But, sadly, their championship stopped there. With an upsurge of violence in Ulster there was a fear of what might happen if Five Nations matches were staged in Dublin, and both Wales and Scotland decided not to play in Ireland that year. With two away victories, Ireland had some justification in feeling that a Triple Crown or even the Grand Slam had been denied them. Perhaps Wales's case was stronger, though, as, by the end of the truncated championship, they had secured three wins.

All interest now had to turn to the game between France and England in Paris, the last to be held at the Stade Colombes, before the move to the new Parc des Princes stadium. The old ground had so often been the graveyard of defeat for the home nations, and England would certainly be haunted by memories of the French performance. The day was warm and mild and France shone, scoring six tries, just as they had done two years earlier. The elegant running full-back Pierre Villepreux, in his final game for his country, had a hand in all six. Beforehand he and his fellow backs, including Jo Maso, Jean-Pierre Lux and Jean-Louis Bérot, had agreed to counter-attack even from their own goal-line, and on one memorable occasion after England had missed a penalty kick the quartet's tactics paid enormous dividends as they went the length of the field. The try provided a fitting send-off for the stadium.

England had conceded their highest-ever score against France, and followed this by allowing Scotland to record their biggest win against them. Deservedly the English took the wooden spoon, with France, who lost to Wales in their closing game, finishing one place above them. But the season had been ruined by events off the field: political unrest had unfortunately carried off the 1972 championship.

1973 – England, France, Ireland, Scotland and Wales share championship

Politics too often have tended to divide the Irish. Rugby football has worked to widen friendships and unite. Rugby-playing Irishmen are just as nationalistic or unionist, or Protestant or Catholic, as their non-rugby neighbours, but they eschew all sectional labels when it comes to pulling on a rugby jersey. The different strands mesh perfectly and men from the farther reaches of Kerry and from the tip of Co. Antrim can scrum down together in a harmonious unit – which is something that gives us all food for thought.

Sean Diffley, *The Men in Green – the Story of Irish Rugby*

It was against a background of mistrust, intolerance and violence that in 1973 the Five Nations overcame political and religious differences and managed to hold out the hand of peace. The decision by Scotland and Wales not to play in Ireland during 1972 had hurt deeply, and England's decision to play in Dublin in 1973 was heartily welcomed by the Irish rugby authorities.

The English team had already been taken apart by Wales in their opening match in Cardiff, with the beefy winger John Bevan scoring two of his side's five tries, one of which went through ten pairs of hands – a classic. To England captain John Pullin it had seemed a major achievement early on to be three-nil ahead for all of five minutes! Wales followed this convincing win, however, with a narrow defeat at Murrayfield to a Scottish side that had previously lost to France in the first game at their new stadium, the Parc des Princes.

Typical of the architecture of the period, the concrete bowl on the edge of Paris's city centre had made an immediate impact on the championship. The noise crashing down from the seemingly vertical stands was highly intimidating for visiting players – this season, it was becoming clear, the place to be was on your own patch.

England's decision to travel to Dublin at least made it possible for Ireland to have home advantage again. The Chairman of Selectors, Sandy Sanders, made it clear that if any players did not want to go then it would not be held against them. But as the game got closer several, including the side's star back, David Duckham, began to have misgivings. 'I refused to go unless my wife went with me – we agreed that if we were going to get shot to bits then we would both get shot to bits. It sounds naïve now, but at the time the threats to the squad were taken seriously. So, protocol was broken and Jean joined the England party – the wife of a player, it was unheard-of!' Security was tight from the moment the team arrived in Dublin – normal arrivals procedure at the airport bypassed so they could be put straight on a bus. The evening before the game they were not allowed to leave their hotel – but the Irish players were staying there too, and some of them joined in to watch a film together.

The English team was safe, but clearly the preparation was far from ideal. 'It was very unsettling,' confirms John Pullin, 'especially for the younger members. There were police and security men everywhere, and when it got to the match it was perhaps no surprise that we didn't play that well.' The fear of a hidden gunman even infected tactics on the field – 'as hooker, throwing into the line-out,' Pullin admits, 'I didn't hang around, because I didn't want to be too exposed. The best thing was to run around to make a moving target – or, better still, get back into the pack! But what I will always remember is the reception the crowd gave us when we came out onto the pitch. It was one of the biggest cheers I've ever heard.'

It was a spontaneous and emotional reaction from the genuinely appreciative Irish supporters. But after the welcome died down Ireland got on with the serious business of beating England, with winger Tom Grace and centre Dick Milliken scoring the Irish tries. John Pullin, the down-to-earth Bristol hooker with a West Country wit, was left to find appropriate words for his speech at the post-match dinner. 'It was a line off the top of my head which seemed to make the most impact. I said, "We may not have been very good, but at least we turned up."'

Ireland were unable to follow up their victory, however, and lost in

Scotland and Wales. In contrast, England did end their record losing run of seven games in the championship by beating France, and at Twickenham met a Scottish side bidding for the Triple Crown. Scotland's captain, the diminuitive but tough Ian McLauchlan, or 'Mighty Mouse' as he was affectionately known, dismisses as 'rubbish' the legend that he played with a broken leg sustained against the Irish. 'I had broken a bone in my leg three weeks earlier, but I didn't feel the injury during the match. Apparently American footballers play with that kind of thing the next week.' But for once his famously passionate team-talk, and the spirit he had helped to develop within Scottish rugby, were not enough. His side's two tries from Billy Steele were cancelled out as England's centre, Geoff Evans, scored late on, adding to flanker Peter Dixon's earlier finish from a rampaging move. The result meant that, if the championship continued true to form, with no side having lost on their own ground that season, then home victories for France and Ireland in the last two matches would lead to a five-country split of the title for the first time.

The boot of Jean-Pierre Romeu was enough to see off Wales in Paris but, when France went to Ireland, for once his kicking fell apart. It was the last championship game for two great forwards, Irish lock Mick Molloy and the French captain, Walter Spanghéro, who could only watch in despair as his fly-half failed with every attempt at goal, even a late conversion which would have given France a draw and the championship. Romeu looked crestfallen, but he had unwillingly helped to create a piece of history that will now never be repeated: 1973 was the only year the Five Nations finished in a five-way tie.

1974 – Ireland's championship

The 1974 championship was the first under a new fixture system. After years of playing the games in the same sequence and spreading them over many weeks, it was decided that two matches would take place on the same day, with five Saturdays being set aside each season. In the interests of fairness, the games would rotate year by year so that countries would play each other in a different order and on different weekends.

However, when Ireland started with a defeat to France in January there was a feeling of déjà-vu. The Irish had grown used to coming close to glory but finishing with nothing to show for their efforts, and it happened again in Paris when Jean-Louis Bérot's long-range penalty won the game in injury time. Worse still for Ireland, it was Bérot's first kick of the afternoon: having missed five attempts on goal, full-back Jean-Michel Aguirre, when offered the chance by his captain, had said, '*Non, merci.*' Two weeks later, against the Welsh in Dublin, it was Ireland's chance to win a game through a late penalty kick, but that opportunity was squandered and they could only manage a draw. The Irish had reached the mid-way point of the season with no tries and just one point from their two matches.

All this was forgotten at Twickenham, however. In an amazing half-hour spell either side of the interval Ireland scored four tries, with two from centre Mike Gibson. 'Johnny Moloney scored his try,' remembers Gibson, 'after a clearance kick from us had been fielded by the English fly-half, Alan Old. Alan's brother, Chris, played cricket for England and Alan always fancied himself as a cricketer. I can see him now – it was one of those "half-chances" on the boundary: he tried to take the ball in one hand, but all he did was set it up in the air for Moloney who had been chasing. John was quick and had under fifty seconds for the four hundred metres, so there was no catching him.' Then Gibson himself got to work. Surely the most gifted player to ever pull on his country's jersey, the intelligent Gibson had it all – sinewy strength, searing speed and a sleight of hand that time and again exposed his opponents – and on that day against England he reigned supreme. From a line-out on the England line the ball was delivered quickly to Moloney and out to the fly-half, Mick Quinn, who made a half-break and linked with Dick Milliken. Gibson got the ball from Milliken, threw a dummy to England wing Peter Squires and was over in a flash. There was more to come. The Irish full-back Tony Ensor picked up an England kick, ran up to the last defender and put Gibson clear with ten yards to go. With a quarter of the game remaining, in front by twenty-six points to nine, Ireland had already equalled their highest ever score against any international side. Gibson even kicked the conversions to his tries – he could do no wrong.

Ireland's next opponents, Scotland, were having mixed fortunes. They had lost on the opening day in Cardiff when Welsh flanker Terry Cobner scored on his debut what was the only try of the match. At Murrayfield England had been the visitors, and seemingly had control of the game when the rangy Rosslyn Park number-eight Andy Ripley lined up the Scots' full-back Andy Irvine and, consuming the ground with his enormous giraffe-like strides, cut through the tackle and found flanker Tony Neary in support to score. Ripley's high-stepping run was reminiscent of his achievements on the athletics track. He was a fine 400-metre hurdler and even today, in his fifties, Ripley is a highly-regarded sportsman, having recently come close to a place rowing in the Boat Race.

In 1974 Scotland needed to find a quick riposte. It came from the dashing 22-year-old Irvine, in only his second championship season, who ducked in and out to pass the English cover and reach the corner for a try which seemed surely to have won the game for his country. But right at the end the Scot had the agony of watching his opposite number, Peter Rossborough, hit a long drop-goal through the posts to give England the lead by fourteen points to thirteen. Again, it looked like England's match – but there was one last twist. When Alan Old tried to clear the England lines David Duckham let his concentration slip and got caught off-side in front of the kicker.

Three minutes into injury time, Duckham had given Scotland a chance to steal the victory. The kick was from forty yards and wide out on the touch-line. Scotland held its breath, but Irvine was in no doubt. 'I quite liked kicking from that side at Murrayfield – there was a very marginal slope so I was kicking slightly uphill, which is always easier. Those sort of kicks are one-in-four or -five chances, but as I ran up that day I actually thought, "This one is going over."' 'It was all my fault and I felt really ashamed,' reflects David Duckham, 'but it's annoying to think a simple error like that turned the whole game.' What was it like to win the game against England in that fashion? 'The word I would use,' laughs Irvine, 'is: *enjoyable*.' To add to his pleasure, it was the only time his mother, not noted for her interest in rugby, attended one of her son's international games. 'The first thing she asked me was who had won? When I told her it was Scotland, she said that was nice.' Irvine's mother never came to another game but she did, he says, appreciate Bill McLaren's television commentary: 'She would say, "Oh, he's a nice man! – he's so kind to you, Andy!"'

The Irvine clan was happy that day, but in Dublin a month later the full-back's two penalty-goals were not enough to beat Ireland. Mike Gibson remembers Willie John McBride's leadership as massively influential: 'You knew you were going to get an honest day's work from him – he was very strong physically and mentally, and totally committed. This led to enormous respect within our team, but also from the opposition.' After their indifferent start, Ireland now had five points from their four games, but they would be reliant on the other sides playing on the final weekend of the championship to make it an Irish year. Their main rivals, the French, were still in with a chance of the title and went to Murrayfield unbeaten. They had followed up their win in Dublin with two draws – first in Cardiff, when a Jean-Pierre Romeu drop-goal in the last minute saved them, and then against England in Paris, where he scored all his side's twelve points, including a dazzling try after a dribble and break up-field from deep inside his own half.

In Scotland, however, Romeu's skill was not enough and France's championship bid was ended in a pulsating match. With half the job done on Ireland's behalf, England still had to beat Wales at Twickenham – something they had not achieved for fourteen years. But the Welsh were without a key man: JPR Williams was missing, and England's hero of the day, David Duckham, cut inside his replacement, Roger Blyth, to score a crucial try. 'Afterwards JPR was quoted in the press, in his typically modest way,' recalls Duckham, 'saying that if he had been playing then he would have stopped me. Knowing JPR, he probably would!'

There was also controversy, and Wales left Twickenham feeling they had been robbed. After England had had an earlier claim for a pushover try turned down, Wales's winger JJ Williams chipped over the top into space and it was a race between him, Peter Squires and David Duckham to get to the ball. As the ball went over the line all three arrived together. 'The referee was miles away and couldn't allow the try,' says Duckham, 'but I admitted later that JJ might have got there first. At the after-match banquet captain John Pullin, who had a great sense of timing, said, "I suppose you'd all like to know if it was a try or not. Well, I can tell you in all honesty that it certainly was ... a pushover try for us!"'

That win was a glorious but isolated moment of success for Duckham, but it did not prevent England from taking the wooden spoon for the second time in three years. 'British rugby was on a high,' he asserts, 'mainly because Welsh rugby was so strong. The success of the 1971 and 1974 Lions was based on that Welsh team. I've often said that British rugby will only be really strong again when rugby in Wales is strong.' As for England, in Duckham's opinion, the talents of a great pack and some gifted runners, and a tremendous team spirit, were undermined by a lack of self-belief – in turn symptomatic of a perennial problem, an inconsistent selection policy.

But the principal significance of the England win was that, at last, Ireland had taken the championship title outright – for the first time since 1951. One of the many talented players for whom this tangible success was long-awaited was hooker Ken Kennedy, who had made his championship debut back in 1965. Another was Mike Gibson: 'It was just sad,' he reflects, 'that we didn't have the opportunity of experiencing the winning of a championship as a unit. On the afternoon itself I was sitting watching on television – England against Wales was the live game, and the result was a bit of a surprise. Then they went over for highlights of the other match – and Scotland beat France. My wife was in the garden, and I walked outside and said to her, "By the way, we're the champions!"' The problem for Ireland and the other nations was that the Welsh were now about to embark on their most prolific period.

1975 – Wales's championship

Wales's new coach, John Dawes, was determined to win back his country's position as the undisputed number one in Europe. At the start of the 1975 championship the Welsh selectors made a crucial decision which, perhaps more than any other, guaranteed their nation a return to the top spot.

Its origins can be traced back to a September day in 1973, when three men played together for their club side for the first time. Sixteen months later, on a wet January day, the Pontypool front-row of Charlie Faulkner, Bobby Windsor and Graham Price ran out against France. Faulkner was a judo black-belt and, like Windsor, was born in Newport in the tough heartland of industrial Wales. Price, the junior member of the trio, was actually born in Egypt but grew up in Wales attending grammar school and UWIST. Bobby Windsor recalls how the relationship was forged: 'Charlie and I went into the steelworks at fifteen, but Pricey came up through a different channel – he was still at school until he was twenty-seven, I think. I don't know what he was qualified to do! Over the years we got to know each other's play so well, when one of us was in trouble the others knew without saying anything. When the Pontypool front-row played for Wales it was a proud moment for the club and coach Ray Prosser, because he was the one who got us all together, got us working and got us there.'

Windsor had already tasted international rugby, but for Graham Price and Charlie Faulkner the match in Paris was their debut. 'The Welsh team hadn't enjoyed the greatest success over the previous couple of years,' says Price, 'and it was decided to pick six players who'd never played in a full international before. A lot of critics did-n't give us much of a chance but, as a front-row, we'd been doing the job at club level for some time. Now Charlie and I had the chance to prove what we could do along with Bobby. As soon as we got there the scrum tightened up and we provided the graft for the stars to play the game.'

Four tries later, Wales had all but made certain of their win, and it was left to Price to see his country to their biggest victory in the French capital since 1911. 'The play had got very loose with the French attacking towards the end of the match, and it broke down on our twenty-five yard line. Lock Geoff Wheel hacked the ball up-field and I just gave chase, only intending to pressurise the French backs so they couldn't run back at us. The way it developed, I got to the ball before they did and kicked it further on. JJ Williams came across from his left-wing position, and I thought we were going to end up with nothing more than a line-out about five yards from their line because the French full-back Michel Taffary was covering. He went to side-foot the ball into touch, but JJ did a sort of sliding tackle and the ball came off the side of his foot and straight into my hands. All I could do was flop over the line and that is exactly what I did.' Price sighs as he tells the story, almost feeling the exhaustion that hit him at the end of that energy-sapping first international. He had covered virtually the length of the pitch in injury time, and provided the per-fect end for Wales and his club. 'They'll never believe it in Pontypool!' exclaimed the BBC's Nigel Starmer-Smith in his television commen-tary, but the other countries soon had to accept what they were see-ing – the emergence of one of the greatest front-rows of all time.

In Wales's next match England were dismissed as, once again, the forwards provided the perfect platform for the backs to express them-selves. Little had changed for the English, who had already suffered defeats by Ireland and France, but Scotland were more successful: having beaten Ireland, their victory built around an impressive dis-play from the pack, they then pushed France to within one point. Against the Scots the Pontypool front row would have to raise their game to an even higher level if Wales were going to continue their winning run. No less than 104,000 people crammed into Murrayfield to witness the occasion – a world record for a rugby international, and still people were turned away. 'The noise coming from the ter-racing was incredible,' recalls Graham Price, whose other vivid mem-ory is the bruises earned that day. 'It was a hard game, and their props, Sandy Carmichael and Ian McLauchlan, were both British

Lions.' So was Bobby Windsor, who was hardly intimidated by the occasion, as the Scottish and Lions fly-half Ian McGeechan well remembers: 'I was caught at the bottom of a ruck, pinned with my head out, and I could see Bobby approaching from fifteen yards away, and he had the biggest smile on his face. I could do nothing – I just lay there, saw him coming and coming and then his boot went up and came right down over the top of my face. But then it stopped and he put his foot to one side and just ruffled my hair!' Wales flanker Trevor Evans scored the only try, and lock Allan Martin missed a chance to win the game with the conversion. The extent of Scotland's achievement can be measured by the fact that it was one of only two occasions when Faulkner, Windsor and Price would be defeated when playing together in the Five Nations – in a partnership that spanned five seasons, from 1975 to 1979.

The Scots celebrated and went to Twickenham for the Triple Crown for the second time in three years and the fourth since 1947, to meet an England side lacking a win and with one stalwart of their 1970s pack, 'Stack' Stevens, in his final championship game. But on the previous three occasions Scotland's mission had ended in failure, and in 1975 their luck was not to change. When Scotland were leading by six points to three England winger Alan Morley scored the only try of the game, judged to have won the race with Andy Irvine for the touchdown. Irvine begs to differ: 'It was very simple, it was either him or me – and it was me. To this day, I swear I got to it first and the referee made a mistake. I spoke to Morley afterwards and he agreed. Whether he was being kind or not, it was pretty heartbreaking.' In controversial circumstances, England had won by a single point.

So Scotland had cruelly missed out on the Triple Crown yet again. Now, moreover, they had lost a share of the championship as well, because Wales had beaten Ireland in Cardiff – and how! Ireland arrived fresh from a good win over France with captain Willie John McBride scoring his first try for his country in his 62nd and penultimate international. The pitch invasion which followed showed the warmth felt by the Irish public towards this colossus from Ballymena. A fortnight later, though, McBride's team met their match, as Wales scored five tries to make it a total of fourteen for the season. It was a coruscating display of attacking rugby, with the stars behind the scrum in devastating form, but it was the Welsh forwards' total dominance which gave so much satisfaction to the supporters of the Pontypool front row. 'I think all the hard work the pack had put in that season paid off in that game,' says Graham Price. 'The Irish were on the wrong end of it – but whatever side had played us that day, the result would have been pretty much the same.'

An extra-special moment was when Charlie Faulkner scored a try – which meant that all three of the Pontypool front row had scored tries in their debut seasons for Wales. While criticism in the media had been suggesting Faulkner was too old, and ineffective in the loose, Graham Price remembers him being 'first everywhere' in the match – 'and we knew he was going to be, because at the previous squad session in Aberavon, Charlie went crazy and ended up scoring about a dozen tries! And when Charlie scored his try I was one of the first up there – I nearly yanked his arm off when I pulled him up!' Faulkner remembers the moment with fondness, too: 'When Graham got his try in Paris, he threw the ball up in the air and I caught it. When it was my turn, I just didn't want to let go of the ball in case somebody kicked it away and they disallowed the try. In Wales they are not so excited by the scrum. They look upon it as a way of starting the game – but nothing could be further from the truth. Without the scrum, any good side will only go to a certain level, no matter how world-class the backs are. But I think the majority of the Welsh people appreciated it at the end of the day.' The art of scrummaging was a subject which in 1975 Wales taught with authority. If others had not done their homework, it was a hard lesson delivered all the way from Pontypool.

1976 – Wales's GRAND SLAM

It was time now for Wales to explode and play the total rugby they had been threatening. France had stopped them in 1969, Ireland in 1970, politics in 1972, Scotland in 1973 and 1975, and England in 1974. Only in 1971 had Wales risen to the dizzy heights of the Grand Slam. In 1976 Wales's ferociously strong pack and poetically gifted backs combined with a competitive spirit to create a team which embarked on an even more glorious period. It was going to take a very good side to beat this matured Welsh vintage.

A man with all the qualities required to be a winner, and more, was full-back JPR Williams. JPR's appearance – the initials alone were enough to strike fear in the opposition's heart – was a statement of pure machismo. Here was the bloodied warrior, his prominent cheekbones bordered by his bushy sideburns and long hair, the socks around the ankles daring others to tackle him. Above all, JPR loved to challenge England and, by the end of his career, he would possess the proud record of never having lost to his country's main rugby enemy in eleven meetings. 'The game against England is always the big one for the Welsh players and fans,' says Williams. 'Losing to Scotland or Ireland never felt quite so bad – or so they tell me. During my time the English didn't seem to want to fight quite so hard for victory as we or the French did. I think the English have a disadvantage being Anglo-Saxon and having to face the Celtic nations – they always seemed totally psyched out when they played against us. It's the classic case of the little boy battling against big brother and refusing to lie down.' On a bitterly cold January day in 1976, Wales reaped the benefits of JPR's liking for the contest as he scored two tries.

It was all far too much for an England team destined for their second whitewash inside five seasons. As England suffered, Wales prospered. Their next opponents, Scotland, had already lost their opening match to France and had not been helped by a wrong decision from the referee, Ken Pattinson of England. It was a windy day in Edinburgh and Andy Irvine needed a placer to hold the ball for his kick at goal. The referee judged that the player had been lying in front of the ball and was therefore off-side when the kick was taken – but there is no such rule! Irvine's successful penalty-goal was disallowed and Scotland were denied.

But this was nothing compared with what happened when the Scots met Wales. Despite having pulled a leg muscle long before fulltime, the idiosyncratic French referee, Dr Cuny, officiating in his first international, simply refused to leave the field, limping behind the action in a bizarre and at times farcical spectacle which clearly annoyed the players. At one stage they had to stand patiently and wait for him to arrive to make a decision on what was a contentious try from Andy Irvine.

Wales went to Dublin to meet an Irish side that had been beaten in France by a record margin. They were not expected to give the Welsh too many problems, but for a while Ireland were very much in it. Then Wales cut loose and the Irish were terminally damaged by an incredible burst of scoring, conceding eighteen points in just over five minutes, with Phil Bennett amassing a total of nineteen points in the match to equal the Welsh record for the championship.

Even so, as Bennett remembers, his performance fell short of captain Mervyn Davies' expectations. The angular Davies, his curly hair held in by his hallmark headband, watched as a high tackle on JPR Williams was penalised. Phil Bennett and Gareth Edwards went to grab the ball quickly – 'but Merv moved in,' says Bennett, 'and said, "Bugger this, kick for goal!" I said, "Let's run it – we're in the mood." But Merv stood his ground and said, "You kick for goal." He was a believer that if somebody broke the law the best way to punish them was to make them pay and kick three points. I took the kick – it wasn't a very hard one – but I missed it. After the game I was feeling very pleased with myself, but Merv said, "You missed the bloody one that counted, though."' Despite spells of brilliance, before this season Bennett's place in the side had not been confirmed. After Barry John's premature abdication, John Bevan was given an opportunity, and there had been calls to cap another fine stand-off, David Richards, but now Bennett was officially the worthy successor to the throne. 'It was so difficult replacing one of the greatest players there had ever been,' he says. 'The one thing you need in any international position is confidence, and when that comes you settle down and relax in your game. In 1976 I was able to think, "Yes, I'm in that side," and having cemented my place I felt the boys and the crowd were fully behind me.'

Ireland had no more joy in their second home game of the season as Scotland won, but it was Wales's next match against France that held everybody's interest. Bennett the new 'king' was a victory away from the Grand Slam. Equally, if France won, they would be well placed, with only England to come in Paris, to take the clean sweep of victories. The Arms Park waited eagerly to celebrate, but the crowd winced as the electrically fast French winger, Jean-François Gourdon, sped in to score after only five minutes. In response, JJ Williams dived over for a try, but it was the boots of Phil Bennett, centre Steve Fenwick and Allan Martin which kept Wales in front. France then scored a second try through their other winger, Jean-Luc Averous, who was deemed to have beaten JPR Williams to the ball, despite JPR feeling he had got there first. This would be the last time, vowed the full-back, that anybody would pass him in the match – and he was true to his word.

For the final fifteen minutes the French attacked incessantly, but they met a man determined to defend his line at all costs. One moment summed up JPR's resistance. Not for the first time that day, Gourdon was flying to the corner: as the Frenchman prepared to beat the cover and go for the flag, JPR took what was arguably his most important defensive decision ever. 'My tackle on Gourdon is one of the most vivid memories I have of my championship career,' says the full-back. 'If I had tackled him around the legs he would have scored the try, and we would have lost the Grand Slam. So I decided to go for the shoulder-barge and put him in the crowd.' Nowadays such a tackle would probably be penalised as illegal – but with one never-to-be-forgotten, emphatic charge Williams had bolted the door, padlocked it and thrown away the key. 'There was tremendous relief and exultation from the players. The crowd down in that corner went berserk after that tackle as everybody sensed we had won the Grand Slam. The challenge won respect from the opposition and adulation from my team-mates.' Welsh rugby followers rank this tackle alongside any piece of artistry from the finer brush-strokes of Williams' colleagues in the back-line.

Tragically, the Grand Slam this great Welsh team had been building towards for five years was to be the last international rugby for their inspirational captain, Mervyn Davies who, less than a month after the triumph, collapsed and suffered a brain haemorrhage during a Welsh Cup game, which forced him to retire. His subsequent brave recovery from his illness was only to be expected.

1977 – France's GRAND SLAM and Wales's Triple Crown

Although Wales had won the Grand Slam in 1976, it was evident that France were building a side of similar qualities. The country that had prevented Welsh domination at the end of the 1960s now looked the most likely to counter Welsh rule at the end of the 1970s. The battle between the two would prove the centrepiece of an epic period in Five Nations history. Wales, aware that they would have to fight hard to retain the title, perhaps took these sentiments a little too literally when they began their championship defence against Ireland.

The Irish were ahead when the respected Scottish referee Norman Sanson lived up to his reputation of being tough on those who crossed the line into violence. Welsh lock Geoff Wheel and Ireland number-eight Willie Duggan became the first men to be dismissed in the Five Nations. Around this time, explains Sanson, there was a general hardening of attitudes against foul play – 'all sorts of posturing by officials with statements that if a player was sent off in an international he would never play for his country again. It seemed a heavy weight of responsibility to put on referees – no matter whether you were right or wrong, if it was a heinous offence or not, then that was the end of their career. But if a player steps across the line-out and lays somebody out without any prior provocation, it seems to me that in any game of rugby they must be sent off. Geoff Wheel had to go. Then Willie Duggan appeared from some distance away, throwing punches at everybody in his way, with the risk of a brawl breaking out, so I thought he deserved to go as well.'

The reaction to the referee's decision was mixed, and many believed Sanson did not receive sufficient support after the incident from the game's administrators. But by modern-day standards, the lack of post-match inquests seems remarkable. 'I don't think a single journalist talked to me after the game,' says Sanson. 'I was not pestered at all for quotes.' He was touched when Phil Bennett, now captain of Wales, even invited him to come and have a drink with the team. 'I spoke to Geoff Wheel,' Sanson continues, 'and although he didn't agree he deserved to be sent off he was a gentleman about it. There was an atmosphere of acceptance and respect then which washed over it all.'

The dismissals had at least left both sides with fourteen men, and it was Wales who came back to score three tries and win by a comfortable margin. In their first match of the season England went one try better in beating Scotland, and a new dawn for English rugby was rather hopefully proclaimed by some of the country's long-suffering supporters. In reality, though, it would be the match between France and Wales in Paris, on only the second weekend of the championship, that would effectively decide the title.

'I think if somebody asked me where the hardest matches of my career have been,' says Phil Bennett, 'I would say, playing the French in Paris. Auckland and Johannesburg were something special, but the French, when they were on song with the crowd behind them – all those huge men took some stopping!' They were certainly not in short supply in the 1977 side: a back row of Jean-Claude Skréla, the Jean-Pierres, Rives and Bastiat; Michel Palmié and Jean-François Imbernon in the second row, and a front row of Robert Paparemborde, Alain Paco and Gérard Cholley – 'What a pack they had!' exclaims Bennett – 'I mean, Jesus creepers!' It was a torrid game: 'I remember Derek Quinnell driving into a ruck,' he recalls. 'He went down and about six Frenchmen trod all over him to get to the ball. I thought, "My God!" – but he was a great gutsy character and he came back with his head cut here, there and everywhere.' The Welsh tried to play the game they wanted to play, building a platform up front, but France blocked JPR out of the game, their half-backs

99

kept going magnificently, and won deservedly.

Those French half-backs were two of the best their country has ever produced: the suave Jean-Pierre Romeu and, at scrum-half, the combative Jacques Fouroux – and this was their last season in the national side. Fouroux has fond memories of the time spent alongside his partner. 'Beyond the game itself, we shared the same view of the rugby of tomorrow, between pragmatism and realism, savouring emotion and an unwavering will to win. At that time France and Wales were the point of reference for European rugby at the same level as the southern nations, and to beat Wales was to be up with the leaders of world rugby. The Welsh, with Gareth, Phil, Fenwick, Gravell, JJ, Gerald and JPR, combined physique with the extraordinary magic of individual technique. It was already rugby of the year 2000.'

After their win against Wales, France went to Twickenham. England had followed up their win over Scotland with victory in Dublin, but the sun quickly set on England's new dawn. They had chances to win the game, but it was left to the French centre, François Sangali, to score the only try of the match to give France victory by a single point. A fortnight later in Paris, it was as if the relief of their narrow escape had galvanised the French to a new freedom of movement against Scotland – four tries meant that only Ireland now stood in the way of a Grand Slam.

In the meantime, England had a chance to bounce back by winning the Triple Crown in Cardiff, but a brilliant reverse pass from Gareth Edwards initiated another JPR Williams try and victory against his old foe. Wales's own Triple Crown bid was set up for their final game at Murrayfield. Scotland had won against Ireland, with both Ian McGeechan and Jim Renwick shining in the centre. McGeechan had moved back to fly-half for the Welsh game and scored a drop-goal, but it was his opposite number, Phil Bennett, who scored the try of the championship to give Wales their victory.

'That game could have gone either way,' says Bennett. 'Scotland were playing superbly and were full of attacking ideas. I remember when they had the ball which led up to the try. When you look at it now, it was only about forty-five seconds, but it seemed as if they'd had it for minutes – there's nothing worse in an international than trying to get the ball back from the opposition.' Eventually, however, Scotland chipped ahead. JPR Williams gathered the ball, took the tackle and the ball went out to Gerald Davies. 'Gerald immediately saw something on,' continues Bennett, 'and his twinkling feet beat the tacklers – great vision by a great player. I passed to centre David Burcher, and then Steve Fenwick delivered a magnificent flick pass to beat the "man and ball" tackle and give me the chance to finish it off.' Now, lo and behold, the last man he had to beat was an old team-mate from the 1974 Lions tour, 'Mighty Mouse' McLauchlan – 'he used to be a right pain in the neck, always getting in the way of second or third phase possession. I used to say, "Mouse, why don't you bugger off back to the ruck or maul!" How the hell he got back I'll never know – no other forward was in sight. But I side-stepped him, thank goodness, and I collapsed underneath the posts with total fatigue. I just felt relief after a long season that we had clinched another Triple Crown. It wasn't my try, though – it was JPR's guts, Gerald's magic, David's support, Steve's quick hands. It was a true team score.'

The best team in the 1977 championship, however, was playing not in Edinburgh but in Dublin. Jean-Pierre Bastiat stormed to the line for the only try of the game, which was enough to reward France with their second Grand Slam. The 'Little General', Jacques Fouroux, again: 'I was very proud to pull off an historic feat with the same fifteen players for the four matches without conceding a single try – unheard-of at the time at international level. In the British press we were nicknamed "the Wild Bunch", and behind that pack I rather had the impression of being the sheep-dog with a flock which sometimes got a little lost.' The Grand Slam was a perfect conclusion to his playing career, and for France the season had ended with the right kind of 'send-off'.

1978 – Wales's GRAND SLAM

Matches were tight, the play was invigorating. All teams knew they had to be on their best form to win, with the emphasis now clearly on attack, not defence. The championship was thriving – it was a halcyon period for the Five Nations.

It was in this spirit that Ireland and Scotland met in Dublin. With only seconds to go the Irish were in front by twelve points to nine, but Scotland were awarded a penalty. The Scottish captain and scrum-half, Doug Morgan, had scored three penalty-goals himself that afternoon: now, feeling he should not settle for a draw but push for the victory, he bravely rejected the chance of another and chose to run the ball from a tap penalty just yards from the Irish line. 'The only chance of taking the Triple Crown was to win the game,' he says now. 'I knew exactly how long there was to go, as the referee had said the next whistle was full-time. I still stand by my decision. In actual fact, had flanker Mike Biggar not dropped the ball, I think we would have scored. When we came off the field having lost, certain sections of the press gave me a hard time, but as time went on more and more people applauded my move. The humorists said I deserved the sportsman of the year award!'

England had started their season with a loss in Paris, where the new French scrum-half, Jérôme Gallion, announced his arrival on the international scene with a strong run to the try-line. He scored again in France's second match at Murrayfield when his team were trailing by thirteen points to nil and looking out of it. Scotland's Andy Irvine was off the field having injured his shoulder scoring a try, and in his absence Gallion pounced on a loose ball to begin his team's thrilling turnaround. Another score from lock Francis Haget, and some accurate kicking from full-back Jean-Michel Aguirre, took the French to a dramatic win.

At a soggy Twickenham England met Wales in weather more suited to ducks than rugby – 'one of those frustrating days,' reflects the great Gerald Davies, 'when a winger was destined not to get the ball.' Phil Bennett outgunned full-back Alastair Hignell by three penalties to two, and Wales won the shoot-out. Davies, slender and rather urbane in appearance with his moustache and collar-length dark hair, provided some of the most aesthetically pleasing moments in Five Nations history. His repertoire included a hitch of the hips and a burst of pace both beautiful and explosive, but for Wales's next match against Scotland he had to swap wellington boots for ice skates: 'It was the coldest day I ever had on the field. The ground was rock hard.' Considering the conditions, however, Wales played some excellent rugby – scoring four tries, including a first international score for centre Ray Gravell and, after a trio of powerful hand-offs, one for his Llanelli team-mate, Derek Quinnell. The weather, though, was still to leave its mark. 'At the after-match dinner,' recalls Davies, 'I went to the gents and looked out of the window to see the snow falling. It got heavier and heavier and in between courses we kept checking to see how deep it was.' By the end of the evening Cardiff had been cut off, and people were coming in off the streets to make temporary beds for the night on the floor. 'I suppose it was every rugby player's dream,' says Davies, 'to be stranded on the evening of a game with all that wine and food!'

Wales's journey took them next to Ireland. The Irish had also experienced problems in Paris in arctic conditions, losing by a point in a game that should never have been played. Luckily, nothing was hurt apart from Irish pride as Jérôme Gallion scored his third try in as many internationals. It was a testament to the impact he had made that Jacques Fouroux had not been missed after his retirement. For the game in Dublin the sun returned and Gerald Davies, without knowing it, was about to play his last championship game for his country. After Steve Fenwick's try and four penalty-goals it was the other Welsh winger, JJ Williams, who sealed a battling win with a late score, but a manic Irish performance had pushed Wales to the limit.

For Davies, though, there would be no Grand Slam game against France. Perhaps he should have ruled himself out of his club's match against Orrell the following week, to rest for the final weekend of the Five Nations, but he felt an equal obligation to his club, especially as it was the first time they had played the northern side in Wales. Davies, the model sportsman, was captain of Cardiff and felt a duty to turn out. He aggravated an injury and had the awful experience of watching Wales go for the Grand Slam without him. 'I have some regrets,' he says now, 'that I had no finale to my career.' The moral he draws is that 'professional sportsmen have to be selfish and think about what is best for them.'

As Wales contemplated the Grand Slam, Scotland landed the wooden spoon by failing to score against England, who won at Murrayfield for the first time in a decade. Lock Bill Beaumont, a big bear of a man in his first season as England captain, was leading his team with distinction and another victory over Ireland ended the Five Nations on a winning note for the English. They had reached the heady heights of mid-table, a remarkable achievement for them in the 1970s. In defeat Ireland could at least enjoy the emergence of a new talent – fly-half Tony Ward had equalled the record for the most points in a championship season.

Meanwhile, in Cardiff, history was being made: Wales meeting France with both countries going into the last game on a Grand Slam, the culmination of a great rivalry that had been boiling up throughout the decade. Wales's captain, Phil Bennett, admits that before the match he had been worried his team would fall short of their goal: before the season a lot of the players had had a hard Lions tour in New Zealand, and come back a little disillusioned with rugby. 'There wasn't the spark of energy in some players that perhaps there should have been,' says Bennett. 'Coming up to the French game, the training on the Sunday was an absolute shambles' – coach John Dawes eventually gave them the afternoon off, astutely realising it would be no good training for the sake of training.

But on the day nobody performed better than the Welsh skipper, who side-stepped his way to the line for Wales's first try and then was on the end of a brilliant overhead pass from JJ Williams to finish off their second. But Bennett takes most satisfaction from a conversion that day. 'It was far out on the left-hand side, and it will always be one of my proudest kicks. I had to get it over because the difference in the forwards' minds between a try, and a try plus the conversion, is vital when they are battling.' Neither will he ever forget the incredible support from the partisan crowd. England's 'Swing Low, Sweet Chariot' and Scotland's 'Flower of Scotland' were rugby anthems that would have their day in a later era, but this was a time when Wales won not only on the fields but in the stands as well. 'We were hanging on and not playing to the best of our ability, but without being sentimental or talking rot, the crowd in those days was worth a six-point start. They had been singing hymns and the arias of Max Boyce and, with ten minutes to go, there was a great anxiety on the faces of my players because we knew we had to win this Grand Slam. Then there was an injury, and the crowd broke out as one into song – "Bread of Heaven" sounded around the ground. When I was a small boy my father used to say to me, "When a Welsh team are tiring they will sing to lift them." I firmly believe they were our sixteenth man.'

France's main weapon, Jérôme Gallion, was tethered by the artful Gareth Edwards at scrum-half, together with the back row of Derek Quinnell, Jeff Squire and Terry Cobner. The Welsh gave everything and, after a bruising second half which saw only a Steve Fenwick drop-goal, they had won their second Grand Slam in three years. Like his half-back partner Gareth Edwards, who had played a record 45 consecutive Five Nations games since 1968, Phil Bennett was making his last appearance for Wales. 'After the win,' he says, 'there was elation in the dressing-room, but I have to say the major emotion was relief. Like in Ireland when we had won the Triple Crown a fortnight earlier, there were scenes of extreme tiredness – the forwards were absolutely out on their feet, their stockings rolled down, and they were too tired to drink champagne. I knew that it was my last game. I'd finished without telling anybody, and for me it couldn't have happened better.'

Wales of the 1970s had become arguably the greatest-ever Five Nations team. Gerald Davies points to a number of elements that, in his analysis, came together to set up such an incredible period of success: a feel-good factor throughout Wales, politically as well as in sport; Wales's adoption of the squad system and appointment of good coaches, which contributed to a healthy and progressive environment; and, with few selection changes and the same players taking part in every match, 'a good sense of "All for one and one for all" – the Welsh national side was like a club. There was a tension,' adds Davies, 'but it was positive – the best teams always have this, an internal competition. It should be an unspoken thing, and it works if people are in tune. But in order to get everything to gel,' he emphasises, 'you need the players. Unquestionably, if I dare say it, there were eight or nine world-class members of that team who made everything work. We had several points of attack: if Gareth didn't have a good day, Phil would, or JPR – there was always somebody to take up the slack. I was lucky to be part of it.' And those who saw Wales play were privileged to watch.

1979 – Wales's Triple Crown and championship

'As the name gets bigger, the gaps get smaller' – words that would have had a familiar ring for the stars of the Welsh team, but also a warning in the press for Ireland's new star, Tony Ward, coming up to the 1979 championship. After a fine debut season Ward was going to be a marked man. Wales were still the team to beat, but had lost players of the calibre of Gareth Edwards, Gerald Davies and Phil Bennett. Could Ward take over from Bennett as the championship's leading playmaker?

France went to Dublin on the opening day to face Ward's Ireland. It should have been an Irish win but for a bizarre incident at the end of the game when, with the scores level at nine points all and the seconds ticking away, Ireland were given a free-kick by referee Roger Quittenton of England. Quittenton, like Scotland's Norman Sanson and Clive Norling of Wales, was one of the most prominent referees of the period. But whereas the modern official sees it as his duty to verbally assist the players, at the end of the 1970s it was not the norm, as Tony Ward found out. He had been living up to his preseason billing, scoring all of his team's points, but now he found himself in a quandary. The French players would be bound to try and charge down his attempt to drop a goal: unsure of the law, he hesitated over whether to retreat to secure a better clearance for the kick.

Ward was left by the referee to make his own decision. In the end he took the kick from too close in, it was blocked and the game finished in a draw. 'All these years later, you still make excuses,' says Ward, but he explains that concussion had left him seeing spots before his eyes, and barely able to pick out his team when he came back after the interval. 'I just made out two team huddles on either side of the half-way line and, without thinking, I actually ran to the group of French players. When I was getting close I saw the socks were the wrong colour, and I just froze!'

A fortnight later it was Ward's full-back colleague, Dick Spring, who was seeing not blue or green but red, and lots of it, as Ireland went to the Arms Park. The new-look Welsh team had come back to beat Scotland at Murrayfield in their first match, thanks to tries from two championship debutants – winger Elgan Rees of Neath, and a scrum-half from Cardiff, the same club as the great Gareth Edwards, Terry Holmes. Against the Irish it was a tactic that takes its name from Tony Ward's club, the skier kick called a 'Garryowen', which put Wales into a winning position. In later years, Spring went on to field many high balls in the world of politics, becoming his country's Deputy Premier and playing an important role in the progress towards an Anglo-Irish peace agreement, but underneath the posts that day he dropped a clanger and Wales pounced to score.

Tony Ward feels it is unfair to focus on Spring's famous blunder: 'That's what people remember him for – but he had the lot, including good hands and a huge left boot trained in Gaelic football. The irony is that he was a confident player and always felt sure he was going to catch everything – but, sadly, not that time.' Ward's total of thirteen points was eclipsed by Steve Fenwick's sixteen, and it was the Welsh who were again one win away from the Triple Crown. Their Grand Slam hopes rested on victory in Paris, but France narrowly won a physical tussle by a single point, despite another powerful try from Terry Holmes. The pendulum of European rugby supremacy was swinging southwards.

Meanwhile, England had started their campaign with a draw against Scotland, for whom the doughty lock, Alastair McHarg, played his 37th and last Five Nations match. Few were predicting great things for an English side which seemed unable to convert the excellent possession won by their forwards into tries, and these fears were confirmed when they lost to Ireland in Dublin. Although England's fly-half, Neil Bennett, scored a consolation try, it was Tony Ward who won the battle of the stand-offs. It seemed almost certain that France would be too much for this England team but, in a season of tight matches, the English produced a one-point victory of their own – they had recovered pride and France had seemingly lost their championship chance.

The third draw of the championship took place at Murrayfield, where Ireland and Scotland could not be separated. In the build-up to the match, however, Tony Ward discovered that there were still limits in those days on how rugby stars could exploit their fame. The boy-wonder of Irish rugby appeared in the *Daily Mirror* as a pin-up, pictured in his swimming attire, relaxing for the game. 'The shot wasn't actually on page three, but it was close enough, and most embarrassing.' News got out at home when a presenter on Ireland's national television channel, RTE, showed the picture in his match preview, and Ward woke up on the morning of the match to find it stuck up on his wall. 'Noel Murphy was the coach at the time,' he recalls, 'and I got a right dressing-down, because at that stage rugby players didn't do things like that.'

The exposure of his half-back partner and room-mate Ward clearly did not affect scrum-half Colin Patterson's play in the match: he scored two tries and Ward himself kicked another penalty-goal, to bring his total score to 33 out of Ireland's 53 points that season. 'At the start of my Five Nations career I had wondered, "What in God's name am I doing playing at this level?"' says Ward. Now, although the gaps had closed, he seemed to have done enough to cement his place in the Irish team. But perhaps his original 'gut-wrenching feeling that you are not ready for it' is perfectly understandable: 'I remember the great Mike Gibson and Willie Duggan had an unusual diet on match day,' Ward recalls. 'At lunchtime they used to drink – or should I say eat – this concoction of raw eggs, honey, sherry and sugar. When you are with such well established players you think, "If this is good enough for these guys, then I have to have some..." I've never been a drinker, so after I had downed this cocktail I convinced myself I was tipsy – at the team meeting, just a couple of hours before my first cap!'

England's joy at having beaten France was short-lived. Wales, despite their loss to France, went to their fifth Triple Crown of the decade with their biggest win over the English since the Five Nations began – although with only a quarter of the game left they were ahead by only four points. Then, in what was meant to be his final Five Nations game, having announced his retirement from international rugby, full-back and captain JPR Williams sustained a cut to his leg. Replacement Clive Griffiths got the call to get ready: 'I thought, this is a waste of time because JPR doesn't get hurt – the week before he'd been in a road accident and collided with a truck on the M4, and the headline in the *Western Mail* was "JPR IN COLLI-SION WITH TANKER, TANKER RECOVERING IN BREAKER'S YARD."' But when Griffiths went down to look his knees turned to jelly: there was no way even JPR was coming back with a hole in his leg like that. 'He grabbed me,' says Griffiths, 'and said, "Relax and play your normal game" – "Relax"! It was Wales versus England for the Triple Crown, the score was seven points to three and he wanted me to relax! But I went on and I did play my normal game because I missed the first tackle!'

Griffiths settled down, however, and Wales cut loose to score four more tries to add to a well-worked first-half effort from their centre, David Richards. As the game opened up, Griffiths started to enjoy himself and, after dummying past England winger Mike Slemen and chipping over full-back Alastair Hignell's head, even found himself racing his own team-mate Elgan Rees to get the touchdown. 'Perhaps I should have been a bit more greedy, with it being my first cap,' says Griffiths – 'I should have pushed him out of the way. I called Elgan "the thief" after that for stealing my try!' At the final whistle he said to himself, 'You've got your first cap: go and get some more' – but then, after his twenty minutes of stardom, rugby league made him an offer too good to turn down. Like Chico Hopkins at the start of the decade, Griffiths never played for Wales again.

The win rendered France's victory over Scotland in Paris irrelevant to the title race, and gave the Welsh another championship. Scotland finished at the bottom of the table, but two narrow defeats and two draws at least justified their claim to the title of 'best side ever to win the wooden spoon.' The 1970s, though, had belonged to Wales – success that would burden subsequent Welsh teams with a heavy weight of expectation.

PART FOUR

1980–1989

If the 1970s was the decade when rugby romantics had been more than satisfied by the union between Wales and the championship, then the 1980s would see a rather messy divorce. It was a long and painful process for the Welsh, with the catalyst being the retirement of so many outstanding players. Wales's problems opened the way for the other nations: France, who had been their major championship rivals during the 1970s, and England and Scotland too, all won Grand Slams and had some of their finest hours during the decade that followed Welsh domination. In addition, Ireland won two Triple Crowns in the space of four seasons. It was only at the end of the 1980s that Wales even threatened to regain their former powers by winning a Triple Crown of their own.

As a competitive tournament, the Five Nations thrived in the 1980s with no single country dominant. Sides now found that, with hard graft, results previously unobtainable in the face of the Welsh and often French flair of the 1970s, were now possible. This even power base further fuelled the public's interest, with the result that the traditionally less-well-supported matches – when France played away from home, for example – also began to attract capacity crowds. The championship was in rude health.

By the end of the decade, however, the Five Nations was being usurped as the leading competition in the world. The World Cup had arrived and, despite initial misgivings about its long-term viability, took the rugby world by storm. It was obvious that this new tournament had become a permanent fixture in the sport's calendar: the Five Nations would have to adjust to having a big brother in the family.

1980 – England's GRAND SLAM

As the decade began, England were well aware that, if they were to recover from the disappointments of the 1970s, then hard work would have to be their top priority. At least 1979 had finished with some grounds for optimism, when, on a dark November afternoon up in Otley in Yorkshire, the Northern Division had memorably beaten the touring All Blacks. The captain of the North that day was Bill Beaumont of Fylde, and in the New Year it was he who took charge of England at Twickenham in their Five Nations opener against Ireland. The family mill in Chorley had clearly taught Beaumont the value of a strong work ethic. His aim was to instil that spirit of the north into his England squad.

Ireland, victorious on their tour to Australia the previous summer, were also confident. Captained by the experienced flanker, Fergus Slattery, they had a set of forwards brimming with talent – but their ace was not in their pack. He was behind the scrum. 'What we aimed to do was get on top up front, just like in the match against the All Blacks,' says Bill Beaumont, 'but having been three-nil up we found ourselves nine-three down! This guy Ollie Campbell was playing at stand-off for Ireland and we'd never heard of him. But we soon learned that he could kick.'

The English needed to concentrate their efforts elsewhere, and now the international shrank to a local northern contest. After scoring a try himself, scrum-half Steve Smith kicked the ball in behind his Northern Division team-mate, Kevin O'Brien, who was playing at full-back for Ireland for the first time. O'Brien had a fly-hack at the ball and missed, and Mike Slemen, another northerner, picked it up and scored. England were now in charge and never looked back, the one black spot being the injury to centre Tony Bond, another member of Beaumont's northern fraternity, who broke his leg.

The long-running tension over selection policy that had so affected England's consistency over the years was revived after the win. Amazingly, the selectors informed Bill Beaumont's second-row partner, Nigel Horton, of his exclusion from the side that would play next in Paris, at the celebration dinner. Horton had only played in the Irish game because of an injury to Maurice Colclough, but it was the manner of his removal which threatened England's growing morale. Roger Uttley, a member of England's back row, remembers consoling his colleague, who had played a great game: 'Nigel's a big bloke, a tough man, but he was in a terrible state, totally distraught and actu-

ally crying.' The senior players were unhappy but, despite this aberration, Bill Beaumont points out that times were changing.
'Chairman Budge Rogers and coach Mike Davis did want to bring a
consistency to selection. For all the time I had played before there
had been a different team each week. It made you frightened to make
a mistake or you'd be dropped. 1980 was different.'

After a good start, England's next opponents were a French team
that had been beaten by Wales. At home, though, they would be a
different proposition: according to Roger Uttley, coach Mike Davis
was so keen for England to do their homework on the opposition that
eyebrows were raised at the team hotel when he produced an overhead projector. 'Some of us thought this was a bit revolutionary...'
ponders Uttley. On the eve of the match the weather looked like playing into England's hands. 'It had been a grim night – snowing up at
Versailles,' says Roger Uttley, 'and when we got down to the stadium
everybody was feeling quite good. For once the French wouldn't have
the sun on their backs. But as soon as we came out of the changing-
rooms and looked through those big glass doors at the Parc des
Princes, the sun came out.'

France sprang into action with a try from their captain, Jean-Pierre
Rives, before England were able to draw breath. In such a position
the English team of the 1970s had frequently capitulated, but
Beaumont's side was of greater resolve. The forwards got on top and
England came back strongly, first with a rather scrappy score from
centre Nick Preston, then John Carleton's first try for his country, and
two drop-goals from John Horton either side of half-time. France
responded, but England hung on to win in Paris for the first time for
sixteen years.

Meanwhile, Scotland had lost to Ireland, but it was England's
meeting with Wales that was most eagerly anticipated. During the
whole of the previous decade the great Welsh side had gone down to
England only once, at Twickenham in 1974. Various personal duels
had been built up by the rugby media, reflecting the increasingly
intense glare being directed on players in the Five Nations – Fran
Cotton against Graham Price at prop; the two Cardiff men, number-
eight John Scott and Terry Holmes, on opposite sides – and the long-
haired Welsh flanker, Paul Ringer, was singled out following his
over-zealous conduct against France a month earlier. Now there was
a hint of war in the air.

'It was a very cold, dank, horribly miserable day,' testifies Roger
Uttley, 'and an atmosphere like something out of *The Lord of the*

Rings. Normally the reception beforehand in the West Car Park is quite genteel, but on this occasion there were people coming up clenching their fists and saying, "Do this for us!", and Welshmen giving it two fingers. We were lining up to do battle – it had that sort of feel. But whereas in days gone by we had always bowed to intimidation, this time there was no stepping back. I remember the first scrum: none of this "crouch, pause and engage." We charged in from five metres.'

Unfortunately, the ominous pre-publicity was fulfilled after only fifteen minutes. Referee David Burnett of Ireland had already given the players his final warning. 'I gathered the lads round,' recalls Bill Beaumont, 'and said, "Anything else and you are going to go."' Two minutes later Paul Ringer – 'a man not physically big who played a very physical game,' in the words of his former Leicester team-mate, the England hooker Peter Wheeler – made a late tackle on the England fly-half, John Horton, and was sent off. The England players slow-handclapped him off the field.

'I think David Burnett thought the sending-off was his decisive action,' says Peter Wheeler, 'but as players we sensed that this was his last decisive action and he wasn't going to send any more off!' Soon afterwards a ball was loose near to the East Stand touch-line and, with red shirts advancing, Roger Uttley attempted to go down on it. 'As the boots came in I felt as if my head was going between the posts,' says Uttley. 'The next thing I could feel the rough edge of flesh where my nose had split and there was blood everywhere. Tony Neary came over and said, "Christ!" My face felt like a football.' Not for the first time in Uttley's courageous career had his craggy features been rearranged, but never with such ferocity.

Amidst the violence, Wales scored a try through Jeff Squire. Then full-back Dusty Hare kicked another penalty-goal to put England ahead. But with only three minutes left, the Welsh hooker, Alan Phillips, charged down a Steve Smith kick, ran for his life and gave the ball to winger Elgan Rees, who scored what seemed to be the winner. Wales, though, as they had done all afternoon, missed the kick, and then dramatically England were awarded a penalty. Hare, the unassuming Newark farmer, was the man with the heavy responsibility of keeping the Grand Slam dream alive: 'I was one of those lucky ones who didn't suffer from nerves on the field. But this was some kick – wide out on the right – and it was clear it was our last chance.' The poor Twickenham playing surface had been further softened by the rain; he was kicking a heavy old-style leather ball; it was virtually dark. 'When I hit it,' says Hare, 'I knew I'd won it. As I ran back the noise of the crowd was deafening.'

England had won, but the scene of carnage in both dressing-rooms showed that the fine line between acceptable and unacceptable brutality had been well and truly crossed. 'I don't know what the stitch count was that day,' says Bill Beaumont, 'but we certainly won that – and if it had been boxing we could well have been counted out!' 'I had to go home and see my two young lads,' adds Roger Uttley, 'my face all swollen and bruised, looking like a freak, thinking they would be scared to death. I really felt it was a very silly game that allowed you to end up like that.'

The Five Nations had rarely seen anything like the violence of that day. What the sport needed now was a match to remind its supporters of the game's finer elements. Thankfully, it was taking place on the same day as the debacle at Twickenham. In Edinburgh, Scotland were playing France and trying to end their eleven-match championship run without a win. Trailing by fourteen points to four with a little over ten minutes to go, they seemed destined to lose yet again. By his own admission full-back Andy Irvine had had a terrible first hour: 'That joker Jim Renwick had offered me his half-time slice of orange and said, "You might as well have this one too, as it's going to be your last" – and by the middle of the second half, after further disasters had befallen me, I thought he was probably right.' Then, dramatically, Scotland broke free, and in the finest one-man salvage operation in the history of the championship Irvine finished off two of the best tries ever seen at Murrayfield. 'That French match was certainly not my favourite game,' says Irvine, 'but the final twelve minutes would count as my favourite moments of rugby ever.'

Scotland were unable to continue this winning form in Cardiff, where the Welsh team, warned by their Union to clean up their act, won by three tries to one. The Scots' single try, however, was another classic, finished by Jim Renwick with the equally talented backs, David Johnston and Keith Robertson, in support. It sent a warning to England, for whom Grand Slam day would be at Murrayfield. The same afternoon Ireland lost narrowly in Paris, but did beat Wales in Dublin on the final day of the championship, when Ollie Campbell took his season's total to 46 points, a new Five Nations record. For Wales, a second loss was a sign of their fading power – would England be the team to take over the Welsh crown?

In Edinburgh, England cut loose for the first time that season and went into a commanding lead. Three tries were scored inside the first half-hour as centre Clive Woodward sliced through the Scottish defence. Winger John Carleton was the main beneficiary of England's freedom, and when the ball sat up for him to collect and race in for his hat-trick try the English looked to be home and dry. 'In the first half we played some great stuff,' says Bill Beaumont, 'and when the whistle went for the interval we just wanted the game to end. But Irvine and Renwick kept coming back at us, and as we had never won anything we had this great fear of failure.'

Both Roger Uttley and prop Phil Blakeway were carrying injuries, but their captain did not dare change a successful team by substituting them. Scotland's brilliant counter-attacks caused hearts to flutter, but Bill Beaumont's exhausted side just hung on, and when the end finally arrived, they were swamped by delirious supporters. For the older members of the team, who had been through the wretched times of the 1970s, the victory signified the end of being treated as second-, and often fifth-, best. It was the one occasion when the gentlemanly Beaumont refused to exchange his jersey with his opposite number. Alan Tomes's request was politely turned down by a man determined to treasure a memento of a very special day.

1981 – France's GRAND SLAM

'In any Five Nations championship, the first game is vital,' declares Clive Woodward, the charismatic centre in England's Grand Slam side and currently the national coach. 'If you lose, draw or don't play well enough, then the whole season can go flat.' Woodward is sure his country should have followed up the 1980 triumph with similar success a year later. But in 1981, on a January afternoon in Cardiff, the English fell at the first hurdle – a slip not entirely unconnected with Woodward: 'Yes, there was a certain player who gave away a penalty in front of the posts...'

With about a minute to go England were leading, recalls Woodward, 'and I was shouting at everybody to stay on side and not to give a penalty away.' Then the Welsh scrum-half, Brynmor Williams, dummied a pass from the base of the scrum and lured the Englishman too quickly up into midfield. 'That kind of pass is now illegal,' Woodward adds – 'so I now say that England won!' – but he had fallen into Williams' trap and been caught off-side. 'I remember the horror on Clive's face,' says Williams, 'his arms hanging in a desperate, embarrassed way.' Steve Fenwick did not strike the ball well, but it went over the bar. England dramatically had a further chance to snatch the win, but Dusty Hare was unable to repeat what he had done to Wales a year before. He missed his final kick and, despite having scored all of England's nineteen points, ended on the losing side. 'I now claim the dubious honour,' says Brynmor Williams, 'of being the only man to win a game for Wales without actually touching the ball.' For prop Fran Cotton, who limped off injured, it was a disappointing end to a fine England career.

Fortunately for Woodward, he was able to make amends just a month later in his team's victory over Scotland at Twickenham. Six tries were scored in the match, three apiece, but none was better than England's first when Woodward gracefully swerved and arched his way past a mesmerised Scottish defence, beating half a dozen attempted tackles. It was a masterclass in side-stepping from a player prepared to experiment and chance his arm. The same could be said of England's new fly-half, Huw Davies. Davies was still a student at Cambridge University, standing in for the injured John Horton: 'Beforehand, John Carleton had told me to enjoy the three or four days of involvement before the international,' he says, 'because the worst bit is the match, in the sense that if things go poorly for you then it's a horrible situation.' But on the day Davies made a big impression, with a scorching run from near the half-way line to bring about the winning score.

Scotland's loss was their second away defeat, as they had already been beaten in Paris. Sandwiched in the middle, though, was a win over Wales at Murrayfield, during which Welsh fly-half Gareth Davies had conceded the championship's first-ever penalty try, a recent addition to the game's law book. Davies had pulled at Andy Irvine's shirt and obstructed his dive on the ball – desperate measures from an increasingly desperate team. The win over England had only served to gloss over the emerging frailties in Welsh rugby. Even the great JPR Williams, who had made his Five Nations comeback that season, could not avoid the axe. After numerous changes, Wales did manage a narrow win at home to Ireland, but it was their opponents who scored the tries. Indeed, Wales finished the season with only two tries to their name, an amazing contrast to their free-scoring habits of the previous decade. Ireland were on their way to the wooden spoon, although their season could have been so different: their biggest margin of defeat was six points, and twice it was by a single point – but they lost all their matches.

Falling on the right side of the results in 1981, however, were

France – a team driven by a committed captain, back-row forward Jean-Pierre Rives, the blond bombshell from Toulouse. Rives, one of the best captains in the championship's history, led by deeds, not words. 'If you beat him to the ball, then you were off-side,' Jacques Fouroux once said of the man he was now coaching. 'It was very easy to captain this French team,' jokes Rives, 'because nobody listened to me. Everyone did what they wanted to do and that was wonderful – great guys, nice fellows, all having a good time on the field. That's the best way for the French, because every time we tried to repeat on the field what we did on the training ground it never worked anyway.' With his hair touching his shoulders and blood frequently pouring from his face during battle, Rives looked more the Norseman than the Frenchman. 'The blood and the hair – that was my image every year. I'm blond but I don't know why; bleeding – that's not my fault, but when I do something I admit it is always messy. When I was a kid my mother would despair: if I was sitting at the table I would put tomato ketchup everywhere. I guess it's a habit I kept on the rugby field, but then it was blood and not ketchup!'

In their victory over Scotland the French showed many similar qualities to the Grand Slam-winning side of 1977. 'In 1977 it was a monster pack,' reflects Rives, 'but this team was a little of everything, a kind of patchwork of players – a good mix.' The pack now included the powerful front row of Pierre Dospital, Philippe Dintrans and a survivor from coach Fouroux's playing days, Robert Paparemborde. Daniel Revallier had joined Jean-François Imbernon in the second-row, and Rives' accomplice in the back row was Jean-Luc Joinel. Behind the scrum fly-half Guy Laporte, in his championship debut, kicked two drop-goals in the win over Ireland in Dublin. In the fiercely-contested match with Wales in Paris full-back Serge Gabernet shared the kicking duties with Laporte, but it was Gabernet's try that sealed the win.

So France went to Twickenham in search of their third Grand Slam. Rives had a premonition that this was to be his day. Whenever the French team played at Twickenham, he explains, they stayed in a hotel near Heathrow Airport, and used to go for a walk in the small square across the road. One year they had played football there with an old Coke can they had found on the ground. 'I remember I put the can in a special place in the square and said, maybe when we come again we will find it. We won that match – and when we returned in 1981 the can was still there! That was my signal we couldn't lose.'

Despite awful conditions, France showed enough faith in their three-quarters – Serge Blanco, Roland Bertranne, Didier Codorniou and Laurent Pardo – to turn the game their way. In a gale-force wind France scored all their sixteen points in the first half when the elements were with them. England were playing well, but four second-half penalty-goals from Marcus Rose, using the wind to full effect, failed to save the home team. 'So we won the game and the Grand Slam because we found a Coke can,' concludes Rives. 'This is how an American company can help France to win a game at Twickenham!'

Rives, never one to acknowledge easily his own personal greatness, looks back at the 1981 season with fondness. 'Most of all I remember the friendship and the good ambience, even between the opposing teams. That is the part of the magic of the Five Nations which appeals to me most. You play games overseas for test series, but for us you are really French in the Five Nations.'

1982 – Ireland's Triple Crown and championship

In 1982 another captain was to have a major impact on the championship. The story goes that when St Mary's College hooker Ciaran Fitzgerald was introduced to the rest of the Irish squad as skipper, he delved into a kit-bag and, in an attempt to concentrate his players' minds on the basics, announced, 'This is a rugby ball.' 'Jaysus!' a voice from the back was heard to reply: 'he's going too fast for us boys!' Fitzgerald, an army captain and a ball of energy, provided the leadership qualities to turn Ireland from a whitewashed team within a year into a side which challenged for all the available honours. France, the Grand Slam holders, would slide the other way.

Ireland's start to the season was delayed by the winter weather. The match against Wales was put back a week, and on the first day of the championship Scotland and England, thanks to the under-pitch heating installed at Murrayfield, took centre-stage. Later in the season, after the match against France in Paris, England prop Colin Smart was to achieve notoriety by drinking after-shave at the post-match reception: following this Calcutta Cup encounter he might have wished for something equally potent. With only seconds to go, he barged into the Scottish back-row forward, Iain Paxton, in an off-the-ball challenge, and gave the home side a chance to level the scores. Up stepped Andy Irvine – for a kick just inside his own half! – and once again his boot was the scourge of England.

Seven days later the snow had gone from Dublin and Ireland,

117

under the guidance of Ciaran Fitzgerald, set about Wales in a determined fashion. In the scrum were experienced men like Fergus Slattery and his back-row partner, John O'Driscoll. Behind the scrum, Ollie Campbell, pale-skinned and almost frail in appearance but with an inner strength and natural ability that set him apart, controlled the match. Campbell continued to keep his great rival Tony Ward out of the fly-half position thanks to his expert tactical kicking, combined with some spectacular breaks, which directly created two of the three Irish tries. Remarkably, winger Moss Finn scored a brace even though he was concussed – and in hospital the next day had the unusual experience of watching the television highlights with no recollection of his performance.

Both the Irish centres, David Irwin and Paul Dean, also had to be taken off injured, Irwin's broken leg signalling the end of his championship and proving costly to Ireland in another way. Until he was in the dressing-room and had been formally deemed unfit to continue, the referee, Mr Short of Scotland, refused to allow a replacement onto the field. In the meantime, Wales made full use of their extra man and scrum-half Terry Holmes grabbed a try. The character of the Irish team was fully tested: inspired by the forwards and aided by Campbell, they recovered to win comfortably. It was a much needed victory: 'Many people forget that we went into the match having lost seven and drawn one of the previous eight games played,' says Ollie Campbell. There was more success to come.

Wales recovered from their defeat with a win at home to France, thanks to full-back Gwyn Evans, who scored a then-world-record-equalling six penalty-goals. On the same day Ireland travelled to Twickenham to meet an England side playing without their captain, Bill Beaumont, who had had to withdraw from the team with a head injury that would ultimately force him to retire from the sport. England's new skipper was the jocular Steve Smith, who nowadays maintains an involvement with the game not only through his club, Manchester Sale, and the sports clothing firm he co-founded with Fran Cotton, Cotton Traders, but also as an ITV pundit. In 1982 he was up against an Irish team playing with the wind behind them, who were 10–3 up by the interval, with full-back Hugo MacNeill scoring the only try. Once again Ollie Campbell was in total charge, but it was actually a mistake of his, when his attempt at a drop-goal was charged down by Steve Smith, that led to the game's defining moment. The ball bounced back to the Irish forwards, and then Campbell got hold of it again. The Irish pack were motoring, so on the England 22-metre line he linked first with Fergus Slattery and then Willie Duggan, who shipped it on to the ginger-haired prop forward from Shannon, Gerry McLoughlin. With the Irish front row of McLoughlin, Fitzgerald and prop Phil Orr in the vanguard, the maul rolled as though it was going downhill – the handbrake was off and there was nothing England could do about it. Full-back Marcus Rose bravely stepped in but was swatted away as McLoughlin's distinctive red head bobbed up and down in the unstoppable surge to the line. The Irish supporters could not conceal their excitement and ran onto the field to celebrate – a famous win was surely theirs. They reached McLoughlin only after captain Fitzgerald had hauled his old college team-mate and front-row partner off the floor.

The victory meant that Ireland went home to play Scotland for the Triple Crown, something they had not won for 33 years, and never at Lansdowne Road. As the crowd gathered, they hoped fervently for a magical moment in Irish rugby history. So did Ollie Campbell. 'I suppose "Stay focussed" would be the current expression – I'm not sure what we used back in 1982. But having been cocooned away upstairs in the hotel room we realised what it all meant when we came down the stairs and walked through reception – people were in a state of high excitement.' As the coach took the players down to Lansdowne Road, Campbell had never felt such an atmosphere or seen such good humour in the crowd.

Later that afternoon Campbell was again the hero, having landed six penalty-goals, plus one drop-goal, to give Ireland all of their 21 points. Even more impressively, this majestic kicking record was achieved on a windy day. In the whole of the East Stand everyone was on their feet – 'They sang "Cockles and Mussels" for what seemed like the duration of the second half,' recalls Campbell – 'they didn't seem to care that it had been a dull game. The incredible silence which greeted John Rutherford's try earlier in the afternoon will live with me forever – that was not on the script. There was almost a presumption that Scotland were just turning up to make up the numbers. When the final whistle was blown I was engulfed by the supporters. I had been weaned by my Dad on the 1948 Irish team and all those great players and suddenly there I was winning Ireland's first Triple Crown at Lansdowne Road. Amazing when you think that Mike Gibson had played all those years and never won one. The beauty of the success was that it was absolutely, completely and totally out of the blue.'

After only three rounds the championship was all but decided, and the rest were left to fight it out for the placings. In Paris England recalled Dusty Hare and won thanks to the nineteen points kicked by the full-back. That win was followed by victory over Wales, while Scotland began to rescue their season with a win over France. On the final weekend the Scots would travel to Cardiff, and Ireland to Paris in search of their Grand Slam.

History did not favour Scotland. They had not won in Wales for twenty years, and it was an amazing 27 matches since the Welsh had lost a championship game at the Arms Park. France had been the last to win there, as far back as 1968 – it was a proud record which Wales had defended with vigour. But this was a Scottish team 'on a mission', as winger Roger Baird explains: 'Coach Jim Telfer took us to stay at the St Pierre Country Club out at Chepstow. The approach for the match was almost like the SAS – we were going to go in, do a job and get out again.'

The game produced the best rugby of the 1982 tournament. The Scottish raid began early when Baird was the instigator of a break-out from defence. 'The ball had been kicked through and our lock, Bill Cuthbertson, got it. I yelled at him, "Give it to me, Bill!" and he said, "No, I'm going for touch." He missed by a mile!' The next thing Scotland knew Wales were coming back at them and had an overlap – but luckily fly-half Gareth Davies' kick ahead bounced nicely for Baird near the left touch-line. He span around the advancing Welsh wing, Robert Ackerman, and soon found himself with just one man to beat. He drew in full-back Gwyn Evans and passed to Iain Paxton – 'I was put squarely on my backside and watched on the turf as the rest of the move unfolded,' recalls Baird, 'as if it was the slow-motion replay' – and from Paxton it went to Alan Tomes, and then Jim Calder to score.

The Welsh crowd were still recovering when Scotland centre Jim Renwick broke away to score another opportunist try. The young guys in the team were really enjoying it and giving it "Yahoo!"' says Baird, 'but Jim Renwick came back and said, "Look here, boys – don't lose your concentration. I've got over forty caps and I still haven't won away from home." That put it into perspective for us – it was important to make sure of a win.' Five tries in Cardiff, even if Wales were falling from their lofty perch, was enough to boost any team: 'Up until then, we had been playing a pretty basic percentage game,' says Baird, 'but this gave us the confidence to expand. A lot of people have said to me since that the match changed Scottish rugby.'

Meanwhile, Ireland had to endure a long month's wait for their tilt at the Grand Slam. When they finally played in Paris, it was against a French side reinforced with experienced players like Robert Paparemborde, recalled at prop. As their captain, Jean-Pierre Rives, put it, that season 'the guillotine had been overused', and now the 1981 champions badly needed to avoid a fourth defeat. All Ireland could muster was three more penalty-goals from Ollie Campbell. After the defeat, says Campbell, 'I remember meeting up with a famous old Blackrock College member, Jimmy Smith, outside the team hotel. It was midnight and we were still bitterly disappointed. Jimmy, who'd had a few drinks but was still just about with it, said that he wanted to make one point, and could I please tell the rest of the team: "The supporters didn't come over to win a Grand Slam – they came over to celebrate winning a Triple Crown." Suddenly, from being depressed, everything was right with the world.' Not an anniversary goes by, he adds, without the squad of that year meeting up – only the Irish can make a party last seventeen years!

1983 – Ireland and France share championship

The green shirt of Ireland had been the jersey to wear in 1982, but for the white colours of England the 1980 Grand Slam was becoming a distant memory. Things were not set to improve: their 1983 season began badly with three tries conceded in defeat at home to France, and the selectors' axe was sharpened. Next stop was Cardiff, where England had not won since 1963. As at Twickenham fly-half Les Cusworth dropped a goal, and also constructed England's only try for John Carleton – the one moment of the game to rise above mediocrity. 'It was a Leicester move,' explains Cusworth, 'called the "Chattanooga Choo-Choo" because Dusty Hare hit the line like a train. Another Leicester man, Paul Dodge, was also involved. It's interesting now seeing all the professionalism and planning that goes into moves in the modern game – but we were doing a lot of that stuff. Where the game was so different was in the amount of preparation. We used to have a couple of sessions on a Thursday morning to run through things, then it was a case of "get out there".'

In the end, though, all England's plotting was only enough to obtain a draw. The Chairman of the Welsh selectors, Clive Rowlands, joked that the replay would be the following Saturday but he, for one, would not be going! On the Monday morning the RFU donned the black cap and Les Cusworth was dropped. It was a very public execution: 'You heard the team selection on Radio Two at eleven o'clock if you were lucky,' says Cusworth. 'There was no follow-up telephone call – all that came in later years – but that was how it was then and you just accepted it.'

While England were looking to their past, the Scots were optimistic following their encouraging performance against Wales the previous season. Their hope was short-lived, though. Ireland's flanker, Fergus Slattery, leapt into the air to deny Jim Renwick a drop-goal in the final minutes at Murrayfield, and the champions narrowly won. In Paris two tries from the French winger, Patrick Estève, squeezed out a victory over Scotland and, to compound their misery, a fortnight later Wales won in Edinburgh. The highlight was a scintillating try started by one Welsh winger, Clive Rees, and finished by his namesake, Elgan. For Scotland, it was off to Twickenham to try and salvage some pride by winning there for the first time since 1971.

The Scottish scrum-half, Roy Laidlaw, had been relieved of the captaincy, handing over to prop forward Jim Aitken. Laidlaw played with a rediscovered freedom and scored a try in the second half which set his side on the road to victory. Like England's score in Cardiff the move was straight off the training ground. 'Laidlaw had this amazing ability to fly away off the back of the scrum,' explains number-eight John Beattie, 'so the forwards created a huge channel – the left-wing forward went away out to one side, and I went a long way to the right. The ball was hooked back strongly and came shooting out, almost three feet from the back of the scrum. This allowed Laidlaw to pick up the ball running and head to the corner flag before England knew where he was.'

Big Tom Smith, on the other hand, the Gala lock winning his first cap, will always be remembered for one of the least dramatic tries in the history of the championship, merely flopping over the line from the line-out. But Scotland had won and ended their dismal run at Twickenham. 'To be fair to England, it wasn't one of their better sides,' adds Beattie, 'but, crucially, we all thought we were going to win. What I will always remember, though, is that we were like little country boys visiting London for the first time. One of our pre-match meals was at McDonald's – I don't think any of us had seen a McDonald's before, let alone eaten there! It was of those low-budget Scottish teams!'

After two wins against Scotland and France, Ireland again had the title on their minds, but a heavy defeat to Wales in Cardiff quickly put paid to such thoughts. The man of that match was the burly Welsh scrum-half, Terry Holmes, whose belligerent play in the early part of the decade was one of the dominant features of the championship. Rugby league and injury robbed him of more appearances for Wales but the young Holmes, who took over from the great Gareth Edwards at both club and international level, was equal to the challenge. Holmes was a bright light in a fading team, and he feels the writing was on the wall for Welsh rugby. 'That day we played emphatically – it was an enjoyable win. But I said at the time we couldn't survive on our club rugby, and since then we have allowed things to drift on, instead of taking a good look at the whole of the game. Our club structure wasn't good enough in the early eighties, and we were kidding ourselves if we thought it was. We were paying a bit for our arrogance.'

France beat Wales to guarantee themselves a share of the championship; in the process Patrick Estève scored his country's single try, to become only the third man to perform the Grand Slam of tries. Ireland joined them at the top of the table after beating England in Dublin. Three years after England's Grand Slam, coach Mike Davis saw his team take the wooden spoon: 'I'm unique,' was his verdict: 'I've turned wine into water.' The season had confirmed the even division of power in European rugby during the 1980s.

1984 – Scotland's GRAND SLAM

England, France and Ireland had all enjoyed major success in the first three years of the decade but it was 1925 since the Scots had won all four matches in a season. Fifty-nine years on, however, they had a team full of fighters, in Jim Telfer a former player who was now a coach prepared to impose his will, and a kindred spirit as captain, Jim Aitken – 'brisk and brusque,' declares Telfer: 'he and I are very similar types of blokes.' Telfer had carved out a name as one of the leading motivators of the time – a reputation he would only add to over the next decade and a half. In 1983 he had been in charge of the British Lions tour to New Zealand, and there, although the series was lost, the seeds of future Scottish success had been sown. 'On the plane home,' recalls Telfer, 'John Rutherford said we would win the Triple Crown. There was a core of Scottish Lions who would be playing together again, and we knew the opposition better – their strengths and weaknesses.' Then in the autumn of 1983 the All Blacks had come to Britain themselves: drawing with them was a solid preparation for Scotland's Five Nations season.

Ironically, it was a man who had been overlooked by the Lions, David Leslie, who put in a world-class back-row display in their first match, against the Welsh. The Scottish skipper, Jim Aitken, went in for his first try for his country and his team were on their way. Next up were the English, in the 100th match between the two nations. England had actually beaten New Zealand at the end of 1983, so they started as clear favourites to win in Edinburgh. But by now Scotland's tactics were sharper, and their play was more vigorous. The mastermind behind the victory was John Rutherford, a tall, elegant fly-half possessed of an easy running style and a kicking boot to die for, whose excellent pick-up led to a try for centre Euan Kennedy. Even though England's normally sure-footed kicker Dusty Hare missed six attempts on goal, Scotland deserved their win by eighteen points to six, and were now one step away from a Triple Crown for the first time in 46 years. Blocking their way were Ireland, who had lost three matches – in Paris, despite the French having their tough prop Jean-Pierre Garuet sent off; at home to the Welsh, when Robert Ackerman scored a magnificent individual try; and at Twickenham.

Scotland against Ireland was the final championship appearance for the Irish second-row, Moss Keane, for ten years a major presence in the Five Nations, but it was a disappointing finale. Scotland scored five tries, two from Roy Laidlaw, whose partnership with John Rutherford – developed while playing for the South Schools, South Under-21s and then Scotland A – had become one of the best pairings in the world, and the axis of the Scottish team. The final whistle went and Scotland had won the Triple Crown. The supporters came running onto the field, and Rutherford's Selkirk club partner, Gordon Hunter, who had come on to win his first cap when Roy Laidlaw had had to leave the field with concussion, collided with a spectator. 'We were celebrating in the dressing-room afterwards,' says Rutherford, 'and I saw Gordon in the corner, distraught. I asked him what was wrong, and he explained the doctor thought that he had fractured a cheekbone. It dawned on the team that we now had a major problem. With a Grand Slam match to play in a fortnight's time we were without both our scrum-halves! After a hasty meeting, Roy's injury suddenly turned from concussion and a mandatory three weeks' ban to athlete's migraine!'

Scotland's last match would be at home to France. Like the Scots, the French had maintained an unbeaten record that year, and after a thrilling final quarter in Cardiff they had won in Wales for the first time since 1968. A crushing victory over England in Paris meant that they too were on course for the Grand Slam. Five of the French backs had scored tries against England, and three other scores were disallowed – France were looking dangerous.

Murrayfield was the venue for the Grand Slam showdown – Wales's victory at Twickenham relegated to a sideshow. Perhaps understandably the match was riddled with tension – Scotland making the more nervous start – but this merely heightened the drama. Despite prolonged spells of French pressure, the score stayed close. The Welsh referee, Winston Jones, in his first international, responded to increasing French frustration by penalising their indiscipline. It turned to anger at the decisions going against them, especially when captain Jean-Pierre Rives, playing his last international, watched his try-scoring scrum-half, Jérôme Gallion, carried off unconscious. With time running out for both sides, Jim Calder burst over from a line-out on the French line for a famous try, and France, feeling he had come through off-side, again claimed justice had not been done.

But what really won the game for Scotland was the kicking of full-back Peter Dods. He was nearly denied his moment of glory when his eye ballooned following a collision with Serge Blanco's knee. Off-target shortly afterwards with a penalty goal he soon had a chance to make amends with another kick. Jim Aitken called Dods over and enquired whether he could see. 'Yes', replied Dods. 'Well, you'd better see this bugger between the posts!' Aitken barked back. With vision restored, Dods kept his nerve and ended with seventeen points in the match, to take his total for the season to fifty and beat Andy Irvine's record.

The unrestrained joy that greeted Jim Calder's try was the release that came after decades of 'nearly's and 'almost's. The team's hooker, Colin Deans, sums up the year. 'I think it's a Scottish trait that you always think you are inferior, and that was something we got over in 1984. We had been pretty green going on that Lions tour but, having toured with the guys from the other nations, we realised they were ordinary human beings.' Scotland had exceeded John Rutherford's prediction on that plane back from New Zealand: not just a Triple Crown but a Grand Slam.

1985 – Ireland's Triple Crown and championship

Scotland's joy was short-lived, however, as the unpredictability of the championship in the 1980s was demonstrated in 1985. The Grand Slam winners would descend while Ireland, the wooden spooners in 1984, would climb the other way. Ciaran Fitzgerald, the man who captained Ireland to their success earlier in the decade, had been recalled in an attempt to repeat those heroics, leading a new, young team determined to make up for experience with 'enthusiasm, fitness, exuberance and enterprise', as Fitzgerald puts it. 'The new coach Mick Doyle said, "Give it a lash." That was our catch-phrase and it served us well.'

First for Ireland it was Scotland away but, despite winger Trevor Ringland's try in the second-half, Scotland managed to kick their way into a winning position. Time was running out and Ireland needed another score quickly. 'It was our last attacking platform, and I told the players to give it one final shot,' says Fitzgerald. Their captain's wish was the team's command – the pack combined with the backs and, after a smart scissors move, Ringland was sent into the corner for his second try. 'It was the defining moment of the season,' Fitzgerald says. 'When we scored that try I knew we had something special. There were so many of the team involved in it, so many pairs of hands. They had licence to run it from anywhere, which in those days was unusual for an Irish team. Often as a captain, when dealing with young people you don't know what to say – it might be the wrong thing and they could freeze. But that team didn't know what freezing meant.'

Ireland returned home to meet the French who had already played two matches in a championship disrupted by the winter weather. At Twickenham the French fly-half, Jean-Patrick Lescarboura, equalled the world record with three drop-goals – an amazing effort in any game. However, after England's scrum-half Richard Harding had dramatically managed to dislodge the ball from Patrick Estève once he had already crossed the English line, the game ended in a draw. After this disappointment, France briefly sparkled against Scotland in Paris, but their victory was unconvincing. In Dublin, however, Ireland were grateful for another draw – centre Michael Kiernan's kicking cancelling out France's tries, the only two of a game in which penalties were always on the agenda. 'It was a savage match,' remembers Fitzgerald: 'a bruising experience for the youngsters – afterwards the guys' bodies were torn apart.'

The bad weather meant Wales had to wait until early March for their first match of the championship. They won an exciting game against Scotland, and hopes were high in Cardiff when Ireland arrived – and even higher after Wales had established forward domination. 'We had a light pack,' says Fitzgerald, 'and we were pushed all over the place – totally outgunned. But what we did do was win the ball back from the opposition and that's where the back row came to the fore. Brian Spillane, Nigel Carr and Phillip Matthews were the trio – marvellous athletes, and in Nigel we had a number seven who suited our side because he was so fast and mobile.' Winger Keith Crossan added Ireland's second try to Ringland's earlier score, and the Irish had defeated Wales for the first time in Cardiff since 1967. The Triple Crown was in their sights for the second time in four years.

Meanwhile, England had beaten Scotland at Twickenham, profiting from another amazing mistake by the opposition. Three Scottish players over-ran a Peter Dods chip and squandered a certain try to deny them what would have been the winning score. Regardless of their good fortune, England were proving to be a gutsy team – they would certainly be no pushover in Dublin. Despite an early English penalty, Irish spirits were lifted when England full-back Chris Martin had a clearance kick charged down and centre Brendan Mullin pounced to score. Ireland could not pull away, however – 'That game was slipping away from us, no doubt about it,' says Ciaran Fitzgerald. 'We were suffering from the sheer power of the opposition's pack.' The match was all square with eighty minutes up when the Irish forced a line-out on England's 22-metre line.

As at Murrayfield, Fitzgerald's young team responded with one of the most exciting finishes in championship history. The captain chose to throw to the tail where Brian Spillane made the catch and lock Donal Lenihan, who had played so well that season alongside Willie Anderson, immediately ripped the ball away and ran straight at England's fly-half Rob Andrew to try and set up a scoring position. Next in the chain to glory was Michael Bradley, who turned and passed to the first green jersey he saw. It belonged not to his half-back partner Paul Dean, but to Michael Kiernan, who found himself standing right in front of the posts, and his drop-goal sailed through to win them the Triple Crown.

'I remember having to come out of the dressing-room again afterwards,' says Fitzgerald, 'because the security guys had asked me to try and calm down the crowd gathering outside. I stood up on one of those slippery seats they used to have at Lansdowne Road, still in my boots, and kept them back from the dressing-room door. I've never known anything like it in rugby.' Wales lost in Paris and won at home to England, but it was Ireland's turn to enjoy tangible success. Fitzgerald, the failed leader of the 1983 British Lions, had proved again that for his country he was one of the best skippers ever. For the second time in his career he had taken Ireland from the bottom of the championship table to the top. They really had 'given it a lash'.

1986 – France and Scotland share championship

Encouragingly, Ireland had won the 1985 championship because they were prepared to use their talented back line. But in 1986 the artisan was just as likely to be rewarded as the artist. It was a year when the boot reigned supreme, as a series of vital kicks at goal shaped the season. The seeds of 'win-at-all-costs' rugby were being sown.

The trend was evident from the first whistle. Against England the Welsh centre Bleddyn Bowen scored the only try of the game, but with pinpoint accuracy Rob Andrew scored all 21 points to secure England's victory. It was a similar story at Murrayfield, where Scotland unveiled a new kicking sensation, Gavin Hastings, who announced his arrival in the championship by scoring all of his team's eighteen points to cancel out two French tries. The clean-cut full-back looked every bit the *Boy's Own* hero. Alongside him in the back line was younger brother Scott, also making his debut for his country and, he confirms, a dream come true: 'As a youngster, I would play rugby on a Saturday morning and rush back to watch the Five Nations matches on the television. If Scotland were at home it meant being dropped off at my grandparents' while the folks went to Murrayfield. We used to say if it was raining Scotland had a chance!' When he was eleven Scott Hastings went to Murrayfield himself to watch Scotland play France, and at half-time was given some soup by their neighbours in the crowd. 'I only found out later that it had been laced with sherry, which might have explained our light-headedness after the match!'

After their victory, Scotland went to Cardiff in joyous mood, but they were brought back down to earth with a bang. This time, the boot that did the damage belonged to a Welshman, Neath's Paul Thorburn. In 1999 he would have another important role for Wales as Tournament Director for the World Cup in his country. Back in

1986 Thorburn's contribution was not in a suit but in the colours of his team. It was an absorbing match, with the lead changing six times, but the most memorable moment came near the end. A Scottish tackle on fly-half Jonathan Davies was adjudged to be late and the Scots were penalised where the ball landed, inside the Welsh ten-metre line. 'Straight away,' says full-back Thorburn, 'I said to our captain David Pickering, "Give me the ball, I want to have a go."' The main aim, he explains, was to take the Scots deeper into their own territory – 'I thought that by having a pot, even if I missed it, the result would be Scotland restarting with a drop-out. The others in the side were probably just glad of the breather.' To the astonishment of the spectators, Wales opted for a shot at goal. 'There was an element of hit and hope about it,' says Thorburn, 'but I remember I gave it a real hoof.' When the ball sneaked over television commentator Bill McLaren was left momentarily speechless: Thorburn says you could almost see the Scots' heads drop. His missile installed him in championship history: when the full distance was later measured it turned out to be no less than seventy yards, eight and a half inches.

For once that season, a stunning try was the highlight of France's win over Ireland in Paris. The record books show that, by the time Philippe Sella finished the move off, there had been, incredibly, 21 passes as the French opened out. At Murrayfield the Scots erased the memory of losing to Wales by beating England with a record score. Captain Colin Deans remembers that the press had written off his new-look team as likely to be trounced by the big England pack – an article in the *Edinburgh Evening News* went as far as to say it was pointless them turning up. That was the spur, says Deans: 'At the Friday night team meeting, John Jeffrey threw the paper across the room.' The standard was set from the first 22 drop-out, he goes on: 'Johnnie Beattie creamed Maurice Colclough – and we just tore into England with a vengeance. We ran and ran and ran, and kept the ball alive all the time, knowing their forwards couldn't play to that type of game.' Backs Matt Duncan, John Rutherford and Scott Hastings all scored tries, and Gavin Hastings, oozing an infectious confidence, kicked the goals, landing eight out of eight attempts to give Scotland their total of 33 points – even in this win the boot was still having its say. 'We were on such a high,' concludes Deans, 'we could have played another eighty minutes quite easily.'

Meanwhile, Ireland's world was turning upside down. After Triple Crown success the year before, they had lost to an increasingly confident Wales. Worse was to come when, in their next match at

Twickenham, the Irish found a new number-eight playing for England, Dean Richards, who scored two tries on his debut and would have had a hat-trick had the ball not been kicked out of a scrum when he was about to score again. Richards, a policeman from Leicester, would make a massive impression on rugby right through to the end of the century. With his socks rolled down and shambling gait he never looked the athlete, but his immense strength, allied to a rugby radar fine-tuned to locate the ball whatever its position, made him a favourite with British supporters.

The championship race was still wide open: should Scotland fail to win in Dublin, France's win in Cardiff now meant one more victory on the final day, at home to England, would give them the Five Nations title. France fulfilled their side of the equation, comfortably beating the English when centre, Philippe Sella, scored a brilliant breakaway try to achieve the Grand Slam of tries that season. But what Sella and France wanted now was to hear that Scotland had lost. Ireland could not oblige, however, and Scotland's victory by a single point was enough to give them a share of the title. The Irish place kicker, Michael Kiernan, who had dropped that goal to secure the 1985 Triple Crown, had a relatively easy chance to win the game, but this time his kick drifted agonisingly wide and consigned his team to the wooden spoon. In the year of the boot, it seemed an appropriate end.

1987 – France's GRAND SLAM

Never before had teams gone into the Five Nations season with anything other than the Grand Slam on their minds. In 1987, an even bigger prize was on offer, as the tournament encountered its first rival as the sport's number-one competition: the Rugby World Cup. 'Before the World Cup, there was nothing comparable with the Five Nations,' says Jamie Salmon, an Englishman who had qualified and played for New Zealand in the early 1980s before returning to play for England. The sporting boycott of apartheid was then excluding South Africa from world rugby, New Zealand had the odd one-off series against Australia or France, 'but the Five Nations was the only tournament that ended up with a table and a winner, and those countries not involved were jealous of it.' Now there was to be a far bigger competition, and Salmon's experiences with the All Blacks had taught him that the Five Nations sides had a lot to learn from how the other side of the world approached rugby: 'The All Black attitude in those days was vastly superior to England's. In New Zealand there was much more intensity and public expectation – rugby was never off the front, let alone the back pages. The way you were expected to train and perform was totally different. Here you always had an opt-out clause that you were doing it for fun and had a shirt to iron on Sunday evening for work.'

England made a terrible start to the 1987 championship on the first day in Ireland. The Irish ran up a total of seventeen points: England, as the saying goes, were lucky to get nil. Neither was it a smooth beginning for the joint champions, France. Despite a victory over New Zealand in the November of 1986, they struggled to beat Wales in Paris. The French still went to Twickenham as favourites, however, and England's new recruit, Jamie Salmon, came up against Philippe Sella, arguably the best centre in the world: 'As an All Black I had played against the excellent Roland Bertranne, but Sella was one of the first players to have a major physical presence in midfield. He combined power, pace and this ability to stand on his feet and hold the ball up until flanker Eric Champ arrived – he was key to their game.' Sella was the perfect blend of rugby brain and body, but even he could not stop France falling 12–3 behind. After a Serge Blanco drop-goal, though, they managed to run up the middle for winger Eric Bonneval to score a fine try. Then Sella himself intercepted a ball between England's scrum- and fly-halves and was away for a try to give France victory – 'the one moment in my rugby life,' he declares, 'when we got the better of England.'

France were now gathering momentum, and beat Scotland in a thrilling match in Paris featuring six tries – three from winger Bonneval, a superb player who was never quite to recover his form after breaking his knee during the subsequent World Cup. They were now only one win away from the Grand Slam and would meet an Irish side already beaten by the Scots.

England, however, hit one of their lowest points of all when they met Wales in Cardiff, in probably the ugliest match ever witnessed in the Five Nations. 'It was then that Anglo-Welsh relations on the field were at an all-time low,' recalls Jamie Salmon; 'it was very unpleasant.' The acrimony preceded the kick-off, when England's captain and scrum-half, Richard Hill, was spat on and abused during the warm-up. 'Hill's planned team talk went out of the window,' says Salmon. 'It just became a verbal tirade against the Welsh – unbeknown to him, the RFU's Don Rutherford was listening to everything. Players like Wade Dooley didn't take much to get them going and the rest of the forwards were fired up like never before. We went out there and at the first line-out all hell broke loose. The whole pack was going ballistic. After that, it was never going to be a pleasant game.' The fists were constantly flying, and following one encounter, during which Phil Davies' cheekbone was smashed by a punch from the giant Lancastrian policeman Dooley, it was amazing that nobody was sent off.

Wales won, but the recriminations went long into the night and beyond. Dooley's punch, Hill's pre-match eruption and other misdemeanours from the front-row forwards Graham Dawe and Gareth Chilcott saw them all banned from England's final match against Scotland. Chilcott was one of the championship's most distinctive characters, with his shaven head, bull-neck and twinkle in his eye.

'It was not a game I'm particularly proud to have been involved in,' he says. 'All we got for the three weeks prior to the game was that it was going to be the "Battle of Cardiff". The newspapers wanted to know what you did for a living, what you ate and drank and how many times you'd been sent off – the pressure was more than I can ever remember at any stage of my international career.' The infamous England-Wales clash in 1980 had been the subject of great attention from the rugby writers, but this match was really the first time that the general press began to get interested in rugby and its personalities. 'We got wrapped up in the media and went out and played into their hands,' continues Chilcott. 'It wasn't so much Wales beating us on the day, it was England losing – yet it takes two to tango, you can't have a bad game without all the players wanting it. But England did go over the top and were looking for bodies rather than ball. The fact that I got banned – well, if you live by the sword, you've got to die by it. But I do think that rugby players, and rugby in general, learnt from that game.'

Now the French, their confidence high, took on the Irish in Dublin. Ireland established a 10–0 lead with early tries from Trevor Ringland and Michael Bradley, but Eric Champ produced his best game of the Five Nations to score two tries, and France had won the Grand Slam under the strong leadership of hooker Daniel Dubroca. This 1987 side had now been together for four years, says Philippe Sella: 'Each year we got better, and after the narrow defeat to Scotland in 1986 we were a year older and wiser. Sometimes in rugby a year can make all the difference.'

The Grand Slam decided, a much-changed England team tried to recover some dignity and prevent Scotland from winning the Triple

Crown, and ended the season with their best performance for some time. The streetwise prop Gary Pearce, who had made his debut against Scotland eight years earlier, was in his final championship match and, along with the equally wily Paul Rendall, had a royal battle with Scotland's Iain Milne and David Sole. A penalty try and a score from Marcus Rose were England's first tries of the championship – after Cardiff it had been a fine recovery. There was still a hint of controversy in the air, however, thanks to the mischievous Jamie Salmon, who was caught coming out of the referee's room afterwards having exchanged jerseys with the match official, Owen Doyle. 'Don Rutherford said, "What are you doing in there?" and I replied with a deadpan look, "I told him if he blew up two minutes early I would swap jerseys with him." Don's jaw dropped, and I swear he thought another massive scandal about to break!'

In the other match that final weekend Wales lost to Ireland, but in Australia and New Zealand later that year it was the Welsh who were the only home nation to reach the last four of the inaugural World Cup. The Five Nations champions, France, represented the northern hemisphere in the final, but New Zealand demonstrated that theirs was the winning way. Attitudes would indeed have to evolve if the five nations were to be winners in a wider contest.

1988 – Wales's Triple Crown; France and Wales share championship

Ten years earlier the Welsh had held the premier position in the championship that France's World Cup Final appearance and Grand Slam win had now confirmed, but in 1988 the signs were that, after nearly a decade of failure, Wales's adventurous approach would see them challenge again.

Wales sat out the opening day of the championship and watched two evenly contested matches – a brave but losing performance by England in Paris and a win for Ireland over Scotland. The Welsh did not have a strong pack and, for their first match away at Twickenham, revealed a side that included four fly-halves: Jonathan Davies was to wear the number ten jersey but the centres, Mark Ring and Bleddyn Bowen, and the full-back, Tony Clement, had all played in the pivotal stand-off role at club level. The result was as fresh and sunny as that February day. On the wing for Wales, and the main beneficiary of his side's attacking policy, was Adrian Hadley of

Cardiff: 'Paul Thorburn had dropped out of the team and that meant my mate Mark Ring would have to kick the goals,' says Hadley, 'so we had no chance with that – we had to run!' After Hadley scored his second try in the same corner as the first, the supporters invaded the pitch. Wales were on their way.

Meanwhile, France had lost their chance of a repeat Grand Slam by going down to Scotland, but then in beating Ireland they regained their high standards of the previous season. For Wales it was Scotland next, and a day of two spectacular scores. The first came when Jonathan Davies received a lobbed reverse pass from his half-back partner, Robert Jones and, under pressure well outside the Scottish twenty-two, set off for the line. He cut back inside with a spry skip and, after a superbly judged grubber kick, controlled the ball to ground it over the try-line. It all happened within a flash. But a wizard was still to weave his spell. From another scrum the ball was fed down the line, Mark Ring went outside Adrian Hadley on the loop and passed to Ieuan Evans. The winger proceeded to beat six bamboozled Scottish defenders on his way to score one of the great tries. 'Merlin the Magician couldn't have done any better!' exclaimed Bill McLaren in his television commentary, and Wales were one victory away from the Triple Crown.

Suddenly, says Adrian Hadley, Wales realised what was possible. 'We were nervous for the Ireland game. You were never going to win by a load over there and, looking back, we tried to play too expansive a game.' Welsh forward Paul Moriarty scrambled a try, after a Jonathan Davies drop-goal but, as the final whistle drew near, Wales still needed three points from somewhere to secure a win. 'It was heart-stopping stuff,' confirms Hadley. In injury time, Wales got their chance. Irish scrum-half Michael Bradley was penalised, and Paul Thorburn, recalled to the side, had a kick for the Triple Crown. The full-back had proved himself to be an excellent pressure kicker, but this was something else. A nation waited nervously, but Thorburn calmly put the ball over. It had been a long wait, but Wales had won their first Triple Crown since 1979.

Now, moreover, they had a Grand Slam match against France in Cardiff, and memories of those epic battles of the 1970s came flooding back. Wales were true to their attacking strategy but encountered the wettest of days at the Arms Park, which inevitably led to a scrappy contest. 'We desperately tried to win it in the last ten minutes,' says Adrian Hadley, 'but we just couldn't get that vital score. Jonathan Davies had a bet on himself that year to score drop-goals in all the championship matches: he tried hard from every angle, but it seemed destined not to be our day.' When the final whistle came Wales had lost by a single point.

But at least Wales had given the championship a feeling of enterprise. The same could not be said of Scotland and England: that year's Calcutta Cup match at Murrayfield was a dour struggle smothered in ill-feeling, which England won in little or no style. 'It was a dreadful game with both sides killing the ball,' confirms John Jeffrey, the blond Kelso farmer and flanker who sat on the bench that day. 'As I watched I said to myself that I wasn't going on unless somebody was really injured. I've never felt like that about an international, before or after – it was a terrible thought, but the game was that bad.'

The atmosphere of Scotland-England matches at that time Jeffrey describes as 'doing Bannockburn once a year – that season the two coaches even had a go at each other after the final whistle.' The bad feeling continued at the after-match reception: the players from both teams were mixed at the top table and, as a fair bit of alcohol had been drunk, one or two scuffles broke out. In those days, recalls Jeffrey, the Scotland players were each presented with a miniature of Drambuie – 'we'd downed those on the bus leaving the ground. My fellow pack-member, Finlay Calder, also had a bottle of Highland Malt and we decided to put that away as well' – all this before consuming any food. 'It was so bad that four of the Scottish team had gone to bed before dinner was served!'

Eventually Jeffrey was instrumental, in partnership with England's Dean Richards, in restoring congenial Anglo-Scottish relations, but his decision not to hit the sack landed him in deep trouble. Richards had arrived late to the dinner to find half a bottle of whisky on the table and Jeffrey announcing that he'd drunk his half and now the number-eight was to do the same. 'I knew full well he hadn't,' says Richards, 'but I decided to take up the challenge.' Then the pair hit on the idea of taking the Calcutta Cup on an impromptu trip around Edinburgh. The famous cup had never seen anything like it. 'We took it into pubs and asked the landlords to keep filling it up. It seemed a good idea because you could put more pints in there than in a glass,' adds the ever-practical Richards. 'The surprising thing was that it came back at all – let's say we weren't always concentrating on where it was, as I'm sure you can understand. Of course, the landlords thought it was great having the Calcutta Cup in their pubs on the night of a Scotland-England match!' At the end of the evening the cup made it back to safety, although not quite in one piece, and if the administrators had a secret chuckle about the episode they didn't show it: Richards got a one-match ban, and Jeffrey in effect got six months, as he was banned from going on the Scots' summer tour. 'That taught him to lie about how much whisky he'd drunk!' says Richards.

Two weeks later, England were hitting the headlines in a more conventional fashion when, for the second year running, they left their try-scoring until the final day of the season. Ireland were hit with an avalanche of six. Winger Chris Oti, the first black player to appear for England since James Peters in 1908, scored a hat-trick in only his second game and on his home debut. Though Wales had finished at the top of the championship table, along with France, they could ill afford the continuing loss of players to rugby league. Try-scoring hero Adrian Hadley and the team's genius of a fly-half, Jonathan Davies, were the next to go, Davies to Widnes for a record deal worth £200,000. The constant drip-feed of talent to the professional code would finally take its toll and, far from heralding a renaissance for the sport in Wales, the success in 1988 would stand in isolation to remind the Welsh public of what could have been.

1989 – France's championship

In 1989, Welsh rugby came crashing back to earth in a championship that generally lacked sparkle. One bright spot was France's exciting comeback from fifteen points down to beat the Irish, including a try from their talented full-back, Serge Blanco. The same weekend, Scotland's victory over Wales was achieved with relative ease, and when Wales lost to Ireland in their next game it was the first time they had been beaten in their opening two championship matches for over twenty years. The champions' misery was exacerbated by a crushing defeat in Paris – leaving only a final-day meeting with England, and a desperate need to avoid a first-ever whitewash.

A confident England arrived in Cardiff unbeaten after three matches. Under the guidance of their new young captain and centre, Will Carling, they had drawn against Scotland and beaten Ireland and France. The Cardiff match, however, revealed there was still considerable bad feeling between Wales and the English, and a second-half brawl involved the majority of the forwards. The only try was instigated by Welsh fly-half Paul Turner, successor to the departed Jonathan Davies. Recommended by Barry John and Phil Bennett,

Turner played for unfashionable Newbridge, and saw his caps as reward for a long career in club rugby. 'Ever since I'd been a little boy I'd dreamed of playing against England at the Arms Park,' he says – 'that was the game all Welsh youngsters wanted to play in. I'd always pictured it as a sunny day, so you can imagine my disappointment to see it pour down. The try came after I had put up a really innocuous kick. The ball went to Rory Underwood on the England wing and, not to put too fine a point on it, he made a real mess of it. He then threw a bad pass to his full-back, Jonathan Webb, and after he could-n't take it the ball was hacked on and our centre, Mike Hall, dived on it to score.' Wales had avoided the dreaded Grand Slam of defeats, and England's appalling record in Cardiff continued, but this was to be Paul Turner's last appearance for his country – he never had his day in the sun.

England's defeat meant that both France and Scotland had a chance of taking the championship. Scotland went to the Parc des Princes on the back of a pulsating encounter against Ireland that pro-duced eight tries, including three for the Scottish winger, Iwan Tukalo. But, like England at the Arms Park, the Scots had a problem with winning at the Parc des Princes and, confronted with such world-class forwards as Jean Condom, Dominique Erbani and Laurent Rodriguez, Scotland had a harrowing experience. The Scottish captain, Finlay Calder, was twin brother of Jim – who had scored the Grand Slam-winning try against France five years earlier – but this, he confirms, was a different kind of day. 'We had been on a bit of a roll that season, but the boys came in at half-time and asked me what we were going to do? I said, "It's every man for himself – let's just get through this." After the match the press put it to me that I'd been naïve with my tactics – but we'd never had the ball!' The French captain and scrum-half, Pierre Berbizier, was highly influential – 'all class and a superb rugby brain,' says Calder: 'he never really got involved at close quarters, although he could tackle when he had to.' Berbizier scored a try to give France their third Five Nations title in four years. 'It was their championship,' concedes Calder, 'and they deserved it.'

As the decade came to an end the Five Nations, reflecting the gen-eral trend in sport, was becoming big business. Its matches were events to be seen at, and demand for seats, from both the paying pub-lic and the corporate sector, was placing a strain on ticket availabil-ity. Far from diminishing the importance of the championship, the 1987 World Cup and the build-up to the second tournament in 1991, the first to be held in the northern hemisphere, were generating even more interest in rugby. These were boom times, with money beginning to flood into the sport – if not the players' pockets.

One man determined not to miss the boat was the former England prop, Mike Burton, who had achieved notoriety in Australia in 1975 as the first Englishman to be sent off in an international. Even as a player Burton was determined to make his name in business and had taken early advantage of sponsorship. 'As amateurs we were all approached by the major boot manufacturers to wear their particular brand. I was the first man to accept £50 for wearing a certain make of boots (I have paid the tax on it!) – but I was the only one that accepted the offer, and I was a prop! Just think what kind of money England's kicker, Bob Hiller, could have made – and what about a dashing back like David Duckham? They were honourable men, though, and didn't take the cash, but in theory the English team could have been bought for £750. It got me thinking about what was possible when I stopped playing.'

Burton hung up his sponsored boots at the end of the 1970s and the next ten years saw his entrepreneurial empire grow. By the end of the eighties he, perhaps more than any other individual, had realised how lucrative rugby had become. 'In 1972, tickets for Five Nations games were priced at £3.50 each. As a player, the Union gave you two and you could buy six more. I soon realised the commercial possibilities! I said to myself, I know a few of these people, and some of the old players, and I could lay my hands on the tickets one way or another...' At the time there were no official facilities at Twickenham for hosting corporate functions, so Burton set up buses in the North Stand Car Park as makeshift hospitality suites for Five Nations games. Soon he had orders for six.

Next Burton branched out from Twickenham and filled a gap in the market by exploiting the attractions of all the Five Nations venues. The weekend rugby package was born. 'When England were over in Ireland it was a wonderful weekend. Golf on the Friday afternoon, plus two nights in a hotel and tickets for the game. And on the Sunday everybody could have time to talk about their headache.' Burton counts off the unique selling-points: 'France had moved from the Stade Colombes to the Parc des Princes – and that was a marvellous venue with all the accessible restaurants and cafés. Cardiff and Edinburgh were ideal because you could walk to the ground from the hotel suites. Twickenham was the only ground which was a long way out from the city centre, but we developed the buses into marquees and business boomed. So each event took on its own personality.'

The roguish Burton has always been happy to take on the establishment, and his activities did not receive universal approval from the conservative home unions. 'I was accused of being a terrible man. But as it turned out, the unions have all done exactly what I did. They've all started up their own hospitality operations – and even struck deals with boot manufacturers!' In any case, argues Burton, the link between the Five Nations and commerce was not a new phenomenon – the relationship was just being taken onto a different level. 'In the 1920s my mate Tommy Voyce, the old England player, used to have most of his business meetings on the Friday before the England-Scotland match – what you did was give a chap a couple of tickets and make sure you had dinner with him on the Thursday night. The grammar school or university boys who'd gone into middle or senior management were able to go to the rugby to reminisce and continue friendships.' The only difference nowadays, concludes Burton, is that hospitality has become more accessible – 'The small firm of industrial cleaners now want a table for ten at a Five Nations match.' The clock could not be turned back, even if some wanted it to be.

PART FIVE

1990–1999

With so much new money coming into the sport it could only be a matter of time before rugby union became professional. Players were finding it difficult to juggle their busy sporting lives with the other professions that occupied them daily; it was not a new problem, but with the demands of modern training schedules, it had got out of hand. The championship was now an excellent passport to national celebrity and its trappings. England captain Will Carling was the prime example of a rugby player whose fame stretched way beyond the confines of his sport. But those who profited were in the minority. The issue of professionalism boiled beneath the surface and accusations of 'shamateurism' mounted.

Many had already been applying professional values to the amateur game, and during the early part of the decade this was an important influence on the championship. Stung by Scotland's famous Grand Slam win in 1990, England responded by taking three Grand Slams in the next five years – a period of success underpinned by not only the skill of the team but also their meticulous organisation.

Off the field, the development of modern, comfortable stadia, to house the fans who would ultimately contribute the money to pay the players, was seen as vital. Twickenham and Murrayfield underwent extensive facelifts at great cost to the English and Scottish Unions. Wales and France went one step further and built new homes for their national sides. With millions of pounds spent on providing an unrestricted view for spectators who demanded more for their outlay on match tickets, and debts to service, a competitive Five Nations was needed more than ever before. But Wales's championship win in 1994 was an increasingly rare act of giant-killing from the Celtic teams, who were in danger of slipping behind. Towards the end of the decade France won back-to-back Grand Slams, with England their main challenger, fueling a concern that the shift to professionalism, formalised in the middle of the nineties, was creating a two-tier championship.

These problems were further highlighted by the advances made in the southern hemisphere, where a smoother transition into professionalism had created a power base that set the standard for the rest of the world. There, the players were contracted to the unions, and a structured season was put in place featuring two new successful competitions, the Super-Twelve – between the best provincial sides from South Africa, Australia and New Zealand – and the Tri-Nations, a triangular international tournament between the three nations. In the northern hemisphere, the clubs claimed that they had first call on the players they had contracted, and this caused unremitting conflict with the unions. The future of the championship itself was even placed in doubt as the five nations argued over television rights, culminating in 1999 in the expulsion of England from the competition for a single day. The final Five Nations, set to become the Six Nations in the year 2000 with the inclusion of Italy, needed to provide a thrilling end to the century in order to kill off premature speculation that the championship was mortally wounded.

1990 – Scotland's GRAND SLAM

In 1990 the word on everybody's lips was not 'professionalism' but 'nationalism'. The rising intensity of Celtic/English rivalry towards the end of the 1980s was unmistakable, and as much a political as sporting issue, but what happened in 1990 would surpass everything. Ten years after Bill Beaumont led England to the Grand Slam, the new decade seemed set to start in a similar fashion, with Will Carling's England overwhelming favourites to brush aside all who lay in their path. The beauty of the Five Nations, however, has always been its unpredictability.

England started well and three late tries against Ireland were enough to see them to a comfortable win. Wales, meanwhile, were heading to defeat at home to France, and their hopes were ended when lock Kevin Moseley followed in the footsteps of Geoff Wheel and Paul Ringer and became the third Welshman to be sent off in the history of the championship. A month later the English referee, Fred

Howard, who had dismissed Moseley for stamping also ordered France's forward, Alain Carminati, off the field at Murrayfield during their defeat by Scotland.

France met England in Paris in what many saw as the potential decider for the season. However, this was an assessment based more on past French glories than the legitimate claims of coach Jacques Fouroux's disparate team, and England responded with one of their best ever performances in the French capital. Will Carling rounded off the win with a try and, after an emphatic victory over Wales, he must have felt sure his team were on course for the Grand Slam.

Lurking in the background, however, Scotland were quietly gathering momentum. They had begun their season with a narrow victory in Dublin and, after that win over France, their prospects looked even brighter. A theme was emerging: the omnipresent back-row of Derek White, John Jeffrey and Finlay Calder was a constant irritant to the opposition. Yet despite Scotland's two early victories, few critics made a case for them coming anything more than a brave second to England. For their tilt at the Grand Slam, Scotland needed to win in Cardiff. Wales had a new coach, Ron Waldron from Neath, and he let everybody know it by playing seven men from his club, including the entire front-row. Despite winger Arthur Emyr scoring the best try of that year's championship, Scotland again squeaked the victory and could look ahead with confidence.

Ireland lost in Paris and headed home to play Wales for the wooden spoon. With their subsequent defeat the Welsh hit rock bottom: their first-ever blank championship season. In contrast, Scotland and England were gearing up for one of the most eagerly awaited international rugby matches for years. The two old enemies were to meet for the Grand Slam, and neither players nor supporters could wait for what many believe the most famous championship game of all time.

Starved of football's defunct Home International championship, and failing to get the same kind of kick from golf's rivalry between Sandy Lyle and Nick Faldo, the British public needed no convincing that Scotland against England on 17 March 1990 was as close to a sporting battle as it could find. The Scots also wanted to teach a lesson to an English rugby side seen north of the border as arrogant and complacent. But the rise in nationalistic fervour had a political undercurrent, and the match build-up spilt over into areas that had little to do with rugby. Governance from London by a party most Scottish people had not voted for was a daily pill increasingly difficult for some to swallow, and the early experimentation with the poll tax in Scotland was a lingering sore. Mr Carling might as well have been Mrs Thatcher, minus the handbag!

These elements, together with the increasing self-belief of the Scotland team, created the perfect conditions for an explosion of national pride. They were captained by prop David Sole, whose gritty leadership qualities had already proved crucial that season – but in the 'blue-hot' atmosphere of Murrayfield the real soul of the Scottish team was going to be tested to the full. 'The most emotional time for me came on the morning of the game,' says Sole. 'At the team meeting coaches Ian McGeechan and Jim Telfer brought everybody to the point of tears. Then, in my final talk to the players two minutes before they went out, I stressed that life would go on come Monday morning irrespective of whether we won or not, but that this was our one opportunity to write our names in the record books. I remember saying last of all, "We are now going out to win a Grand Slam."'

England had already burst from their dressing-room into a cacophony of noise. Now the Scottish captain takes up the story: 'Murrayfield used to have a very gentle sloping exit from the changing rooms, so if you started jogging at the top of the tunnel, by the time you came out you were sprinting, and there would be a huge roar. In 1990 we decided to walk.' It seemed to take an age before Scotland emerged and then, with their chests thrust forward and backs ramrod-straight, Sole's men paced out with a slow and methodical stride. It was as if the team were aware that this moment in rugby history already belonged to them. As they emerged, the usual cheer went up, but then it died down – the crowd realising, says Sole, 'that we were making a very clear statement of intent.' The second roar just about took the roof off the stands, and the noise filled the stadium for the full eighty minutes.

Fly-half Craig Chalmers put Scotland into an early lead with a successful kick at goal. England's response was to score an excellent try through centre Jeremy Guscott but, imprisoned by the ferocious Scottish tackling, they could not show the freedom of movement so evident earlier in the year. The decisive score came for Scotland shortly after half-time, when John Jeffrey fed scrum-half Gary Armstrong. The nuggety Armstrong, so inspirational throughout the championship, found Gavin Hastings with a clever and well-executed pass. Hastings chipped and up went winger Tony Stanger. The 21-year-old from Hawick capped an amazing debut season by plucking the bouncing ball out of the sky to score a try that sits at the pinnacle of Scotland's Five Nations history. England flailed and scrambled to respond, and when Rory Underwood seemed odds-on to score he was dramatically scythed down by Scott Hastings in a tackle that finally destroyed English ambitions. At the sound of the final whistle the English players sank to their knees in despair, and ecstatic fans poured onto the pitch.

The whole of Scotland celebrated on a day when its rugby players sparked unrestrained national joy. 'When the result came over the tannoy we realised what a great thing it was to be part of,' says David Sole, 'but you also wanted to be everywhere else in the country to witness the experience. At Pittodrie, where Aberdeen were playing Hearts in a crucial soccer match, the biggest roar came when the announcer gave the score from Murrayfield! We even found out they announced the result in the very staid atmosphere of Jenners department store on Princes Street, and all the Edinburgh ladies with their blue rinses let out a cheer!'

Some have argued that an over-zealous reaction from a section of supporters took national pride a step too far. This was probably true, but such passion was not new to the championship – the tournament had always been built on the desire to beat England. Behind the aggression on the pitch, moreover, as Scotland coach Ian McGeechan confirms, there was mutual admiration among the players. 'To be fair to the Scottish team, they played it down and there was no cock-crowing. At the end, the first thing Finlay Calder did was go over to the England hooker, Brian Moore, because he was a mate from the Lions tour to Australia, and he knew how devastated Brian would be.'

So why did Scotland record one of the biggest upsets in the history of the championship? 'I have to say first,' responds flanker Finlay Calder, 'that had Dean Richards been playing against us we would never have won, not in a million years. He was a man who could choke a game to death.' But England had been un-nerved and unsettled by the atmosphere at Murrayfield that day – 'when you play a game of rugby,' comments Calder, 'you know in the first three or four minutes whether or not you are going to win.' The unsung heroes like backs Sean Lineen and Iwan Tukalo contributed memorably, as did forwards Kenny Milne and Damian Cronin, and even players like lock Chris Gray, on the margin of selection for Scotland, or prop Paul Burnell in only his second championship season – 'this was a day when our journeymen played out of their skins,' confirms Calder. 'In short, the 1990 Scotland side was a ripe team.'

1991 – England's GRAND SLAM

The defeat at Murrayfield in 1990 hurt England as much as it thrilled Scotland and haunted their thinking for years. England resolved to become even more 'professional' in their approach – managers and coaches would plot the downfall of the opposition with military-style precision, while sport psychologists and dieticians moved in to join the fitness gurus and video analysers. Defeat could no longer be glorious and gallant – the win-at-all-costs mentality had taken over. The move towards the formal payment of players was inevitable.

England headed off to their by now regular winter training camp in the sun to prepare for the 1991 Five Nations, knowing that in World Cup year nothing short of outright victory in the championship would suffice if they were to be considered as realistic contenders for rugby's biggest prize. Wales were lying in wait on their return, with a proud 28-year-old unbeaten record against England in the Principality. This match would undoubtedly reveal the character of the English squad.

Nothing was left to chance in England's painstaking preparations – as the players ran out for training one day the management even unexpectedly blasted out a recording of 'Land of My Fathers'! A man with a huge responsibility was the side's goal-kicker. 'That game in Cardiff is the most vivid memory that I have of the Five Nations,' says Simon Hodgkinson. 'The team walked from the hotel to the ground together in a display of unity, and nobody said a word. Then Richard Hill went ballistic in the changing-room – we had to keep calming him down. None of us went onto the pitch beforehand to warm up. It was the most intense I had ever felt before a match.' The metronomically accurate Hodgkinson knew the English game plan depended on him – a year on from the Murrayfield defeat the team had changed little, but there was a noticeable shift in policy. The aim now was to maximise the forward power and grind the opposition into submission, forcing penalties for Hodgkinson's boot.

The full-back practised kicking for hour after hour to play his part. During one session in the week before the game he had feared the worst. 'I was very nervous and kicked terribly – I couldn't land anything.' But Hodgkinson need not have worried: on the day his team's strategy worked to a tee. After a robust start from Wales, the English forwards proved too powerful and, in their frustration, Wales repeatedly fell foul of the referee. "It was a simply electric first twenty minutes,' says Hodgkinson, 'but after that it was quite obvious who was going to win and the crowd quietened down. I can remember winger Nigel Heslop smiling all the time, and I kept shouting to him that it wasn't all over.' But the ball was, again and again – the Nottingham man scored a championship record of seven penalty-goals – and with a solitary try, from back-row forward Mike Teague, England dispelled their Cardiff hoodoo.

The English celebrations were muted, however, by the extraordinary events which followed the final whistle. A message delivered to the waiting media announced that the team would not be giving post-match interviews. The controversy had its origins in a dispute between the players and the RFU over the regulation of their potential earnings from off-field activities, and rumours were circulating that the squad had made a formal request for payment for BBC interviews. Coach Geoff Cooke laments that his team's achievement was overshadowed by what he describes as 'one of those ridiculous situations which escalated from nothing into a major diplomatic incident. We had taken a huge weight off our shoulders, and we just wanted to be on our own for a while. I remember Rory Underwood sitting in the corner of the dressing-room, almost in tears, and when the Welsh press officer came in I felt it was still too early and said, "Look, for God's sake go – we're not speaking to the media."'

It was then that Cooke's problems began. With the press banging on their hotel-room doors, the hotel manager had to take the team through the kitchens to get to the after-match reception – to find RFU officials apoplectic with rage. 'Of course I regret what happened now,' admits Cooke – 'but on match day it was definitely not to do with money. It was almost a militant thing – the players were not getting anything and felt they were being pushed around.' The gloss had been taken off one of England's greatest-ever wins, but the episode served to underline the players' growing desire for official payment for their services.

While all this was happening in Cardiff, a new and victorious French management team were attending their first press conference in Paris. Former players Daniel Dubroca and Jean Trillo had taken over from Jacques Fouroux, promising an expansive style of rugby more in line with the French tradition. Despite their predictions there were no tries in a dour and at times dirty match. The lightest moment came before kick-off when 'Roses of Prince Charlie' was played to the Scottish team instead of 'Flower of Scotland'! Scotland recovered to beat Wales and Ireland, who had drawn in Cardiff. In the other matches, France showed greater flair to win in Ireland, and England avenged their 1990 defeat by beating the Scots at Twickenham. At the Parc des Princes France dismissed Wales, with Serge Blanco scoring a scintillating try in the opening seconds of his final home championship match. 'I'm same age as Jesus Christ when he was crucified,' he cheekily declared afterwards, having ended the game with an imperious conversion from wide out on the touch-line: 'what better time to go?' The Five Nations had rarely seen a player of such talent, and Blanco, always the showman on the field, also confirmed himself as a fine ambassador for the sport by immediately giving away his special commemorative medal to a disabled fan.

In Dublin, England were looking for their first Triple Crown in eleven years. They got it, but not without a scare. Trailing inside the last ten minutes, they seemed destined to repeat their Murrayfield experience, but a try from Mike Teague and another world-class finish from Rory Underwood saw them home. One year on, the team had another opportunity to take the Grand Slam. Either England or France would win the championship, and now their showdown could take place.

The English side had gone through the whole championship unchanged for the first time since 1960, and at Twickenham those familiar faces found themselves in a familiar situation when France produced a piece of rugby gold. Simon Hodgkinson missed a kick at goal and, from underneath their own posts, the French started a counter-attack that will live long in the memory. A young, dishevelled winger called Philippe Saint-André was making his Twickenham debut: 'I watched it all – Berbizier to Blanco, to Lafond, to Sella, who switched with Camberabero, who was incredible as he kicked to himself and kicked again.' Now Saint-André himself came across the pitch, picked up the ball and ran the final ten metres 'to score the try of all tries.' From posts to posts – a champagne score had been uncorked. 'If I had missed the ball,' says Saint-André, who would one day become his country's most capped winger, 'I would never have played for France again! Even now, before England against France, we always watch it on French television because it is a creative try, lots of hands and part of the French culture.'

Shocked, England gathered in a huddle. Resolved to work their way back into the match, they managed to earn a respectable lead with a try from Underwood and, once again, Hodgkinson's crucial kicking. Nerves were jangling when the French backs Franck Mesnel and Didier Camberabero scored tries, but the frustrations of recent years melted away as England hung on to achieve the Grand Slam.

Their professional approach had paid dividends. It was the forwards who had made the difference: the props, Jason Leonard and Jeff Probyn, the vigorous young pup and the gnarled old dog; the pit-bull between them, Brian Moore; the rock-like second-rows Wade Dooley and Paul Ackford, and the model back row of Mike Teague, Dean Richards and Peter Winterbottom. The rugged Winterbottom, first selected in 1982, had experienced many lows. Of them all perhaps he had the most cause to celebrate.

1992 – England's GRAND SLAM

In the autumn of 1991 England fell agonisingly short of their World Cup dream, losing to Australia in the final – a defeat ascribed to their tactical move away from a forward-dominated game in favour of running the ball. Now the 1992 Five Nations season was all about proving their doubters wrong. Winning one Grand Slam had been a major achievement: to follow with another in immediate succession would put them alongside Wavell Wakefield's great English team of the 1920s, the only other to perform this feat.

England had a new coach – Geoff Cooke having moved to team manager – but Dick Best was the only new boy in the England set-up. 'I remember looking around the room at my first team meeting – there were all these immortal names. After some quick mental arithmetic I realised there were over three hundred caps in there – I thought, "What am I going to say to these guys?" It seemed that anything less than a Grand Slam would be deemed a failure. But we wanted to adjust their game – we recognised that they had bullied and battered their way to a Grand Slam and we had to think how to improve on it. I told them, "We don't want to change everything, but we need to play a faster game." Brian Moore immediately responded, "Why, what's wrong with us winning?"' Cooke and Best felt that the only way to alter the style was to introduce some new personnel, and brought in the up-and-coming back-row forwards Tim Rodber and Ben Clarke. They also made the 'monumental decision', in Best's words, to drop Dean Richards for the opening match against Scotland.

It was not England's first return to Murrayfield since that fateful day in 1990, as they had won their World Cup semi-final against the Scots there, a bruising and tight affair. Edinburgh was also an appropriate starting-place for Dick Best, who in 1990 had been 'Under-21

Brothers in arms – the Pontypool front row. From the left: Graham Price, Bobby Windsor and Charlie Faulkner.

Mike Gibson of Ireland – a brilliant all-round back whose total of 56 championship appearances is a Five Nations record.

Charlie Faulkner scores for Wales against Ireland in 1975 to secure the championship title. Mike Gibson is making the tackle and JJ Williams is ready to start the celebrations.

'Thou shalt not pass' is the message from Wales's talismanic full-back JPR Williams to the French winger Jean-François Gourdon at the Arms Park in 1976. Many saw this as the moment when the Grand Slam was won.

Welsh flanker Paul Ringer is sent off in the battle of Twickenham in 1980. The injured party, England's fly-half John Horton, receives treatment.

Bill Beaumont leads by example as England go to their first Grand Slam in 23 years with victory at Murrayfield in 1980. Fellow pack member Roger Uttley is in support.

Flanker Jim Calder crashes over for Scotland against France in the Grand Slam decider in 1984.

A warrior in familiar pose – France's captain in the early 1980s, Jean-Pierre Rives.

Scotland's wonderfully talented full-back, Andy Irvine.

Bill McLaren – a broadcasting legend.

Murrayfield 1990, and try-scorer Tony Stanger, a former pupil of McLaren, sends the Scottish nation delirious and scuppers England's own hopes of a Grand Slam.

The English dressing-room in joyous mood a year after the Murrayfield nightmare. France are beaten at Twickenham in 1991 and the Grand Slam moves south.

A third Grand Slam in five years for Will Carling's England in 1995.

The clown about to wear the crown: Thomas Castaignède's dramatic drop-goal seals victory against England in Paris at the start of the 1996 championship.

Almost as important as the rugby: pre-match preparations of a different kind in the car park at Twickenham.

Commercialism starts to move in *(left)*. The Five Nations trophy, first played for in 1993.

Commercialism has arrived *(right)*. Paint from the sponsor's pitch logo lends Ireland hooker Keith Wood a different complexion at Lansdowne Road against France in 1999.

Scotland celebrate their dazzling victory in Paris to become the last champions of the Five Nations, although they did not know it at the time.

A day later Scott Gibbs dives in for his stunning try against England at Wembley in the dying seconds of the final Five Nations game on 11 April 1999. Neil Jenkins' match-winning kick handed Scotland the title in a never-to-be-forgotten finale to the championship.

coach, B-team coach, general dogsbody and bottlewasher – the nationalistic pride was so strong I thought, "God, one day I'm probably going to be England coach – how am I going to cope with all this?" and two years later I was there!' The irony of what happened in the match was not lost on Best, always one to look for the humour in life. Just when England were struggling, the new cap Rodber was knocked out, which meant that the mighty Dean Richards came on anyway. From then on, says Best, 'the ball seemed to migrate to him, and we came away with a fairly comfortable win!'

Best's new Welsh counterpart, Alan Davies, also had a winning start as Wales celebrated victory in Dublin – their first championship win for three years. Ireland's misery was multiplied at Twickenham when they encountered an England side happier to express themselves. Full-back Jonathan Webb, who was to amass a record 67 points in the championship that season, started the scoring with a try after only 23 seconds, and his team crossed the Irish line six times. England won by 38 points to nine, and those who had accused the 1991 Grand Slam winners of lacking ambition were being made to eat their words by the 1992 successors. On the same afternoon, France were scrapping their way to a narrow win in Cardiff, but the tension in that game was just a foretaste of what was to come in Paris a fortnight later when England returned to the scene of another World Cup knock-out tie. If that quarter-final had been a spicy *hors d'oeuvres*, then the subsequent championship meeting was a sizzling main course.

'I remember they called the teams out together,' says England's scrum-half, Dewi Morris, 'and we were lining up against each other in the tunnel, which is something you don't really want to do, and in the game there were cheap shots and knees in the back all the time.' The match was scarred by acts of violence, and in Morris's recollection when one of the French props was sent off Brian Moore and Jeff Probyn stood laughing – 'I thought, "It's not going to get any better now."' By the end France had been reduced to thirteen men, with two of their front-row, Vincent Moscato and Gregoire Lascubé, having been dismissed for foul play. At the end of the match, Irish referee Stephen Hilditch had to be escorted from the field surrounded by security men. The relationship between France and England on the rugby field had been stretched to the limit. Amidst the mayhem, the English had managed to maintain some discipline, with four tries – Dewi Morris among the scorers – and victory the reward for their cool heads.

Now only Wales were standing in their way. The match was a special occasion for Wade Dooley – the England forward was winning his fiftieth cap. With his wife having made a big effort to be there to watch – despite being due to give birth the next day – and Terry Waite, just released from captivity in the Lebanon, sitting alongside her, Will Carling let Dooley lead the side out. But his team-mates saw to it, as Dooley remembers, that the honour was enhanced. 'Down in the tunnel, Will had thrown me the ball. I ran onto the pitch, waiting to hear the clatter of studs behind me, and the next thing I knew I was stood in the middle of Twickenham on my "Jack Jones". What a moment!' When Will Carling challenged Welsh full-back Tony Clement after only a minute of the match to score the opening try, everybody knew that the result was beyond doubt. England threatened, but never managed to cut loose, and it was left to Wade Dooley to cross for a late sentimental score and prompt the crowd into a standing ovation. England had achieved their second Grand Slam in two years.

A victory over Wales by 24 points to nil was unheard-of in modern times. Winger Simon Halliday and, among the pack, the uninhibited Mickey Skinner and the quietly purposeful Martin Bayfield, had all been successful additions to the team, and for Dewi Morris, who had sat on the bench throughout the 1991 season, the experience was well worth waiting for – 'thinking about the win still gives me the shivers now!' But at the end of the match England's Grand Slam acclaim was tempered by further criticism of the team's failure to follow a more adventurous path to success. 'They had some of the best players in the British Isles,' says the then-Scottish coach, Ian McGeechan, 'and they were probably playing the least sharp-edged rugby. It was safety-first and structured, and although it won a Five Nations it actually didn't take our game on. The Grand Slam was almost the be-all and end-all.' 'You never saw New Zealand throw caution to the wind and play any old style,' responds Wade Dooley. 'They made sure they had the game won first before chucking the ball around. We did score some great tries, and we were appreciated by the true English supporter and the purist.' What cannot be disputed is that this England team created a surge of interest in the game – Dooley realised even the forwards had become household names when he went back up north and found 'little old dears coming up and asking me questions about rugby in Blackpool town centre'! 'I'd like to think,' he concludes, 'that the side from 1990–1992 was the team which kick-started English rugby again.'

So was this a truly great England team? Built around one of the most outstanding packs of all time, they manufactured a strategy to suit their strengths, and the players delivered what no other England team had done for nearly seventy years: back-to-back Grand Slams. 'The result against Scotland in 1990 changed the course of Five Nations history,' says Geoff Cooke – 'it was a crushing defeat which hardened our resolve. But I honestly believe it didn't stifle our play over the next two years, and the video evidence proves that we played some excellent rugby in the Grand Slams that followed. It's just that the loss made us even more determined to win.' Cooke's major legacy was an efficient organisation and dedication – the dominant memory of England in the early nineties. 'When I took over,' he says, 'rugby was founded on the tradition of ale, dirty songs and training just twice a week, even at international level. I told the players to think of themselves as Olympic athletes first and rugby players second. There were to be no excuses, and if they performed badly it was down to them.' Effectively the side had been transformed into a 'professional' outfit long before the sport had taken any formal steps away from amateurism.

The other four nations were left to squabble for crumbs at the foot of England's table. Scotland beat Ireland and France but then went to Cardiff and lost. On the final day of the championship, the French back Sebastien Viars scored a record individual championship points tally of 24 in the demolition of Ireland to condemn them to the bottom spot. During the course of the season the Irish had conceded 116 points; England, by contrast, had scored 118.

1993 – France's championship

The inexorable move towards a professional game was further demonstrated in 1993. Not only was this the first season that five points were awarded for the scoring of a championship try, the latest step taken to encourage running rugby: a trophy was also to be awarded to the winners of the Five Nations. The days of sharing the prize had gone. The modern sporting world demanded a winner. Traditionalists saw it as the glorifying of victory, something against the amateur ethos, and took solace in the fact that the trophy was not to be sponsored – yet!

In 1993 many believed it was up to England to lose the championship, but this was an ageing English team and the others were determined to strike back. France had first crack and, if luck ever plays a part in sport, then England certainly had their fair share that day. 'Touch wood,' goes the saying: England rattled the posts. Jonathan Webb's penalty rebounded into the hands of winger Ian Hunter, who raced past a French defence left cruelly flat-footed. As England led by the slenderest of margins, Jean-Baptiste Lafond tried his luck with a drop-goal, only to see the ball come back off the cross-bar and France's hopes die. Somehow, England's were still alive.

Welsh invincibility against the English in Cardiff had of course ended in 1991, and a different aura now surrounded this fixture. 'The singing at the Arms Park had deteriorated over the previous few seasons, with more and more tickets going to hospitality and businesses based in England,' says Welsh winger Ieuan Evans. 'But for this game the atmosphere had returned, and the crowd responded because *we* responded.' Tipped as unstoppable favourites, the English met a determined Welsh team. In a charged atmosphere, England seemed to weather the early storm, but on the verge of the interval Welsh forward Emyr Lewis chipped up field. It appeared Rory Underwood had plenty of time to deal with the bouncing ball but, as time seemed to stand still, so, inexplicably, did Underwood. Before he could wake himself, the thrusting Ieuan Evans was steaming up on the outside like a train out of Cardiff station. The Arms Park exploded in noise as Evans hacked on and, as the ball crossed the try-line, steadied his hands before pushing the ball into the earth with an emphatic shove. 'The groundsman said the following day that there was a big hole where I had landed on the ball,' remembers Evans. 'I told him it definitely wasn't my fault, and we concluded that some supporters had dug up the pitch – that turf is now probably in somebody's garden!'

Following the break, Wales hung on. Dewi Morris was unlucky not to have been awarded a try after he seemed to stretch successfully for the line to ground the ball, and when England were awarded a penalty with little left on the clock they took a highly questionable decision to reject a kick at goal. To add insult to injury, had the old scoring method still been in operation, the match would have finished as a draw. Wales were worthy of their success, though, and there was a growing feeling that, if matched for power, this England team did not have the solutions.

The Welsh were unable to consolidate their win and tamely lost to Scotland without scoring a point. The Scots were also full of inconsistencies: after starting their season with victory over Ireland, they had continued their awful run in Paris by losing to France. In a bizarre move, the French coach, Pierre Berbizier, had been sacked and then re-instated just before the start of the championship but his team were looking increasingly assured.

England's selection policy was now under scrutiny – were the old guard good enough to keep the successful times going? For the main part, they survived the chop, but for the game against Scotland at Twickenham it was deemed time for a change in the pivotal number ten position. Bath's Stuart Barnes versus Rob Andrew of Wasps as England fly-half had been a running debate for almost a decade. The maverick Barnes had made his England debut in 1984 but lost out on many possible caps by ruling himself out of selection, and Andrew's more conservative style was more suitable for England's controlled approach.

For the 1993 Calcutta Cup match, however, this all changed. 'I remember sitting at my desk in the building society where I was the manager,' says Barnes, 'and somebody told me Geoff Cooke was on the phone. My initial reaction was, "Oh, no, I've been dropped from the bench."' Barnes, now into his thirties, was entrusted with the task of uncaging the England back line. On the eve of the match, he decided to retire to his hotel room and relax with a bottle of wine. Jeremy Guscott, his club team-mate, heard music drifting along the corridor and knocked on his door. 'I had been fairly vociferous about what I thought England lacked,' says Barnes, 'and I was determined to play the game against the Scots that I played every week for my club. Jerry came in and had a drink and we decided that it was just another game for the Bath midfield.'

When match day arrived, Barnes delivered and the England backs were released in a moment of brilliance. A high pass from Dewi Morris deep inside English territory caused the fly-half to look up at the advancing Scottish back-row. Barnes assessed the risk and, with a dart and a scurry like an animal sensing its one chance for freedom, he left the would-be hunters firing into the air. Within a split second, Guscott was on his shoulder and, two perfectly timed passes later, Rory Underwood was in. A memorable moment for television viewers that weekend, after Tony and Rory Underwood had both benefited from England's expansive strategy to score tries on the wings, was the sight of their mother, Mrs Anne Underwood, dancing a jig of delight. For once, Stuart Barnes was the toast of English rugby, though modestly he claims that 'apart from one or two more breaks, I didn't play that well – but I excelled in the areas it was easy for one-dimensional journalism to assess as "Barnes runs and Andrew kicks".' The next day, when Barnes went into an off-licence to buy a bottle of wine, the man behind the counter said, 'Thanks for yesterday,' and gave him a case. 'Believe me,' says Barnes, 'that was the highlight of the weekend!'

In Cardiff, another fly-half was making an impact. Ireland's new discovery Eric Elwood had orchestrated the end of an eleven-match sequence without a Five Nations victory. Now it was next stop Dublin for England. 'I recall watching a news programme on RTE the night before the game,' says Mick Galwey, the durable forward who had been restored to the Ireland pack, 'and an English player said they fully expected to win.' On a March day made for chaos on the rugby field Ireland roared like the elements and their forwards outplayed the English eight. 'The weather conditions were good for rugby,' confirms Galwey – 'well, Irish rugby anyway!' Eric Elwood was a match-winner for the second time in a fortnight and his penalty-goals, plus two drop-goals, put Ireland into an unassailable position. It was left to Galwey to provide the perfect ending by crashing over for a late try to seal the win – 'there was no stopping me from five yards!' Lansdowne Road erupted into song, the players were chaired off the field and the festivities began. The party ended up at Kitty O'Shea's on the Sunday morning, from where Galwey had to find his way to the Far East to play for Ireland in the Hong Kong Sevens. The flight left on the Monday morning, and when they arrived, he confirms, 'the party seemed to start all over again.'

So, after two Grand Slams, England's fortunes had changed and the French took the title, having beaten Scotland, Ireland and, in their final match, Wales, to become the first country to be awarded the Five Nations Trophy. Perhaps, though, with their back-row of the highest quality – Marc Cecillon, Philippe Benetton and Laurent Cabannes – they should have achieved more. 'It was great,' agrees their lock from Dax, Olivier Roumat, 'but my first thoughts were of Twickenham and Lafond's drop-goal attempt which hit the woodwork. Had that sailed through we would have been drinking Grand Slam champagne!'

1994 – Wales's championship

Wales's win over England proved yet another false dawn, and later that year even their loss to Canada was no longer viewed as a shock result. A triumph over Scotland in January 1994 on a filthy, wet

Cardiff day, however, gave the Welsh an altogether sunnier outlook, and they celebrated three tries in a championship match for the first time in six years. For their next match away to an Irish side easily beaten by France, Wales were favourites – then an unusual experience – and narrowly won after Eric Elwood missed a simple penalty-kick near the end.

It was appropriate, then, that, with a Welsh resurgence at last a distinct possibility, a young man called Scott Quinnell should play such an important role in his team's vital third fixture at home to France. As it happened, his father Derek, the former Welsh great, was watching his son from the stand and, though Wales had not beaten the French for twelve years, early in the game Scott made it his match. The ball came loose at a line-out, the strapping forward grabbed it and, just as his father had done in 1976 against Scotland, with a mixture of hand-offs, dummies and brute force put his head down for the corner.

When Scott Quinnell went over, however, Wales's decision for this match to alter their team's kit, from red socks to green, almost backfired. 'The touch judge nearly flagged him out,' explains coach Alan Davies, 'because he thought Wales had red socks!' But it was a Frenchman's red ankles that had strayed into touch, and the platform was laid for a famous win. Quinnell junior was playing alongside now-established players like hooker Garin Jenkins and lock Gareth Llewellyn, in a pack growing in experience, and for the most senior Welsh forward, Phil Davies, first capped in 1985, there was at last some reward. 'It had been a long wait, and the sense of pride and purpose on that day was overwhelming,' he says now. 'There was a confidence about this Welsh team that ran through the whole side and management.' It was three in a row for Wales and the expectation was growing all the time. The final stop would be Twickenham and a tilt at the Grand Slam.

The English had started with a win in Scotland, but only by their fingertips – Rob Andrew's, to be precise. Ever since the 1991 World Cup, when the RFU had bowed to the growing commercialism in the game by signing a deal with a sports clothing manufacturer, England's strip had been changing: the plain white shirt with the single red rose had been 'modernised'. Now, against Scotland, the latest alteration would actually influence the result of a Five Nations match. After Scotland's young fly-half, Gregor Townsend, thought he had won the game with a late drop-goal, a ruck formed inside the Scottish half. The hands went in and the New Zealand referee, Lindsay

McLachlan, blew his whistle to award a penalty to England. The Scottish crowd groaned, and video evidence later showed that, once again, kit changes had confused the officials. There was a blue cuff to the offending arm – but out of sight there was also a big red stripe going up the sleeve, the rest of which was white. England's new strip, masquerading as a Scottish jersey at the wrist, had fooled the referee! The upshot of this much-publicised mistake was a suggestion that referees and touch judges should be wired for sound and in constant contact during matches, so that, if one official missed an incident, another could alert him – a practice now commonplace in most top games, but it came too late for Scotland in 1994.

The penalty still needed kicking, however, and the man to do it was Jonathan Callard. The Bath full-back had shot to fame when, on his England debut in 1993, he had booted his country to victory against New Zealand. Could he do it again? 'Will Carling handed me the ball,' says Callard, 'and said, "Get on with it, it's easy." "Easy for you," I thought. I walked away and couldn't face it initially. Then it's all a bit of a blur – but I do remember a Scottish ball-boy hurling the kicking tee at me as if to say, "Take that, you b******." When I did strike it I thought, "Oh, no – I've pushed it wide!" but there was a little curl which brought it back in for some reason – and I've never curled the ball in my life. As it went over, I heard the final whistle and apparently I went delirious, running towards the tunnel – I can't understand how footballers have rehearsed celebrations!'

Callard had carved his notch in the championship's history. 'I've only won five caps, but I wouldn't swap those five for fifty in view of the moments I've had. Even now, if I go to a rugby club in Scotland they all say, "You're the one who did that – it was never a Scottish hand." To this day they still argue – it's like Maradona and the hand of God!' During a television interview following the drama the devastated Scottish captain, Gavin Hastings, broke down in tears: it was obvious the wounds would take time to heal. Indeed, after a draw against Ireland and a loss to France – their first win at Murrayfield since 1978 – Scotland ended the season with the wooden spoon.

England's next match was against Ireland at Twickenham, where none of the other Five Nations sides had tasted success for six years. It soon became clear nobody had explained this to the Irish winger Simon Geoghegan. 'Bambi on benzedrine' was one description of the blond winger's running style as he bobbed his way to the line to help his country to a famous victory. England recovered to win in Paris, where Rob Andrew's classy kicking triumphed over the indifferent performance of France's centre Thierry Lacroix and the only try of the match, scored by flanker Abdelatif Benazzi. Victory by sixteen points over Wales, the English now knew, would give them the Five Nations crown.

This was the 100th rugby match between England and Wales, and Her Majesty the Queen was present at the rapidly metamorphosing Twickenham to grace the occasion. Work that began at the start of the decade was now nearing completion, and in late 1995 the ground would boast an all-seated capacity of 76,000, with the spectators watching from a three-tiered horseshoe comprising the East, North and West stands. But the game never lived up to its stage or its billing: the English took an early stranglehold and never let go, though the Welsh winger and former Olympic hurdler Nigel Walker scored a late consolation try. 'It was weird,' says Ieuan Evans, captain that day, who recalls the occasion with mixed emotions. 'We didn't perform – a lot of the boys had never played at the new-look Twickenham, with the crowds way up in the gods, and I think they were overawed. There was a sense of anti-climax, and a feeling of a job only part-well done.' Nevertheless, England's winning margin of seven points had not been enough – and it had handed the championship to Wales.

Wales had fallen short of a first Grand Slam since 1978 and, inevitably, those who lamented the passing of the glory years made unfavourable comparisons between the nearly men in 1994 and the winning sides of the 1970s. Evans has always felt such parallels unfair. 'It always happens, whatever sport you're in – who's the best? Michael Jordan or Magic Johnson in basketball, Carl Lewis or Jesse Owens on the track or, in Welsh rugby, who's the next Gareth Edwards, Barry John or Gerald Davies? I was brought up on the great era and these players were always my heroes, but I found it difficult to be cast as the next Gerald. It's a pressure-cooker in South Wales at the best of times, and these comparisons made it hard to live up to expectations. It didn't make you lose, but it was a hindrance.'

Ultimately the failure of the 1994 Welsh team to emulate their illustrious predecessors would be the downfall of Alan Davies and his coaching partner, the former international lock, Robert Norster. 'We had refused to tell the committee how many games we would win that season,' says Davies, 'but we said we would have a positive try count in every match – our research had shown that this was the way to success in the Five Nations. We delivered and won the championship, but Robert and I were doomed.'

1995 – England's GRAND SLAM

Job changes were also in the air in the England camp as the close of the 1994 season signalled the end of Geoff Cooke's spell as England manager. After a tour of South Africa that summer, coach Dick Best also parted company with the team. Both had records to be proud of but, looking back, Best believes there was still plenty of work to be done. 'We realised that to compete on a global stage we had to get away from the forward-dominated game and the tactic of the Carling "crash ball". As the months went on, although we were beating New Zealand and South Africa in one-off matches, those teams, along with Australia, were starting to play a totally different game. They were liberating the ball much more than we did.'

England were now under the guidance of Jack Rowell, a large man with a big reputation in business and rugby. The company director had masterminded Bath's great period of success in the 1980s and early 1990s, taking them to five league titles and seven cup wins. In a tense start to the 1995 championship, Rowell's new team faced the prospect of a third consecutive defeat at the hands of Ireland, and arrived at Lansdowne Road fully expecting the day's weather to be matched by the ferocity of the Irish play. 'It was the worst wind I've ever played in,' recalls fly-half Rob Andrew. 'In those conditions it's just a war, and a question of how well you can cope with the Irish rampaging at you. I could hardly stand up facing into the teeth of the gale, but we were so controlled and played brilliantly up-front.' That England stood firm, scoring three tries, and dictated events boded well for the rest of their season.

The only black spot for the English had been the first 'yellow card' in international rugby – an adoption of football's long-established means of warning a player that another serious misdemeanour would lead to a sending-off. It was shown to Ben Clarke for stamping on Simon Geoghegan, but in Paris a more grievous offence had taken place. The French lock Olivier Merle headbutted Welsh prop Ricky Evans, who in falling to the ground broke his leg. Merle was not sent off but, with cameras positioned at all angles, players were now aware that few incidents would go undetected. It was left to television replays to expose his crime, as a consequence of which he was dropped and missed the match that was expected to settle the championship: England versus France, already being billed as 'Le Crunch'.

France, facing their eighth consecutive defeat against England, produced a stroke of genius with shades of their 1991 Twickenham try –

once more covering virtually the length of the field before Sebastien Viars put the ball down for a beguiling score. But with two tries from Tony Underwood the result was never seriously in doubt. 'Not to put too fine a point on it, we thrashed France,' says Rob Andrew, who was looking at what would be a third Grand Slam in five years. 'We were playing with such confidence that season – but I think we probably peaked during the Five Nations and never really produced that controlled form in the World Cup later in the year.'

Meanwhile, Scotland had beaten Ireland and now readied themselves for a journey to Paris and a fixture that had ended in defeat ever since 1969. When Philippe Saint-André scored his second try late in the game nobody expected the tide of history to turn in Scotland's favour. But captain Gavin Hastings had other ideas and, with his troops inside French territory, he emerged on the shoulder of Gregor Townsend. Townsend could sense the presence of his skipper and, with a terrific sleight of hand straight from the card schools of the western saloons, delivered a reverse pass of the highest calibre to allow Hastings to burst away. Hastings pinned his ears back and galloped over the line. In the dying seconds, the game was Scotland's.

This celebrated win came towards the end of Hastings' playing days and he feels it gave his Five Nations career a certain symmetry. 'Remember my international debut was against France in 1986 when I played with my brother Scott. From the kick-off I kicked the ball straight into touch and, instead of the scrum back on the half-way line, they took a quick line-out and scored inside the first minute. It was not the most promising of starts – but eighty minutes later we had won by a point, with me scoring six penalty-goals, all of our side's points. Eight years later, Scott and I won our fiftieth caps together, also against France at Murrayfield. We lost that day and I had come to realise that in international sport winning meant everything. Now we had won in Paris and ended Scotland's nightmare. It was a great way to finish there, and the speech I gave that night was somewhat memorable, too. The French translation described how I "made love to my wife in celebration" prior to the dinner – it went down well with our hosts, who were certainly approving of that, if not the match result!'

England's relentless progress towards the Grand Slam continued in Wales, where they put on another confident display. The main talking-point after this match was not the result – predictable for most of the game – but the sending-off of Welsh prop forward John Davies for a stamp on Ben Clarke. After Davies was ordered from the field there was an almost comical delay in play as Hemi Taylor, normally a back-row player, reluctantly moved up to cover in the front row and the Welsh captain, Ieuan Evans, was forced to ask his opposite number, Will Carling, if he could bring a specialist prop off the bench to ensure that the scrum did not dangerously collapse. Carling agreed and the game continued safely. The incident highlighted an important lacuna in the laws, and within weeks the sport's governing body had taken remedial action. The next round of matches was illuminated by a breathless score from Scotland number-eight Eric Peters in the victory over Wales in Edinburgh. The Welsh went on to lose to an Ireland side already beaten by France, but the Scots had advanced to within one match of their own Grand Slam. As in 1990 it was England who stood in their way – but this time the venue was Twickenham.

In the end the game fell a long way short of the hype. There were no tries, just kicks at goal, and lots of them. In Rob Andrew England had a match winner, his total of 24 points equalling the individual record for a Five Nations game and his seven penalty-goals matching Simon Hodgkinson's effort against Wales four years earlier. Afterwards the England hooker, Brian Moore, accused Scotland of trying to ruin the game by spending all of the match off-side. Scottish voices retorted that Moore should take a look at his own tactics. 'It was a disappointing and frustrating game,' says Rob Andrew, 'and although it was great to be part of history and win a third Grand Slam it was a bit of an anti-climax. I can remember everybody trying to come off upbeat about the whole thing, but it had been one of those afternoons when we had tried to finish off in style and, typically, Scotland didn't let us play.'

In truth, both sides had lacked ambition, but it was England's extra power that had seen them through. Rugby was fast becoming a big man's game and the extra muscle of the English meant that new stars like scrum-half Kyran Bracken and lock Martin Johnson only knew of England as the favourites. But the ageless Andrew, ten years in the England team, had seen the long-term change from losers into winners. 'Back in the 1980s the two centres for one match, Bryan Barley and Rob Lozowski, had never even met, let alone played alongside each other – the first thing they did together was not pass a rugby ball but shake hands! English rugby was a shambles, and I saw it go through the first moves towards fitness-testing for the 1987 World Cup, then the drive to professionalism in the nineties. In the days when we didn't train much together and had a few beers, the seriousness of the Five Nations games was no less, but what changed was the level of fitness and preparation time. The Friday lunchtime get-together became Thursday, then Wednesday – and now it's the whole week.' The greater resources in the English game were being better utilised, league rugby for the clubs, inaugurated at the end of the 1980s, was now established, and there seemed a real danger that for the first time the Five Nations might cease to be truly competitive.

1996 – England's Triple Crown and championship

The 27 August 1995 was the day when the International Rugby Board announced that the sport was officially to become professional – an inevitable but giant step into the unknown, with nobody quite sure what the ramifications would be. One certainty, however, was that the countries with the greatest financial clout would attract the better players to their domestic game. In the context of the Five Nations England and France looked best placed to strengthen their hands. The English were rebuilding their side, while France had broken their abysmal run of losses to England with victory in South Africa in the third place play-off at the 1995 World Cup. Amidst persistent media categorisation of the championship as a two-horse race, the two countries met in Paris in the opening round of the first professional Five Nations season.

Northampton stand-off, Paul Grayson, chosen to play in his first championship match together with his club half-back partner, Matt Dawson, had the additional burden of taking over from Rob Andrew. 'At the time, people said, "Do you feel under pressure?"' recalls Grayson, 'but my view was that I was getting a go at playing for England – the pressure comes only if you establish yourself. As I came out of the tunnel, the noise was so intense it filled my chest and I could sense the vibration throughout my body. It's a stunning thing to "feel the noise", but we were told to use that to our advantage and not to be afraid of it.'

A draw was nearly the final result as Grayson's late drop-goal levelled the scores, but an identical riposte in the last minute from France's new star back, Thomas Castaignède, secured a dramatic win. As the ball precariously wobbled over the crossbar, the baby-faced assassin Castaignède announced his arrival on the international scene by jigging his way back to his team with high-stepping, fist-punching, tongue-sticking-out cheekiness – the lasting image of that year's championship. He had ruined England's day, and their repeat-Grand Slam ambitions into the bargain.

Surely now, France would continue towards a Grand Slam of their own? Scotland's victory in Dublin on the opening Saturday of the championship was well-earned, but there was little to suggest they would reproduce such success against the French at Murrayfield two weeks later – only a fortnight before the tournament began the Scotland A team, a full-strength side in all but name, had lost to Italy. But in a stirring victory the Scots again proved themselves the team to keep the ethos of Five Nations equality alive. Winger Michael Dods, whose brother Peter had kicked Scotland to a Grand Slam over France twelve years earlier, finished with a new record of nineteen points for the fixture, scoring all of his side's tally. The French could only muster fourteen points between them, and suddenly Scotland, led by flanker Rob Wainwright, were being talked of as Grand Slam winners in 1996.

Scotland went on to beat Wales and then, at Murrayfield, faced an England side less than convincing in their own defeat of the Welsh. Against all the pre-season odds, the English went north with only one thing on their minds – to stop the enemy from winning the Grand Slam for the first time since 1990. As in that famous year, Scotland announced an unchanged team for the fourth championship match in a row, but it was the make-up of the England side that caused Scottish hearts to sink. Dean Richards was recalled, on a special assignment. 'I wasn't the fastest around the pitch or the greatest with ball skills,' concedes the Leicester number-eight, 'but I think Jack Rowell wanted somebody who could give it a push and a shove in the right direc-tion.' Richards was true to his word: after six penalties from Paul Grayson, England had squeezed the life out of the opposition. By the time Richards had to leave the field injured he knew that Scottish hopes had been smashed. At the final whistle he leapt off the bench, arms aloft, and saluted the victory. His big toothless grin filled the nation's television screens. 'I know,' he says: 'it's a hideous picture, isn't it!'

Scotland had been denied, but the widely predicted two-tier cham-pionship had not materialised. The season ended with another result that had not been foretold as, after defeat by Ireland, Wales prevented a second successive whitewash with a win over France in Cardiff. This meant England needed to beat the Irish at Twickenham on the same afternoon to become champions. Though their defence was bet-ter in London than on their previous away trip when they were well

and truly beaten in Paris, Ireland lost again. In an effort to rekindle
former glories they had gone overseas and brought in a new coach,
New Zealander Murray Kidd. But Kidd and Ireland ended up with a
wooden spoon.

England won the title having only scored three tries throughout the
season. Twenty-three points from the boot of Paul Grayson, a record
for the fixture with Ireland, made sure the trophy stayed in Will
Carling's hands. For Carling, who had announced his intention to
retire from the England captaincy, his last game in charge had ended
prematurely when he fell and twisted his ankle some metres away
from the action. Carling's patriotic leadership had not always
endeared him to the opposition, and his contemporary approach
sometimes rankled with the RFU hierarchy – particularly when he
famously referred to its committee members as 'old farts'. But when
he was stretchered off it was clear what the English public thought of
his reign – he received a standing ovation from a grateful
Twickenham crowd. The Five Nations had helped make Carling into
English rugby's most successful leader of all time and one of sport's
most recognisable figures. In *My Autobiography* Carling recognises
the momentous changes in rugby which followed the success of his
England team in the 1990s, and the extent to which this affected his
own fortunes.

> By the age of 22, I was driving around in a top-of-the-range
> Mercedes. Rugby has also enabled me to set up my own com-
> pany. Insights has evolved as a business and now provides
> motivational and leadership seminars for managers and busi-
> ness executives. Then there are the invitations to film pre-
> mieres, tables at top restaurants and the chance to meet people
> like John Cleese and Hugh Laurie. All of that has been fantas-
> tic and never, for one moment, would I opt for the days when
> I was an impoverished young man beginning to forge a career
> in the army or working for an oil company. Anyone who states
> that the problems which notoriety can bring far outweigh the
> advantages is talking nonsense.

Carling's private life – his friendship with the late Diana, Princess of
Wales and the break-up of two high-profile relationships – was
microscopically analysed by the media. When his public image
plunged from hero to zero, however, perhaps the former England captain wondered about those words. In the 1990s the rugby celebrity,

his fame and fortune stretching far outside the boundaries of sport, had been well and truly born. New Zealand's Jonah Lomu, the man-mountain who dominated the 1995 World Cup, is the other prime example of the player becoming public property. In the professional age, the attention and money heaped on the main attraction were set to simply grow and grow.

1997 – France's GRAND SLAM and England's Triple Crown

The money men had moved in. High-flying businessmen such as Sir John Hall at Newcastle and Saracens' Nigel Wray had invested mil-lions in their clubs expecting the sport to flourish. The Welsh wel-comed back such luminaries as Scott Gibbs from rugby league – with the advent of professionalism he was now free to return, though the transfer cost Swansea £250,000, a fee partly subsidised by the WRU. For all involved in rugby, cash was needed to pay the new wage bills and service the bank loans, and the sale of television rights was a quick fix. In a revolutionary move, the RFU decided to go it alone and signed a deal giving satellite broadcaster BSkyB exclusive rights to show England home games live. Previously the Five Nations had only ever been shown on the BBC – but years of tradition were set aside to enable Sky to gain a foothold. The sum of £87.5 million over five years was a massive increase on previous agreements. The RFU's chief negotiator, Tony Hallett, justified the move on the grounds that England had more clubs and more mouths to feed and were also a bigger attraction to viewers and sponsors, and therefore deserved a larger share of the television revenue. Ireland, Scotland and Wales took exception, arguing that the English had sold an asset which did not fully belong to them. The Celtic nations also claimed that England had gone behind their backs, and that they would be noth-ing without the matches against their Five Nations rivals. That the French had for many years negotiated their own television contract complicated matters further. The gloves were off in the committee rooms for all-out war – in the opinion of Vernon Pugh, Chairman of the WRU, England were about to forfeit their right to a place in the championship. Not since the 1930s, when France had been expelled, had the Five Nations known such political turmoil.

Other issues catalysed by the move to professionalism were also lurking in the muddy waters. The English clubs were threatening to break away from their Union, there was talk of an unofficial Kerry Packer-style international 'rugby circus' similar to that which had threatened cricket at the end of the 1970s and, in Parliament, the Broadcast Bill threatened to take away the rugby establishment's right to decide television contracts by making the Five Nations a 'listed' sporting event that by law had to be broadcast on the terrestrial channels. The threat to exclude England from the championship was perceived as all too real: prompt action was required. A backlash of anti-RFU feeling up and down the country led the RFU committee to call for a compromise. Fear of losing the competition spurred the disputing parties to reach agreement, the RFU treasurer, Colin Herridge, ironically brandishing a sheet of paper to claim 'Peace in our time'. The RFU vowed never again to strike out on their own and sign an individual agreement on Five Nations television coverage, and agreed to donate somewhere in the region of £25 million from the BSkyB deal to the Celtic nations. In the months that followed, Ireland, Scotland and Wales sealed their own television contracts with the BBC at a further benefit to the game of £40 million. A truce, albeit an uneasy one, had been negotiated between the home unions and the Five Nations was saved. This had merely been round one, though, in an on-going fight that would dog the rest of the decade and do much to damage the image of the game in the northern hemisphere. In sharp contrast elsewhere was the positive development of the new Tri-Nations tournament between Australia, New Zealand and South Africa, quickly establishing itself as the bench-mark against which the Five Nations would be judged.

One way for the home unions to redress the increasing imbalance in playing standards between the hemispheres was to turn to rugby league. The Welsh in particular began the 1997 Five Nations season with a team boosted by a number of returnees – as well as Scott Gibbs there was Allan Bateman and Scott Quinnell. After years of haemorrhaging talent, the new money on offer in union helped Wales to beat Scotland. The Welsh crossed for four tries and fly-half Neil Jenkins became their leading points scorer in Five Nations history. Meanwhile, France posted their highest-ever away score in the tournament, 32 points, with victory in Ireland, as winger David Venditti scored a hat-trick of tries. After staying in contention for an hour the Irish ran out of steam and the fitter French team scored twenty points in the last quarter.

In the next round of matches England gave Scotland their heaviest defeat since the Five Nations began, while Ireland pipped Wales to victory in Cardiff: this season, it was clear, the Five Nations was separating into two 'divisions'. The pattern seemed to be confirmed when England took Ireland apart in Dublin – six more English tries and the biggest-ever winning margin, forty points, in the history of the championship. Ironically, the man with the task of turning Irish fortunes around was an Englishman, former Bath coach Brian Ashton, who had been imported as the new coaching adviser to replace Murray Kidd and continue the trend towards foreign coaches in the championship. For Ashton, watching his old partner at club level, Jack Rowell, leave Dublin a happy man, it was a difficult day. 'When you play against the country you were born in and coaching in eight weeks previously, you are torn in a whole variety of ways. It was odd – almost as if it wasn't happening, something I was reading about.' Wales bravely tried to upset the French in Paris in a thrilling match of seven tries, but it was France who went to Twickenham to decide the championship.

After sixty minutes the English, now captained by centre Phil de Glanville, were twenty points to six up. Flanker Lawrence Dallaglio had stormed to the try-line and it looked for all the world to be England's match and the third leg of a Grand Slam. What followed was one of the greatest comebacks of the Five Nations. First Laurent Leflamand pounced on a chip through from his inspirational fellow back Christophe Lamaison. Then Lamaison himself bounded over to finish off another attacking move and, inevitably, it was Lamaison again who won the game with a penalty-goal five minutes from time. The Brive centre had the set: a try, a conversion, a drop-goal and a penalty-goal and his eighteen points was a new French record for the fixture. Never before had England lost such a lead in an international. Their play in the last quarter of the game was as dire, however, as the first hour had been impressive – but to dwell on their inadequacies would detract from France's scintillating performance. On the same day Ireland crashed to defeat against Scotland, but the overriding feeling was that the Scots would not have it so easy in Paris two weeks later, when France would go for the Grand Slam.

Saturday, 15 March 1997 was a historic day as two great Five Nations grounds said farewell to the tournament. The Parc des Princes had been the home of French rugby for 25 years, but the French authorities had decided to transfer games to the newly-constructed Stade de France, which was also to host soccer's World Cup Final in 1998. For Wales it was not a permanent move away from the National Stadium in Cardiff, but when they returned the famous ground would be transformed into another state-of-the-art arena, at a cost of over £100 million. Again, a World Cup was the motivation behind the building works – this time, the Rugby World Cup of 1999. In both cities it was set to be an emotional farewell.

The chance of a perfect goodbye – victory over England – disappeared for Wales when the England centre Jeremy Guscott came off the bench, where his talents had been under-used for the majority of the season, magically to create two second-half tries. Jonathan Davies had come back from rugby league to wear the Welsh number-ten jersey for one last time, but was not to finish his career as a winner in Cardiff. 'I knew I wasn't the same player as when I went,' asserts Davies. 'I was that little bit older than the others who'd been up north, and I returned more for the romantic side. But to play again for Wales was also to prove people wrong, those who said I couldn't do it again, so it was very much a personal triumph. I remember making a couple of important tackles, especially when I caught Jerry Guscott from behind!'

A consolation for the Welsh supporters, even as England were piling on the agony towards the end, was the final try at the old stadium, scored by scrum-half Robert Howley. Jonathan Davies was left with the conversion. 'I thought, "This is going to be the last kick at the Arms Park – don't miss the damn thing!" That ground was extra special for me because of my family roots. Also, you don't get many national venues right in the heart of a city. Because of this, the atmosphere would build all morning in the streets outside, and then, when you got inside, the supporters were so close to the game that there was always a lot of noise. But I've never been one to let history stand in the way of progression. I'm sure when the new stadium is up and running it will have a special feeling all of its own.' The final curtain was dropping not only for Davies and the old ground but also for Will Carling and Rob Andrew, the latter having come on late in the game for one final international fling. It was the Englishmen who went out on a winning note, but at the end of the match the three men embraced.

There was little surprise when the news came through that France, in their fiftieth and final match at the Parc des Princes, had chalked up 47 more points as the Scots played the supporting role. It was France's highest-ever Five Nations score, and the dazzling length-of-the-field try finished off by flanker Olivier Magne was, for the French, a fitting end. The Parc des Princes had witnessed the country's fifth Grand Slam.

The 1997 Five Nations had been saved in the committee rooms, but events on the field had raised a new question: how could the tournament prosper if the big two could not be beaten? A close result when a Celtic country played England or France now seemed like a one-off, which for Brian Ashton meant time to start worrying. 'Professionalism had been taken on board in England and France,' he explains, 'and for a variety of reasons hadn't been in the other nations.' The varying domestic structures of the game were a key factor: 'there was a definite gap appearing.' A further concern, he adds, was that the new laws introduced in the mid 1990s to keep the ball alive had ignited rugby down under, but the game hadn't changed drastically in the northern hemisphere. 'It was fairly obvious from the Tri-Nations,' says Ashton, 'that the players in the southern hemisphere had the necessary fitness and technical skills to play the game at a higher level.'

1998 – France's GRAND SLAM and England's Triple Crown

Despite its problems, the championship was given a facelift for the start of the 1998 season when France hosted England at their grand new home, the Stade de France. With the construction of Wales's Millennium Stadium well under way and, with the English and Scots now well accustomed to their modern surroundings, it was only the Irish who would end the century in a ground that had changed little over the years. Inside their futuristic bowl of a stadium the French supporters roared their side to victory. Under their new coach Clive Woodward England had drawn with New Zealand at the end of 1997, so this loss in Paris was a backward step. Woodward could only be envious of the French performance. 'France played some of the rugby I like to see,' is his simple verdict. 'We had the personnel with pace, but they simply didn't show it.' 'This is how the modern game should be played,' said his French counterpart, Jean-Claude Skréla, the former flanker: 'there were fifteen men playing well and their efforts totalled more than fifteen.'

Skréla's comments summed up how rugby was evolving, with backs expected to do the work of forwards and vice-versa. The French side included many such players, none better than the dynamic props from Toulouse, Franck Tournaire and Christian Califano. France, carrying the standard for 'total rugby', went on to

Murrayfield and demolished Scotland, who had overcome Ireland by a mere point on the first weekend. The French scored seven tries with winger Philippe Bernat-Salles crossing for two of them. France became the first away side to top fifty points in a championship game, and it seemed almost irrelevant that this was only the second French win in Scotland since 1978. Some urgent questions had to be answered by the Celtic nations.

Almost as alarmingly, on the same day England were also re-writing history in amassing an astonishing total of sixty points against Wales at Twickenham – another Five Nations record. Eight tries were scored by the home team but, despite the torrent of points, even English supporters felt a sense of emptiness. Their team's win was well merited but, as a contest, the match had ended long before the referee had blown for the final time. Such one-sidedness was almost unheard-of since the earliest years of the championship, and for the Welsh it was the stuff of nightmares. Captain Robert Howley had led his team out in a championship game for the first time, but recalls the day with anguish. 'I'll never forget the build-up to that match, because we shot our ourselves in the foot. There was a lot made of the fact that "one on one" we were a better side than England. At half-time Lawrence Dallaglio shouted across the dressing-rooms, "That was for blabbing off in the press." We started well and Allan Bateman scored twice, one of them a superb length-of-the-field try, but then for the next hour we were blown apart by England's driving line-out and scrum. It had been a heartbreaking match to play in. At the end I got all the players together and said that we had to be accountable and responsible for our actions. Going back over the Severn Bridge the following day we were ready to accept the criticism from the press and the supporters. I had great self-belief as a player and a captain but because of the slaughter started questioning that. That it couldn't get much worse was the most positive outcome I could think of at the time.'

Mercifully, the following set of games provided a badly-needed twist of the unexpected. This season the kick-off times were staggered to suit live television coverage, a long overdue move which enabled the viewer to watch both the day's matches in their entirety. But what all spectators, either in the armchair or at the ground, really desired was an Irish performance in Paris that would make a mockery of the pundits' lopsided forecasts.

Ireland had yet another new man at the helm: the forthright New Zealander Warren Gatland, who had taken over from Brian Ashton.

Gatland was immediately rewarded as Ireland, without a win against France for fifteen years, nearly caused a major upset. The Irish forwards, including the experienced lock, Paddy Johns, and his Saracens team-mate, prop Paul Wallace, were in inspirational form, and when another prop, Nick Popplewell, came on to join the fray for his last international appearance, it seemed that his long career would end with a glorious victory. But Denis Hickie's breakaway try, Ireland's first in Paris since another winger, Freddie McLennan, had scored eighteen years earlier, was cancelled out by a late try from the French hooker and captain, Raphael Ibañez, to give the home side victory by only two points. Ireland had at least gained the respect that Warren Gatland craved. 'They were so disappointed not to win, but I told them I was proud of their performance. We may not be the greatest or the most talented, but we walked off with heads held high.' England and France, he adds, simply have so many more players to choose from – 'France can drop seven guys and replace them – and in fact they regularly do that! I wanted to establish that if anyone was going to beat us they would have to play well for the full eighty minutes.'

Wembley Stadium had become the temporary home of Welsh rugby, and there Wales met Scotland – two more sides trying to regain lost reputations. Hordes of loyal followers made the trip up the M4 motorway, and were able to return celebrating a win. Wales followed with victory over Ireland in Dublin, but neither match convinced the doubters that the corner had been turned. England reminded the Scots that there was still plenty of work for the Celts in recording their highest total at Murrayfield, with Paul Grayson becoming the first English player in a Five Nations match to score a try, conversion, penalty-goal and drop-goal. Playing the game on a Sunday curtailed the supporters' celebrations, but in truth the party had been pooped by the clear anticipation of the result. Whatever the reason, there were fewer sore heads at work on the Monday morning!

The final weekend saw England predictably beat Ireland to win their fourth consecutive Triple Crown, to equal the record of the great Welsh side of the 1970s. In doing so they took their points total for the season to a championship record of 146. Just as inevitably, the Five Nations Trophy was awarded the following day to France, when Raphael Ibañez went up the famous Wembley steps as a Grand Slam captain following a devastating 51–0 victory over Wales. It was the biggest winning margin since the Five Nations had begun; for the first time in their history, moreover, the Welsh had failed to score against

France. It had all looked too easy as the French ran in seven tries, two of which went to their star full-back, Jean-Luc Sadourny. But the man who really twinkled at Wembley was Thomas Castaignède, in a virtuoso display. Only England in 1913–14, 1923–24 and 1991–92 had won back-to-back Grand Slams: now Castaignède's side could be added to this illustrious list. 'It felt so good to be inside the stadium – magical. But we were not so much a French national team – more a club team. This was the real face of French rugby. Against Ireland it was not a happy face. This was the new face, a face of fun and movement and self–belief.' Ten thousand travelling French supporters concurred. They had witnessed a team who that season, despite a temporary blip against the Irish, had taken Five Nations rugby to a new level.

Nearly ninety years after joining the championship, France were now in a position to go for a unique third Grand Slam in a row. After 1999, there would be a further hurdle: the five nations had ratified Italy's inclusion in the championship. 'This is an historic day for northern hemisphere rugby,' announced Allan Hosie, the Chairman of the Five Nations Committee, 'from a playing, commercial, social and cultural point-of-view.' However, both on and off the pitch the future Italy had fought so hard for was looking far from certain.

1999 – Scotland's championship

1999 began with the shocking and incomprehensible news that England were to be thrown out of the Five Nations. The issue of television revenue at the heart of the discord between the unions earlier in the decade had never gone away, and now the RFU wanted further clarification from the Five Nations Committee on how that money would be divided in future years. Allan Hosie gave the RFU a deadline to honour the previously signed agreement, but the hour passed, England had failed to comply, and they ceased to be a member of the championship.

How matters had been allowed to reach such a point was almost beyond belief. The players' wishes had been ignored, the supporters who had booked tickets and hotels had been treated with contempt and the broadcasters, sponsors and travel companies stood by ready to litigate. For the overwhelming majority, the prospect of a championship without the English was equivalent to watching rugby played without a ball. Within 24 hours of the expulsion the Chairman of the

RFU's Management Board, Brian Baister, along with the former England captain, Bill Beaumont, were meeting Allan Hosie in Glasgow. Beaumont's presence was vital, despite his modest estimation of his role: 'My involvement was just to get everybody back at the table again, because the Five Nations is part of the fabric of our rugby life.' He got up at an RFU committee meeting and said, 'Look, this is the position, lads: unless we move rapidly there is a distinct possibility we could be out of the thing for good.'

After a meeting at Hosie's offices, the three men adjourned to the now-infamous Drum and Monkey pub, the humble setting where the Five Nations was saved. After a couple of hours and pints England were re-admitted into the championship. 'It showed how stupid things had got,' says Beaumont, for whom it was mission accomplished. But solving the dispute, as Beaumont's exchange with Allan Hosie shows, had drawn on long-lasting personal friendships. 'I said, "Crikey, Allan, we can't throw this all away! I've got a photograph of you in my office refereeing a game I'm playing in!"' To everybody's relief, the century finished with a Five Nations to remember for all the right reasons.

France's hopes of winning their record third Grand Slam in a row were almost dashed at the outset as Ireland showed great spirit in Dublin. It took Thomas Castaignède's last-minute penalty-goal to win the game for France – and even then the Irish fly-half, David Humphreys, had a chance to snatch victory with another kick at goal. But it went agonisingly wide, and his team lost by a point. The match had also had some particularly colourful moments. This was the first year that the championship had a title sponsor, Lloyds TSB, and the Irish authorities had allowed the sponsor's logo to be painted in the centre of the pitch: after heavy rain the dye rubbed off onto the players, leaving Irish hooker Keith Wood daubed like an Indian war-chief!

Against Wales in Edinburgh Scotland continued the year's kaleidoscopic theme, unzipping their orange track-suits to reveal a new blue and purple strip – another change symbolic of the era. The early administrators of the SRU might have gasped in horror, but their modern counterparts were more concerned with coaxing the crowds back to Murrayfield after a disappointing attendance for the autumn international against South Africa – perhaps a sign that the supporters' patience had been eroded by the predictable results. A large Welsh presence ensured a full house, however, and witnessed a Scottish win in a pulsating match that will be remembered for the fastest try in the history of the championship – centre John Leslie crossing the line in under ten seconds. Along with his brother Martin in the pack, Leslie had been recruited from New Zealand, their father Andy having captained the All Blacks in the 1970s, but their grandfather's birthplace, Linlithgow, making them eligible for Scotland. Wales had adopted a similar policy with Shane Howarth, an ex-All Black, installed at full-back thanks to his Cardiff-born grandfather. Howarth was under the direction of Wales's new Kiwi coach, the thoughtful Graham Henry, who made his name guiding the Auckland Blues to two Super-Twelve titles. With former Waikato team-mates Warren Gatland of Ireland and the assistant England coach, John Mitchell, in the second year of their Five Nations roles, the New Zealand influence on the championship was strong. The respected Mitchell believes the southern hemisphere input was a timely addition: 'There were a lot of quality players in the championship, but it gave them technical and tactical knowledge they hadn't been offered before. Also, a New Zealander's passion for the game is quite different to other people's, because a lot of us have been doing it since five years of age. These ingrained attitudes allowed us to adapt to professionalism better than others. Losing is not part of our vocabulary. When we do lose we take it very hard – in fact it's a matter of life and death!'

England had already been installed as favourites to win the championship without yet having taken the field. Nevertheless, Scotland, their experienced lock Doddie Weir out with an injury picked up against the Welsh, still went to Twickenham feeling they had a realistic chance of victory, something they had not achieved since 1983. Both sides scored three tries, and in the end the English scrambled home with a three-point winning margin. In Dublin England played a potentially dangerous Irish side that had beaten Wales at Wembley but, inspired by captain Lawrence Dallaglio and with locks Martin Johnson and Tim Rodber in towering form, they muscled their way to another win. John Mitchell knew what his side yearned for: 'The Triple Crown in 1998 was like a glass of champagne without any fizz. It was nice to achieve and something not too many New Zealanders are involved in, but what you want is the premier accolade, and that is the Grand Slam.'

What was really required to restore the championship's competitive edge was a Celtic victory over one of the 'big two'. It came in Paris in unforgettable fashion when, in one of the greatest matches of all time, Wales banished the memories of their earlier two defeats with a performance of stunning quality. The Welsh won with a combination of skill and bravery – their backs, marshalled by Neil Jenkins, breaking through time and again to set up some startling scores. The try finished off by lock Craig Quinnell bears comparison with any from a previous era, and to top it all he was hauled from the ground by his brother Scott, who five years earlier had scored a vital try against the French. France, too, played their part, in particular full-back Emile Ntamack, who became the first player to score a hat-trick of tries in the history of the Five Nations and still end up on the losing side. Dramatically, they had a kick to win the game at the death, but Thomas Castaignède failed to repeat his Dublin success and Wales rejoiced at the sight of a scoreboard which read, France 33 – Wales 34.

It was a seminal moment for the championship, and especially for the rejuvenated Welsh captain Robert Howley. After the home nations' impressive performances against the South African tourists at the end of 1998 he had predicted the closest Five Nations for some time, and he had used the memory of Wales's humiliation by France's half-backs twelve months earlier to good effect. 'I spoke to Neil Jenkins about the way Thomas Castaignède and Philippe Carbonneau had run the show that day. I keep a scrapbook, and in one of the clippings prior to the Wembley game the French pair said they were out to prove they were the best. Before the Paris re-match we read those comments and vowed to have the game of our lives. The word used by Graham Henry prior to the game was "boldness", and if we were going to beat France on their own park we had to play their style of rugby, but better than they did. Half an hour after the game we were still shaking with the elation and emotion – we couldn't stop hugging and kissing each other.'

There was another glimpse of a bright future for the championship in England's victory over France, when the nineteen-year-old centre Jonny Wilkinson became the new boy-wonder of English rugby, landing seven penalty-goals from seven attempts to put his name alongside Simon Hodgkinson and Rob Andrew. A year earlier Wilkinson had become the youngest player to appear for his country since H.C.C. Laird in 1927, and now his cool display enabled England to go to Wembley to meet Wales for the Grand Slam, while Scotland's exciting win over Ireland meant they still had a chance of the championship title should they win in Paris and England slip up. The last Five Nations weekend promised much, but surely nobody could have predicted the final instalment of the 89-year story.

In 25 astonishing minutes of the first half at the Stade de France the Scots scored a spectacular five tries. One year after their humiliation at home to France, it was an attacking display on a par with anything the championship had ever witnessed and, with the French also crossing the line three times in the first period, a stunned Paris crowd must have wondered if it was all really happening. It was Scotland's new-found self-belief that was the decisive factor as they recorded their highest-ever score against France: 36 points. The French had now lost three matches in a season for the first time in thirty years. For Jim Telfer, his final Five Nations game as Scottish coach was the ideal farewell. 'It was the best I've ever seen Scotland play. I don't think anyone could deny that our brand of rugby was entertaining. We were supposed to be wooden spoonists, and I think there was only myself and the rest of the squad who felt we were going to do as well as we did. Of all the teams I've coached, this one created something special out of nothing.'

The Five Nations had been turned on its head. Scotland's full-back, Glenn Metcalfe, another New Zealand import, had cut the French defence to ribbons just as his fellow ex-Kiwi, Shane Howarth, had done for Wales earlier in the season. New stars like the athletic lock Scott Murray flourished in the positive environment while the old man of the team, centre Alan Tait, again reaped the benefit of playing alongside the wonderfully creative John Leslie and Gregor Townsend. Tait's two tries against France took his season's tally to five and Scotland's to sixteen, but nobody could match the feat of fly-half Townsend, whose own score added him to the illustrious list of those who had achieved a Grand Slam of tries in the championship.

And what of the Grand Slam itself? Could Wales deliver the title to their Celtic cousins by bloodying England's nose in their own backyard at Wembley? The pre-match singing from Max Boyce and Tom Jones had some echoes of the past, but this was a new Wales, freed like Scotland from the shackles of doubt that had dogged them in recent years. England used all their might to carve out three first-half tries, with their back row of Lawrence Dallaglio, Richard Hill and Neil Back again outstanding, but they were never able to pull away because for Wales Neil Jenkins kicked like a dream. Despite their territorial dominance, at half-time England were only in front by 25 points to 18. After the interval, Jenkins unlocked the near-perfect English defence with a pass borrowed from Barry John's kit-bag and Shane Howarth scored the try to bring Wales right back into the game.

In injury-time, it appeared that England had done enough, and the

Grand Slam, record fifth consecutive Triple Crown and final Five Nations title seemed all but theirs. Awarded a controversial penalty after what was judged an illegal tackle by England's Tim Rodber, the Welsh banged the ball into touch and dug deep for one last attempt. On the English twenty-two the impressive lock, Chris Wyatt, soared into the air and spooned the ball to Robert Howley. Scott Quinnell grabbed the ball and the initiative and charged at England's defence. Then in stepped Scott Gibbs and, five missed tackles later, he had smashed his way to the line with a score fit for a Five Nations finale to drag England's sweet chariot to the wrecker's yard. Neil Jenkins had the conversion to win the game, but Gibbs says he knew instantly they had done enough: 'When Neil was lining up to kick I didn't feel any nerves at all – I had total faith in his ability.' Jenkins, unfazed, obliged with his customary confidence despite the pressure of the kick – one he would normally expect to get, but this was not a normal situation. Just as in Paris only a few weeks earlier, Wales's margin of success was a single point. This time the scoreboard read, Wales 32 – England 31. Jenkins had notched up a total of 22 in the match and 64 for the season, both championship records for Wales.

So for the first time since 1990 the championship went to Scotland. The Celts had combined to restore an even distribution of power. Both England and France, who had hoped for so much, were left with nothing – England had lost to a Celtic nation for the first time in five years, and France's astonishing decline had resulted in the wooden spoon. Unpredictable and unimaginably exciting – that was the season of 1999. Looking back at Five Nations history, that is just as it always was and, surely, how the Six Nations always will be.

CONCLUSION

So where does the Five Nations go from here? In one respect it is quite simple – to the Six Nations, as Italy's inclusion in the year 2000 comes ninety years after France came on board. But is the tournament fit to sail a course through another century of rugby? At the end of the 1998 season the answer to that question might well have been, 'No'. The smoother transfer into professionalism in Australia, New Zealand and South Africa was 'trophy-full and argument-free' – northern hemisphere rugby was being beaten both on and off the pitch.

The man who steered Scotland to the 1990 Grand Slam, Ian McGeechan, also played in the championship with distinction and coached the last three British Lions teams. Once the game went professional, McGeechan feels, it was inevitable there would be a gap between the 'haves' and the 'have-nots' of Five Nations rugby. 'The more organized the game became,' he argues, 'the more it favoured those countries with large numbers of players – there are more in Yorkshire alone than in either Scotland or Ireland. Previously, when it was an amateur game, two of the most disorganised unions were England and France, and that helped to level things out. They always thought they could choose a better side, made those changes and therefore prevented continuity. It was only when Geoff Cooke said, "Right, these are the players, and I don't care if somebody thinks he's better" – and stuck with them, that England came strong. And France, probably the most talented country in the championship, became much more organised so they didn't fall apart.'

Celtic passion and togetherness created motivated and tight-knit squads all through the history of the Five Nations. The lack of numbers to choose from actually helped by promoting security, which in turn led to a freedom of expression on the field and success – for Ireland in 1948, for example, Wales in the 1970s and Scotland in 1990. In the professional world of the late 1990s, however, these qualities were not enough on their own and the Five Nations, the last bastion of tradition in the sport, found that its stock was falling.

Moreover, the chance to see the southern hemisphere nations on a more regular basis further emphasised the growing gulf between the two halves of the rugby world. Aside from the British Lions, individual victories by the five nations over the sport's leaders were becoming increasingly rare, even taking into account the rise in the number of international matches being played. More worryingly for the Celtic countries, the size of the defeats had reached embarrassing proportions and criticism was growing. 'In the last decade of the Five Nations, the game became more global,' adds Ian McGeechan. 'We watched the southern hemisphere games live on television, when at one time you only ever saw the sides on tour, and the nature of the spectator and viewer changed accordingly. There used to be the rugby traditionalist, brought up on it at school and part of a network almost, whereas modern spectators were from a slightly different background. They saw the game differently and became more educated observers – far more critical of play than the old rugby fan used to be. The sport responded by becoming more of a spectacle. The standard was not the Five Nations any more, it was the world game, and tactically that is now what we are pushing towards.'

The greater tendency for the new supporters to criticise was based on the sound principle that they paid the players' wages. In return for the high price of admission to games both entertainment and competition were demanded, and the fear was that if people could predict the result fewer would turn up. Then along came the 1999 championship, an epic year when the Celtic countries struck back and the anticipation returned before each and every game. It was as if the fruits of professionalism in the northern hemisphere were belatedly ripening, and perhaps it was no coincidence that this was in part inspired by a southern hemisphere influence, both in coaching talent and players. The result was the most invigorating of recent seasons, and one which put an end to the question marks hovering over the future of the tournament.

Italy's inclusion now comes at the perfect time to give the competition a further boost. 'I think for the credibility of developing northern hemisphere rugby, Italy deserve to be in,' agrees Ian McGeechan, 'as they have produced a consistent level of performance. It's not an exclusive old boys' club, and if you want to take the game on there have to be more countries playing. They may not get seventy or eighty thousand crowds initially, but France didn't when they came in.' The plan for a second division of European competition has already been revealed, and in future years the vision surely has to be one of promotion and relegation between the two 'leagues', although this is inevitably some way off. A move that could be implemented immediately, however, is to increase the number of points awarded for a win in the Six Nations, and introduce bonus points for tries scored. This would send out a positive message to both players and supporters.

A more controversial change currently being debated concerns the structure of the season. Many in the game argue that the championship should be relocated to the end of the domestic year, with the matches being played back-to-back over a five-week period in April and May. It is an idea well received by Ian McGeechan: 'It would be a terrific end to the season, and not something thrown in as part of it. It would lend perspective to the whole year without counter-demanding on clubs or other events – the championship then becomes even stronger.' Currently, players return home to their clubs from international duty and are asked to turn out either tired or carrying injuries. As professionals they perform, but the situation is far from ideal for either club or country. Moving the tournament would also prevent a critical drop in revenue for the clubs mid-season, and would allow a national coach to take charge of his squad for a two-month period. Tours to the southern hemisphere would follow the Six Nations with players better prepared for having operated as a unit in a tournament of comparable intensity to the World Cup.

In response, the traditionalists retort that the competition has always been there to warm the winter heart, allowing a fortnightly jaunt around the capitals when the days are short and the nights are long. Certainly to lose those familiar weekends, which provide a mounting drama in the New Year when championship rugby is often the focal point of the nations' sporting interest, is a potential hardship. However, in a recent survey in *Rugby World* magazine, 46% of fans said they would be in favour of a switch to the end of the season. Ian McGeechan believes that the majority of supporters could be won over for the sake of the sport as a whole: 'Because we are now professional, it is very important what the spectator thinks and wants to do. But at the moment the grounds are oversold and people can't get enough tickets. What might happen if you play the championship over five weeks is that people pick and choose to a greater extent, and say, "I'll have this home game and this away game". The market place would be opened for others.'

The issue needs to be addressed with the utmost urgency, with all stakeholders – players, spectators, administrators, broadcasters and sponsors – being consulted. It must be remembered that the greatest traditions move with the times, and indeed the championship has always done that – not just enduring the passage of years, but thriving on it. The challenge and responsibility for the current custodians is to continue to marry the important traditions with contemporary needs. They must recognise that the tournament cannot stand in isolation – however magnificent, it is now part of world rugby. 'We have to be more open-minded,' says Ian McGeechan. 'Tradition is fine, it is very important to me, and I have always been committed to international rugby – but the Six Nations has to have a modern place. By challenging everybody else to change all the time and saying the championship never will, it almost becomes the dinosaur you never want it to be. You must be able to see it evolve, so that in the end it is still the flagship encouraging our best players to play their best rugby.'

In a world where too many sporting fixtures have no meaning, the Six Nations must have a prominent place. It is an electric environment in which to play or watch rugby, a perfect way of settling local rivalries, with each nation having a unique style of hosting the event. No country has ever dominated the championship, and it is to be hoped that no nation ever will. Only in the last decade has the future been placed in doubt, primarily because of the speed of the professional revolution. The future is bright, however, because the tournament will always mean so much to so many, and that is why we can look forward to another ninety years of championship history.

FIVE NATIONS –
FIFTEEN PLAYERS

This book has recounted the history of the Five Nations through the stories of the players whose deeds have made the tournament such a wonderful success. So who are the greatest fifteen players to have graced the championship? That, of course, is an impossible question to answer – but it does not make it any less fun to speculate! We have all done it on a beer mat, but here the unenviable task falls to Ian McGeechan, who must put his expertise into action and choose his all-time Five Nations team.

At the outset, Ian wanted to stress a number of points. 'If it's a team that would be successful today then, with the best will in the world, the older stars would not get in – they wouldn't live with the way the modern game is played. The grounds and the playing surfaces are better, and the skills required are much more demanding now. But I've tried to choose those who were outstanding in their time – given the same conditions, the quality players of previous decades would still succeed in today's environment. These players brought something absolutely special, magical almost, to their era in the Five Nations – they saw the rugby differently, moved the game on and influenced not only their team but also the championship.'

Full-back
'It came down to four: Pierre Villepreux, Serge Blanco and Andy Irvine came close, but I've chosen JPR WILLIAMS – he was like a rock, and had such an tremendous influence. His style of play had

really not been seen before: he was an outstanding attacker and the most devastating defensive full-back. Under a high ball or running back out of defence, who else would you want?'

Wings

'GERALD DAVIES was a class above everybody. He could side-step off both feet, had acceleration and also played in the centre – he was probably one of the most gifted runners I've ever seen. Like JPR, he did things I still remember today. The others – well, Ian Smith and Ken Jones were great players and match winners, and Ieuan Evans had a major impact on Wales even when his team was not playing well. Then there's Andy Irvine again, who would not only be my second-best full-back but also my third-best wing. But to partner Davies it's DAVID DUCKHAM. The thing about him was that if somebody even mentioned his name, people got excited.'

Centres

'I can't go past MIKE GIBSON in the centre. He was so outstanding and intelligent, and his work-rate and ability to make and score tries over such a long period of time are unparalleled. His partner would have to be PHILIPPE SELLA. Again, you would always look to see if he was playing – over one hundred internationals and so consistently good. The combination: Gibson the total competitor with the vision, alongside the physical presence of Sella who could handle that vision. I should also mention Jim Renwick, Jeff Butterfield and my boyhood hero – Lewis Jones. I used to stand on the terracing at Leeds Rugby League, watch him every week with his little 'hitch-kick' and just try to touch him at the end of the match. But he left the Five Nations too soon.'

Fly-half

'I would love to have seen this fellow at first-hand. When people talk about the Ireland of the 1950s they talk about JACK KYLE with reverence, as if he was a god. They say that if you didn't mark him spot-on, then he'd beaten you. He knew instinctively when something was wrong in the opposition's defence. Kyle was one of those players, like Cliff Morgan, Barry John and Phil Bennett, about whom you'd think, "How do we stop them?" John Rutherford was another.'

Scrum-half

'I had a nightmare on this one! Haydn Tanner, Pierre Berbizier, Jacques

Fouroux and Dickie Jeeps were the centre-pieces of their teams. A scrum-half must have the respect of the forwards and they certainly did. In the end, though, it had to be GARETH EDWARDS, because he had everything: power, pace and a great pass, especially those reverse passes into the middle of the field. His legs weren't particularly big, but from the waist upwards he was massive – he was an athlete.'

Props

'For me these are the real characters. Syd Millar was unbelievable, and Fran Cotton had great hands for a big man and was a wonderful scrummager. Like Fran, Robert Paparemborde could operate on either side, and his modern successor Christian Califano needs mentioning too. Hughie McLeod was a very influential player for his country – but above all others GRAHAM PRICE was the prop ahead of his time. He used to do anything he liked with his opposite number, and then he'd be out in the open scoring tries from seventy metres. At loose-head, it's impossible to ignore IAN McLAUCHLAN, despite his size. He was a great ball player and, more than anybody, was instrumental in giving Scotland a different character in the 1970s, which led into the Grand Slams of the 1980s and 1990s.'

Hooker

'I've great respect for Brian Moore's attitude to the game, and John Pullin was an Englishman who stood out in a losing side. Three other great talents were Bryn Meredith of Wales and the Frenchmen Philippe Dintrans and Daniel Dubroca. But it comes down to a choice between two complete rugby players and masters of their position – Scotland's Colin Deans and England's PETER WHEELER. I've chosen Wheeler because he got lower in the scrum than any hooker I've ever seen, and all other aspects of his game were world-class.'

Locks

"The problem is again who to leave out. England's Grand Slam second-rows of the early 1990s, Wade Dooley and Paul Ackford, would never let you down. I also believe Ackford was one of the most underrated players of all time – he moved lock play onto a different level. Gordon Brown was a fine exponent, but probably had his best days for the Lions and not in the Five Nations. France's Benoit Dauga and Jean Condom, plus Moss Keane and Bill Beaumont, were all very gifted. In the end I've chosen an Irish/English combination: WILLIE JOHN McBRIDE had such an overwhelming presence in the game;

alongside him MARTIN JOHNSON – history will show what a great player he was, too.'

Flankers

'I must mention two of the Scotland Grand Slam side in 1990, Finlay Calder and John Jeffrey – men you would want with you at any time. A Scot from a previous generation, Doug Elliot, and others like Michel Crauste and Jean Prat, were clearly outstanding in their time. Neil Back came very close, and it's a joy to see him fulfilling his potential, while Fergus Slattery had non-stop energy and Tony Neary was also a great player. I've gone for two more men who could operate on either flank – PETER WINTERBOTTOM and JEAN-PIERRE RIVES, who both had a huge impact on the teams in which they played.'

Number-eight

'This came down to four players and, as with so many of the other positions, I couldn't really get it wrong because somebody else would be waiting in the wings to do an equally impressive job. I'd love to see how Wavell Wakefield would play with all these stars around him – I bet he'd adapt. But because I'm relying on hearsay I've centred my selection on three more modern players: Jean-Pierre Bastiat, so powerful; Dean Richards, who could read a game like no other; and MERVYN DAVIES, whose bravery and skill were exceptional. Davies gets my vote, but it was a tough call.'

Finally, in a team of captains, I would choose WILLIE JOHN McBRIDE as skipper, closely followed by Rives, Johnson and McLauchlan.

Ian McGeechan
Northampton, 1999

So there you have it, the Five Nations team to beat all others: J.P.R. Williams, T.G.R. Davies, P. Sella, C.M.H. Gibson, D.J. Duckham, J.W. Kyle, G.O. Edwards; J. McLauchlan, P.J. Wheeler, G. Price, M.O. Johnson, W.J. McBride (capt.), J-P. Rives, P.J. Winterbottom, T.M. Davies – five Welshmen, four Englishmen, three Irishmen, two Frenchmen and a Scot. How many Italians, or other nations for that matter, will feature in another ninety years' time?

STATISTICAL APPENDIX

MATCH BY MATCH SCORES

1910

1 Jan	St Helen's, Swansea	Wales	49	France	14
15 Jan	Twickenham, London	England	11	Wales	6
22 Jan	Inverleith, Edinburgh	Scotland	27	France	0
5 Feb	Arms Park, Cardiff	Wales	14	Scotland	0
12 Feb	Twickenham	England	0	Ireland	0
26 Feb	Balmoral Showgrounds, Belfast	Ireland	0	Scotland	14
3 Mar	Parc des Princes, Paris	France	3	England	11
12 Mar	Lansdowne Road, Dublin	Ireland	3	Wales	19
19 Mar	Inverleith	Scotland	5	England	14
28 Mar	Parc des Princes	France	3	Ireland	8

1911

2 Jan	Stade Colombes, Paris	France	16	Scotland	15
21 Jan	St Helen's	Wales	15	England	11
28 Jan	Twickenham	England	37	France	0
4 Feb	Inverleith	Scotland	10	Wales	32
11 Feb	Lansdowne Road	Ireland	3	England	0
25 Feb	Inverleith	Scotland	10	Ireland	16
28 Feb	Parc des Princes	France	0	Wales	15
11 Mar	Arms Park	Wales	16	Ireland	0
18 Mar	Twickenham	England	13	Scotland	8
25 Mar	Mardyke, Cork	Ireland	25	France	5

1912

1 Jan	Parc des Princes	France	6	Ireland	1
20 Jan	Twickenham	England	8	Wales	0
20 Jan	Inverleith	Scotland	31	France	3
3 Feb	St Helen's	Wales	21	Scotland	6
10 Feb	Twickenham	England	15	Ireland	0
24 Feb	Lansdowne Road	Ireland	10	Scotland	8
9 Mar	Balmoral Showgrounds	Ireland	12	Wales	5
16 Mar	Inverleith	Scotland	8	England	3
25 Mar	Rodney Parade, Newport	Wales	14	France	8
8 Apr	Parc des Princes	France	8	England	18

1913

1 Jan	*Parc des Princes*	France	3	Scotland	21
18 Jan	*Arms Park*	Wales	0	England	12
25 Jan	*Twickenham*	England	20	France	0
1 Feb	*Inverleith*	Scotland	0	Wales	8
8 Feb	*Lansdowne Road*	Ireland	4	England	15
22 Feb	*Inverleith*	Scotland	29	Ireland	14
27 Feb	*Parc des Princes*	France	8	Wales	11
8 Mar	*St Helen's*	Wales	16	Ireland	13
15 Mar	*Twickenham*	England	3	Scotland	0
24 Mar	*Mardyke*	Ireland	24	France	0

1914

1 Jan	*Parc des Princes*	France	6	Ireland	8
17 Jan	*Twickenham*	England	10	Wales	9
7 Feb	*Arms Park*	Wales	24	Scotland	5
14 Feb	*Twickenham*	England	17	Ireland	12
28 Feb	*Lansdowne Road*	Ireland	6	Scotland	0
2 Mar	*St Helen's*	Wales	31	France	0
14 Mar	*Balmoral Showgrounds*	Ireland	3	Wales	11
21 Mar	*Inverleith*	Scotland	15	England	16
13 Apr	*Stade Colombes*	France	13	England	39

(1915–1919 no championship)

1920

1 Jan	*Parc des Princes*	France	0	Scotland	5
17 Jan	*St Helen's*	Wales	19	England	5
31 Jan	*Twickenham*	England	8	France	3
7 Feb	*Inverleith*	Scotland	9	Wales	5
14 Feb	*Lansdowne Road*	Ireland	11	England	14
17 Feb	*Stade Colombes*	France	5	Wales	6
28 Feb	*Inverleith*	Scotland	19	Ireland	0
13 Mar	*Arms Park*	Wales	28	Ireland	4
20 Mar	*Twickenham*	England	13	Scotland	4
3 Apr	*Lansdowne Road*	Ireland	7	France	15

1921

15 Jan	*Twickenham*	England	18	Wales	3
22 Jan	*Inverleith*	Scotland	0	France	3
5 Feb	*St Helen's*	Wales	8	Scotland	14
12 Feb	*Twickenham*	England	15	Ireland	0
26 Feb	*Lansdowne Road*	Ireland	9	Scotland	8
26 Feb	*Arms Park*	Wales	12	France	4

12 Mar	*Balmoral Showgrounds*	Ireland	0	Wales	6
19 Mar	*Inverleith*	Scotland	0	England	18
28 Mar	*Stade Colombes*	France	6	England	10
9 Apr	*Stade Colombes*	France	20	Ireland	10

1922

2 Jan	*Stade Colombes*	France	3	Scotland	3
21 Jan	*Arms Park*	Wales	28	England	6
4 Feb	*Inverleith*	Scotland	9	Wales	9
11 Feb	*Lansdowne Road*	Ireland	3	England	12
25 Feb	*Twickenham*	England	11	France	11
25 Feb	*Inverleith*	Scotland	6	Ireland	3
11 Mar	*St Helen's*	Wales	11	Ireland	5
18 Mar	*Twickenham*	England	11	Scotland	5
23 Mar	*Stade Colombes*	France	3	Wales	11
8 Apr	*Lansdowne Road*	Ireland	8	France	3

1923

20 Jan	*Twickenham*	England	7	Wales	3
20 Jan	*Inverleith*	Scotland	16	France	3
3 Feb	*Arms Park*	Wales	8	Scotland	11
10 Feb	*Welford Road, Leicester*	England	23	Ireland	5
24 Feb	*Lansdowne Road*	Ireland	3	Scotland	13
24 Feb	*St Helen's*	Wales	16	France	8
10 Mar	*Lansdowne Road*	Ireland	5	Wales	4
17 Mar	*Inverleith*	Scotland	6	England	8
2 Apr	*Stade Colombes*	France	3	England	12
14 Apr	*Stade Colombes*	France	14	Ireland	8

1924

1 Jan	*Stade Pershing, Paris*	France	12	Scotland	10
19 Jan	*St Helen's*	Wales	9	England	17
26 Jan	*Lansdowne Road*	Ireland	6	France	0
2 Feb	*Inverleith*	Scotland	35	Wales	10
9 Feb	*Ravenhill, Belfast*	Ireland	3	England	14
23 Feb	*Twickenham*	England	19	France	7
23 Feb	*Inverleith*	Scotland	13	Ireland	8
8 Mar	*Arms Park*	Wales	10	Ireland	13
15 Mar	*Twickenham*	England	19	Scotland	0
27 Mar	*Stade Colombes*	France	6	Wales	10

1925

1 Jan	*Stade Colombes*	France	3	Ireland	9
17 Jan	*Twickenham*	England	12	Wales	6

24 Jan	Inverleith	Scotland	25	France	4
7 Feb	St Helen's	Wales	14	Scotland	24
14 Feb	Twickenham	England	6	Ireland	6
28 Feb	Lansdowne Road	Ireland	8	Scotland	14
28 Feb	Arms Park	Wales	11	France	5
14 Mar	Ravenhill	Ireland	19	Wales	3
21 Mar	Murrayfield, Edinburgh	Scotland	14	England	11
13 Apr	Stade Colombes	France	11	England	13

1926

2 Jan	Stade Colombes	France	6	Scotland	20
16 Jan	Arms Park	Wales	3	England	3
23 Jan	Ravenhill	Ireland	11	France	0
6 Feb	Murrayfield	Scotland	8	Wales	5
13 Feb	Lansdowne Road	Ireland	19	England	15
27 Feb	Twickenham	England	11	France	0
27 Feb	Murrayfield	Scotland	0	Ireland	3
13 Mar	St Helen's	Wales	11	Ireland	8
20 Mar	Twickenham	England	9	Scotland	17
5 Apr	Stade Colombes	France	5	Wales	7

1927

1 Jan	Stade Colombes	France	3	Ireland	8
15 Jan	Twickenham	England	11	Wales	9
22 Jan	Murrayfield	Scotland	23	France	6
5 Feb	Arms Park	Wales	0	Scotland	5
12 Feb	Twickenham	England	8	Ireland	6
26 Feb	Lansdowne Road	Ireland	6	Scotland	0
26 Feb	St Helen's	Wales	25	France	7
12 Mar	Lansdowne Road	Ireland	19	Wales	9
19 Mar	Murrayfield	Scotland	21	England	13
2 Apr	Stade Colombes	France	3	England	0

1928

2 Jan	Stade Colombes	France	6	Scotland	15
21 Jan	St Helen's	Wales	8	England	10
28 Jan	Ravenhill	Ireland	12	France	8
4 Feb	Murrayfield	Scotland	0	Wales	13
11 Feb	Lansdowne Road	Ireland	6	England	7
25 Feb	Twickenham	England	18	France	8
25 Feb	Murrayfield	Scotland	5	Ireland	13
10 Mar	Arms Park	Wales	10	Ireland	13
17 Mar	Twickenham	England	6	Scotland	0
9 Apr	Stade Colombes	France	8	Wales	3

1929

30 Dec	(1928) Yves du Manoir Stadium, Paris	France	0	Ireland	6
19 Jan	Twickenham	England	8	Wales	3
19 Jan	Murrayfield	Scotland	6	France	3
2 Feb	St Helen's	Wales	14	Scotland	7
9 Feb	Twickenham	England	5	Ireland	6
23 Feb	Lansdowne Road	Ireland	7	Scotland	16
25 Feb	Arms Park	Wales	8	France	3
9 Mar	Ravenhill	Ireland	5	Wales	5
16 Mar	Murrayfield	Scotland	12	England	6
1 Apr	Stade Colombes	France	6	England	16

1930

1 Jan	Stade Colombes	France	7	Scotland	3
18 Jan	Arms Park	Wales	3	England	11
25 Jan	Ravenhill	Ireland	0	France	5
1 Feb	Murrayfield	Scotland	12	Wales	9
8 Feb	Lansdowne Road	Ireland	4	England	3
22 Feb	Twickenham	England	11	France	5
22 Feb	Murrayfield	Scotland	11	Ireland	14
8 Mar	St Helen's	Wales	12	Ireland	7
15 Mar	Twickenham	England	0	Scotland	0
21 Apr	Stade Colombes	France	0	Wales	11

1931

1 Jan	Stade Colombes	France	3	Ireland	0
17 Jan	Twickenham	England	11	Wales	11
24 Jan	Murrayfield	Scotland	6	France	4
7 Feb	Arms Park	Wales	13	Scotland	8
14 Feb	Twickenham	England	5	Ireland	6
28 Feb	Lansdowne Road	Ireland	8	Scotland	5
28 Feb	St Helen's	Wales	35	France	3
14 Mar	Ravenhill	Ireland	3	Wales	15
21 Mar	Murrayfield	Scotland	28	England	19
6 Apr	Stade Colombes	France	14	England	13

(1932–1939 France not in the championship)

1932

16 Jan	St Helen's	Wales	12	England	5
6 Feb	Murrayfield	Scotland	0	Wales	6
13 Feb	Lansdowne Road	Ireland	8	England	11
27 Feb	Murrayfield	Scotland	8	Ireland	20

12 Mar	Arms Park	Wales	10	Ireland	12
19 Mar	Twickenham	England	16	Scotland	3

1933

21 Jan	Twickenham	England	3	Wales	7
4 Feb	St Helen's	Wales	3	Scotland	11
11 Feb	Twickenham	England	17	Ireland	6
11 Mar	Ravenhill	Ireland	10	Wales	5
18 Mar	Murrayfield	Scotland	3	England	0
1 Apr	Lansdowne Road	Ireland	6	Scotland	8

1934

20 Jan	Arms Park	Wales	0	England	9
3 Feb	Murrayfield	Scotland	6	Wales	13
10 Feb	Lansdowne Road	Ireland	3	England	13
24 Feb	Murrayfield	Scotland	16	Ireland	9
10 Mar	St Helen's	Wales	13	Ireland	0
17 Mar	Twickenham	England	6	Scotland	3

1935

19 Jan	Twickenham	England	3	Wales	3
2 Feb	Arms Park	Wales	10	Scotland	6
9 Feb	Twickenham	England	14	Ireland	3
23 Feb	Lansdowne Road	Ireland	12	Scotland	5
9 Mar	Ravenhill	Ireland	9	Wales	3
16 Mar	Murrayfield	Scotland	10	England	7

1936

18 Jan	St Helen's	Wales	0	England	0
1 Feb	Murrayfield	Scotland	3	Wales	13
8 Feb	Lansdowne Road	Ireland	6	England	3
22 Feb	Murrayfield	Scotland	4	Ireland	10
14 Mar	Arms Park	Wales	3	Ireland	0
21 Mar	Twickenham	England	9	Scotland	8

1937

16 Jan	Twickenham	England	4	Wales	3
6 Feb	St Helen's	Wales	6	Scotland	13
13 Feb	Twickenham	England	9	Ireland	8
27 Feb	Lansdowne Road	Ireland	11	Scotland	4
20 Mar	Murrayfield	Scotland	3	England	6
3 Apr	Ravenhill	Ireland	5	Wales	3

1938

15 Jan	Arms Park	Wales	14	England	8
5 Feb	Murrayfield	Scotland	8	Wales	6
12 Feb	Lansdowne Road	Ireland	14	England	36
26 Feb	Murrayfield	Scotland	23	Ireland	14
12 Mar	St Helen's	Wales	11	Ireland	5
19 Mar	Twickenham	England	16	Scotland	21

1939

21 Jan	Twickenham	England	3	Wales	0
4 Feb	Arms Park	Wales	11	Scotland	3
11 Feb	Twickenham	England	0	Ireland	5
25 Feb	Lansdowne Road	Ireland	12	Scotland	3
11 Mar	Ravenhill	Ireland	0	Wales	7
18 Mar	Murrayfield	Scotland	6	England	9

(1940–1946 no championship)

1947

1 Jan	Stade Colombes	France	8	Scotland	3
18 Jan	Arms Park	Wales	6	England	9
25 Jan	Lansdowne Road	Ireland	8	France	12
1 Feb	Murrayfield	Scotland	8	Wales	22
8 Feb	Lansdowne Road	Ireland	22	England	0
22 Feb	Murrayfield	Scotland	0	Ireland	3
15 Mar	Twickenham	England	24	Scotland	5
22 Mar	Stade Colombes	France	0	Wales	3
29 Mar	St Helen's	Wales	6	Ireland	0
19 Apr	Twickenham	England	6	France	3

1948

1 Jan	Stade Colombes	France	6	Ireland	13
17 Jan	Twickenham	England	3	Wales	3
24 Jan	Murrayfield	Scotland	9	France	8
7 Feb	Arms Park	Wales	14	Scotland	0
14 Feb	Twickenham	England	10	Ireland	11
21 Feb	St Helen's	Wales	3	France	11
28 Feb	Lansdowne Road	Ireland	6	Scotland	0
13 Mar	Ravenhill	Ireland	6	Wales	3
20 Mar	Murrayfield	Scotland	6	England	3
29 Mar	Stade Colombes	France	15	England	0

1949

15 Jan	Stade Colombes	France	0	Scotland	8
15 Jan	Arms Park	Wales	9	England	3

191

29 Jan	Lansdowne Road	Ireland	9	France	16
5 Feb	Murrayfield	Scotland	6	Wales	5
12 Feb	Lansdowne Road	Ireland	14	England	5
26 Feb	Twickenham	England	8	France	3
26 Feb	Murrayfield	Scotland	3	Ireland	13
12 Mar	St Helen's	Wales	0	Ireland	5
19 Mar	Twickenham	England	19	Scotland	3
26 Mar	Stade Colombes	France	5	Wales	3

1950

14 Jan	Murrayfield	Scotland	8	France	5
21 Jan	Twickenham	England	5	Wales	11
28 Jan	Stade Colombes	France	3	Ireland	3
4 Feb	St Helen's	Wales	12	Scotland	0
11 Feb	Twickenham	England	3	Ireland	0
25 Feb	Stade Colombes	France	6	England	3
25 Feb	Lansdowne Road	Ireland	21	Scotland	0
11 Mar	Ravenhill	Ireland	3	Wales	6
18 Mar	Murrayfield	Scotland	13	England	11
25 Mar	Arms Park	Wales	21	France	0

1951

13 Jan	Stade Colombes	France	14	Scotland	12
20 Jan	St Helen's	Wales	23	England	5
27 Jan	Lansdowne Road	Ireland	9	France	8
3 Feb	Murrayfield	Scotland	19	Wales	0
10 Feb	Lansdowne Road	Ireland	3	England	0
24 Feb	Twickenham	England	3	France	11
24 Feb	Murrayfield	Scotland	5	Ireland	6
10 Mar	Arms Park	Wales	3	Ireland	3
17 Mar	Twickenham	England	5	Scotland	3
7 Apr	Stade Colombes	France	8	Wales	3

1952

12 Jan	Murrayfield	Scotland	11	France	13
19 Jan	Twickenham	England	6	Wales	8
26 Jan	Stade Colombes	France	8	Ireland	11
2 Feb	Arms Park	Wales	11	Scotland	0
23 Feb	Lansdowne Road	Ireland	12	Scotland	8
8 Mar	Lansdowne Road	Ireland	3	Wales	14
15 Mar	Murrayfield	Scotland	3	England	19
22 Mar	St Helen's	Wales	9	France	5
29 Mar	Twickenham	England	3	Ireland	0
5 Apr	Stade Colombes	France	3	England	6

1953

10 Jan	Stade Colombes	France	11	Scotland	5
17 Jan	Arms Park	Wales	3	England	8
24 Jan	Ravenhill	Ireland	16	France	3
7 Feb	Murrayfield	Scotland	0	Wales	12
14 Feb	Lansdowne Road	Ireland	9	England	9
28 Feb	Twickenham	England	11	France	0
28 Feb	Murrayfield	Scotland	8	Ireland	26
14 Mar	St Helen's	Wales	5	Ireland	3
21 Mar	Twickenham	England	26	Scotland	8
28 Mar	Stade Colombes	France	3	Wales	6

1954

9 Jan	Murrayfield	Scotland	0	France	3
16 Jan	Twickenham	England	9	Wales	6
23 Jan	Stade Colombes	France	8	Ireland	0
13 Feb	Twickenham	England	14	Ireland	3
27 Feb	Ravenhill	Ireland	6	Scotland	0
13 Mar	Lansdowne Road	Ireland	9	Wales	12
20 Mar	Murrayfield	Scotland	3	England	13
27 Mar	Arms Park	Wales	19	France	13
10 Apr	Stade Colombes	France	11	England	3
10 Apr	St Helen's	Wales	15	Scotland	3

1955

8 Jan	Stade Colombes	France	15	Scotland	0
22 Jan	Lansdowne Road	Ireland	3	France	5
22 Jan	Arms Park	Wales	3	England	0
5 Feb	Murrayfield	Scotland	14	Wales	8
12 Feb	Lansdowne Road	Ireland	6	England	6
26 Feb	Twickenham	England	9	France	16
26 Feb	Murrayfield	Scotland	12	Ireland	3
12 Mar	Arms Park	Wales	21	Ireland	3
19 Mar	Twickenham	England	9	Scotland	6
26 Mar	Stade Colombes	France	11	Wales	16

1956

14 Jan	Murrayfield	Scotland	12	France	0
21 Jan	Twickenham	England	3	Wales	8
28 Jan	Stade Colombes	France	14	Ireland	8
4 Feb	Arms Park	Wales	9	Scotland	3
11 Feb	Twickenham	England	20	Ireland	0
25 Feb	Lansdowne Road	Ireland	14	Scotland	10
10 Mar	Lansdowne Road	Ireland	11	Wales	3

17 Mar	Murrayfield	Scotland	6	England	11
24 Mar	Arms Park	Wales	5	France	3
14 Apr	Stade Colombes	France	14	England	9

1957

12 Jan	Stade Colombes	France	0	Scotland	6
19 Jan	Arms Park	Wales	0	England	3
26 Jan	Lansdowne Road	Ireland	11	France	6
2 Feb	Murrayfield	Scotland	9	Wales	6
9 Feb	Lansdowne Road	Ireland	0	England	6
23 Feb	Twickenham	England	9	France	5
23 Feb	Murrayfield	Scotland	3	Ireland	5
9 Mar	Arms Park	Wales	6	Ireland	5
16 Mar	Twickenham	England	16	Scotland	3
23 Mar	Stade Colombes	France	13	Wales	19

1958

11 Jan	Murrayfield	Scotland	11	France	9
18 Jan	Twickenham	England	3	Wales	3
1 Feb	Arms Park	Wales	8	Scotland	3
8 Feb	Twickenham	England	6	Ireland	0
1 Mar	Stade Colombes	France	0	England	14
1 Mar	Lansdowne Road	Ireland	12	Scotland	6
15 Mar	Lansdowne Road	Ireland	6	Wales	9
15 Mar	Murrayfield	Scotland	3	England	3
29 Mar	Arms Park	Wales	6	France	16
19 Apr	Stade Colombes	France	11	Ireland	6

1959

10 Jan	Stade Colombes	France	9	Scotland	0
17 Jan	Arms Park	Wales	5	England	0
7 Feb	Murrayfield	Scotland	6	Wales	5
14 Feb	Lansdowne Road	Ireland	0	England	3
28 Feb	Twickenham	England	3	France	3
28 Feb	Murrayfield	Scotland	3	Ireland	8
14 Mar	Arms Park	Wales	8	Ireland	6
21 Mar	Twickenham	England	3	Scotland	3
4 Apr	Stade Colombes	France	11	Wales	3
18 Apr	Lansdowne Road	Ireland	9	France	5

1960

9 Jan	Murrayfield	Scotland	11	France	13
16 Jan	Twickenham	England	14	Wales	6
6 Feb	Arms Park	Wales	8	Scotland	0

13 Feb	Twickenham	England	8	Ireland	5
27 Feb	Stade Colombes	France	3	England	3
27 Feb	Lansdowne Road	Ireland	5	Scotland	6
12 Mar	Lansdowne Road	Ireland	9	Wales	10
19 Mar	Murrayfield	Scotland	12	England	21
26 Mar	Arms Park	Wales	8	France	16
9 Apr	Stade Colombes	France	23	Ireland	6

1961

7 Jan	Stade Colombes	France	11	Scotland	0
21 Jan	Arms Park	Wales	6	England	3
11 Feb	Lansdowne Road	Ireland	11	England	8
11 Feb	Murrayfield	Scotland	3	Wales	0
25 Feb	Twickenham	England	5	France	5
25 Feb	Murrayfield	Scotland	16	Ireland	8
11 Mar	Arms Park	Wales	9	Ireland	0
18 Mar	Twickenham	England	6	Scotland	0
25 Mar	Stade Colombes	France	8	Wales	6
15 Apr	Lansdowne Road	Ireland	3	France	15

1962

13 Jan	Murrayfield	Scotland	3	France	11
20 Jan	Twickenham	England	0	Wales	0
3 Feb	Arms Park	Wales	3	Scotland	8
10 Feb	Twickenham	England	16	Ireland	0
24 Feb	Stade Colombes	France	13	England	0
24 Feb	Lansdowne Road	Ireland	6	Scotland	20
17 Mar	Murrayfield	Scotland	3	England	3
24 Mar	Arms Park	Wales	3	France	0
14 Apr	Stade Colombes	France	11	Ireland	0
17 Nov	Lansdowne Road	Ireland	3	Wales	3

1963

12 Jan	Stade Colombes	France	6	Scotland	11
19 Jan	Arms Park	Wales	6	England	13
26 Jan	Lansdowne Road	Ireland	5	France	24
2 Feb	Murrayfield	Scotland	0	Wales	6
9 Feb	Lansdowne Road	Ireland	0	England	0
23 Feb	Twickenham	England	6	France	5
23 Feb	Murrayfield	Scotland	3	Ireland	0
9 Mar	Arms Park	Wales	6	Ireland	14
16 Mar	Twickenham	England	10	Scotland	8
23 Mar	Stade Colombes	France	5	Wales	3

1964

4 Jan	Murrayfield	Scotland	10	France	0
18 Jan	Twickenham	England	6	Wales	6
1 Feb	Arms Park	Wales	11	Scotland	3
8 Feb	Twickenham	England	5	Ireland	18
22 Feb	Stade Colombes	France	3	England	6
22 Feb	Lansdowne Road	Ireland	3	Scotland	6
7 Mar	Lansdowne Road	Ireland	6	Wales	15
21 Mar	Murrayfield	Scotland	15	England	6
21 Mar	Arms Park	Wales	11	France	11
11 Apr	Stade Colombes	France	27	Ireland	6

1965

9 Jan	Stade Colombes	France	16	Scotland	8
16 Jan	Arms Park	Wales	14	England	3
23 Jan	Lansdowne Road	Ireland	3	France	3
6 Feb	Murrayfield	Scotland	12	Wales	14
13 Feb	Lansdowne Road	Ireland	5	England	0
27 Feb	Twickenham	England	9	France	6
27 Feb	Murrayfield	Scotland	6	Ireland	16
13 Mar	Arms Park	Wales	14	Ireland	8
20 Mar	Twickenham	England	3	Scotland	3
27 Mar	Stade Colombes	France	22	Wales	13

1966

15 Jan	Twickenham	England	6	Wales	11
15 Jan	Murrayfield	Scotland	3	France	3
29 Jan	Stade Colombes	France	11	Ireland	6
5 Feb	Arms Park	Wales	8	Scotland	3
12 Feb	Twickenham	England	6	Ireland	6
26 Feb	Stade Colombes	France	13	England	0
26 Feb	Lansdowne Road	Ireland	3	Scotland	11
12 Mar	Lansdowne Road	Ireland	9	Wales	6
19 Mar	Murrayfield	Scotland	6	England	3
26 Mar	Arms Park	Wales	9	France	8

1967

14 Jan	Stade Colombes	France	8	Scotland	9
4 Feb	Murrayfield	Scotland	11	Wales	5
11 Feb	Lansdowne Road	Ireland	3	England	8
25 Feb	Twickenham	England	12	France	16
25 Feb	Murrayfield	Scotland	3	Ireland	5
11 Mar	Arms Park	Wales	0	Ireland	3
18 Mar	Twickenham	England	27	Scotland	14

1 Apr	Stade Colombes	France	20	Wales	14
15 Apr	Lansdowne Road	Ireland	6	France	11
15 Apr	Arms Park	Wales	34	England	21

1968

13 Jan	Murrayfield	Scotland	6	France	8
20 Jan	Twickenham	England	11	Wales	11
27 Jan	Stade Colombes	France	16	Ireland	6
3 Feb	Arms Park	Wales	5	Scotland	0
10 Feb	Twickenham	England	9	Ireland	9
24 Feb	Stade Colombes	France	14	England	9
24 Feb	Lansdowne Road	Ireland	14	Scotland	6
9 Mar	Lansdowne Road	Ireland	9	Wales	6
16 Mar	Murrayfield	Scotland	6	England	8
23 Mar	Arms Park	Wales	9	France	14

1969

11 Jan	Stade Colombes	France	3	Scotland	6
25 Jan	Lansdowne Road	Ireland	17	France	9
1 Feb	Murrayfield	Scotland	3	Wales	17
8 Feb	Lansdowne Road	Ireland	17	England	15
22 Feb	Twickenham	England	22	France	8
22 Feb	Murrayfield	Scotland	0	Ireland	16
8 Mar	Arms Park	Wales	24	Ireland	11
15 Mar	Twickenham	England	8	Scotland	3
22 Mar	Stade Colombes	France	8	Wales	8
12 Apr	Arms Park	Wales	30	England	9

1970

10 Jan	Murrayfield	Scotland	9	France	11
24 Jan	Stade Colombes	France	8	Ireland	0
7 Feb	Arms Park	Wales	18	Scotland	9
14 Feb	Twickenham	England	9	Ireland	3
28 Feb	Twickenham	England	13	Wales	17
28 Feb	Lansdowne Road	Ireland	16	Scotland	11
14 Mar	Lansdowne Road	Ireland	14	Wales	0
21 Mar	Murrayfield	Scotland	14	England	5
4 Apr	Arms Park	Wales	11	France	6
18 Apr	Stade Colombes	France	35	England	13

1971

16 Jan	Stade Colombes	France	13	Scotland	8
16 Jan	Arms Park	Wales	22	England	6
30 Jan	Lansdowne Road	Ireland	9	France	9

6 Feb	Murrayfield	Scotland	18	Wales	19
13 Feb	Lansdowne Road	Ireland	6	England	9
27 Feb	Twickenham	England	14	France	14
27 Feb	Murrayfield	Scotland	5	Ireland	17
13 Mar	Arms Park	Wales	23	Ireland	9
20 Mar	Twickenham	England	15	Scotland	16
27 Mar	Stade Colombes	France	5	Wales	9

1972

15 Jan	Twickenham	England	3	Wales	12
15 Jan	Murrayfield	Scotland	20	France	9
29 Jan	Stade Colombes	France	9	Ireland	14
5 Feb	Arms Park	Wales	35	Scotland	12
12 Feb	Twickenham	England	12	Ireland	16
26 Feb	Stade Colombes	France	37	England	12
18 Mar	Murrayfield	Scotland	23	England	9
25 Mar	Arms Park	Wales	20	France	6

(truncated championship)

1973

13 Jan	Parc des Princes	France	16	Scotland	13
20 Jan	Arms Park	Wales	25	England	9
3 Feb	Murrayfield	Scotland	10	Wales	9
10 Feb	Lansdowne Road	Ireland	18	England	9
24 Feb	Twickenham	England	14	France	6
24 Feb	Murrayfield	Scotland	19	Ireland	14
10 Mar	Arms Park	Wales	16	Ireland	12
17 Mar	Twickenham	England	20	Scotland	13
24 Mar	Parc des Princes	France	12	Wales	3
14 Apr	Lansdowne Road	Ireland	6	France	4

1974

19 Jan	Parc des Princes	France	9	Ireland	6
19 Jan	Arms Park	Wales	6	Scotland	0
2 Feb	Lansdowne Road	Ireland	9	Wales	9
2 Feb	Murrayfield	Scotland	16	England	14
16 Feb	Twickenham	England	21	Ireland	26
16 Feb	Arms Park	Wales	16	France	16
2 Mar	Parc des Princes	France	12	England	12
2 Mar	Lansdowne Road	Ireland	9	Scotland	6
16 Mar	Twickenham	England	16	Wales	12
16 Mar	Murrayfield	Scotland	19	France	6

1975

18 Jan	Parc des Princes	France	10	Wales	25
18 Jan	Lansdowne Road	Ireland	12	England	9
1 Feb	Twickenham	England	20	France	27
1 Feb	Murrayfield	Scotland	20	Ireland	13
15 Feb	Parc des Princes	France	10	Scotland	9
15 Feb	Arms Park	Wales	20	England	4
1 Mar	Lansdowne Road	Ireland	25	France	6
1 Mar	Murrayfield	Scotland	12	Wales	10
15 Mar	Twickenham	England	7	Scotland	6
15 Mar	Arms Park	Wales	32	Ireland	4

1976

10 Jan	Murrayfield	Scotland	6	France	13
17 Jan	Twickenham	England	9	Wales	21
7 Feb	Parc des Princes	France	26	Ireland	3
7 Feb	Arms Park	Wales	28	Scotland	6
21 Feb	Lansdowne Road	Ireland	9	Wales	34
21 Feb	Murrayfield	Scotland	22	England	12
6 Mar	Twickenham	England	12	Ireland	13
6 Mar	Arms Park	Wales	19	France	13
20 Mar	Parc des Princes	France	30	England	9
20 Mar	Lansdowne Road	Ireland	6	Scotland	15

1977

15 Jan	Twickenham	England	26	Scotland	6
15 Jan	Arms Park	Wales	25	Ireland	9
5 Feb	Parc des Princes	France	16	Wales	9
5 Feb	Lansdowne Road	Ireland	0	England	4
19 Feb	Twickenham	England	3	France	4
19 Feb	Murrayfield	Scotland	21	Ireland	18
5 Mar	Parc des Princes	France	23	Scotland	3
5 Mar	Arms Park	Wales	14	England	9
19 Mar	Lansdowne Road	Ireland	6	France	15
19 Mar	Murrayfield	Scotland	9	Wales	18

1978

21 Jan	Parc des Princes	France	15	England	6
21 Jan	Lansdowne Road	Ireland	12	Scotland	9
4 Feb	Twickenham	England	6	Wales	9
4 Feb	Murrayfield	Scotland	16	France	19
18 Feb	Parc des Princes	France	10	Ireland	9
18 Feb	Arms Park	Wales	22	Scotland	14
4 Mar	Lansdowne Road	Ireland	16	Wales	20

4 Mar	Murrayfield	Scotland	0	England	15
18 Mar	Twickenham	England	15	Ireland	9
18 Mar	Arms Park	Wales	16	France	7

1979

20 Jan	Lansdowne Road	Ireland	9	France	9
20 Jan	Murrayfield	Scotland	13	Wales	19
3 Feb	Twickenham	England	7	Scotland	7
3 Feb	Arms Park	Wales	24	Ireland	21
17 Feb	Parc des Princes	France	14	Wales	13
17 Feb	Lansdowne Road	Ireland	12	England	7
3 Mar	Twickenham	England	7	France	6
3 Mar	Murrayfield	Scotland	11	Ireland	11
17 Mar	Parc des Princes	France	21	Scotland	17
17 Mar	Arms Park	Wales	27	England	3

1980

19 Jan	Twickenham	England	24	Ireland	9
19 Jan	Arms Park	Wales	18	France	9
2 Feb	Parc des Princes	France	13	England	17
2 Feb	Lansdowne Road	Ireland	22	Scotland	15
16 Feb	Twickenham	England	9	Wales	8
16 Feb	Murrayfield	Scotland	22	France	14
1 Mar	Parc des Princes	France	19	Ireland	18
1 Mar	Arms Park	Wales	17	Scotland	6
15 Mar	Lansdowne Road	Ireland	21	Wales	7
15 Mar	Murrayfield	Scotland	18	England	30

1981

17 Jan	Parc des Princes	France	16	Scotland	9
17 Jan	Arms Park	Wales	21	England	19
7 Feb	Lansdowne Road	Ireland	13	France	19
7 Feb	Murrayfield	Scotland	15	Wales	6
21 Feb	Twickenham	England	23	Scotland	17
21 Feb	Arms Park	Wales	9	Ireland	8
7 Mar	Parc des Princes	France	19	Wales	15
7 Mar	Lansdowne Road	Ireland	6	England	10
21 Mar	Twickenham	England	12	France	16
21 Mar	Murrayfield	Scotland	10	Ireland	9

1982

16 Jan	Murrayfield	Scotland	9	England	9
23 Jan	Lansdowne Road	Ireland	20	Wales	12
6 Feb	Twickenham	England	15	Ireland	16
6 Feb	Arms Park	Wales	22	France	12

20 Feb	Parc des Princes	France	15	England	27
20 Feb	Lansdowne Road	Ireland	21	Scotland	12
6 Mar	Twickenham	England	17	Wales	7
6 Mar	Murrayfield	Scotland	16	France	7
20 Mar	Parc des Princes	France	22	Ireland	9
20 Mar	Arms Park	Wales	18	Scotland	34

1983

15 Jan	Twickenham	England	15	France	19
15 Jan	Murrayfield	Scotland	13	Ireland	15
5 Feb	Parc des Princes	France	19	Scotland	15
5 Feb	Arms Park	Wales	13	England	13
19 Feb	Lansdowne Road	Ireland	22	France	16
19 Feb	Murrayfield	Scotland	15	Wales	19
5 Mar	Twickenham	England	12	Scotland	22
5 Mar	Arms Park	Wales	23	Ireland	9
19 Mar	Parc des Princes	France	16	Wales	9
19 Mar	Lansdowne Road	Ireland	25	England	15

1984

21 Jan	Parc des Princes	France	25	Ireland	12
21 Jan	Arms Park	Wales	9	Scotland	15
4 Feb	Lansdowne Road	Ireland	9	Wales	18
4 Feb	Murrayfield	Scotland	18	England	6
18 Feb	Twickenham	England	12	Ireland	9
18 Feb	Arms Park	Wales	16	France	21
3 Mar	Parc des Princes	France	32	England	18
3 Mar	Lansdowne Road	Ireland	9	Scotland	32
17 Mar	Twickenham	England	15	Wales	24
17 Mar	Murrayfield	Scotland	21	France	12

1985

2 Feb	Twickenham	England	9	France	9
2 Feb	Murrayfield	Scotland	15	Ireland	18
16 Feb	Parc des Princes	France	11	Scotland	3
2 Mar	Lansdowne Road	Ireland	15	France	15
2 Mar	Murrayfield	Scotland	21	Wales	25
16 Mar	Twickenham	England	10	Scotland	7
16 Mar	Arms Park	Wales	9	Ireland	21
30 Mar	Parc des Princes	France	14	Wales	3
30 Mar	Lansdowne Road	Ireland	13	England	10
20 Apr	Arms Park	Wales	24	England	15

1986

17 Jan	Twickenham	England	21	Wales	18
17 Jan	Murrayfield	Scotland	18	France	17
1 Feb	Parc des Princes	France	29	Ireland	9
1 Feb	Arms Park	Wales	22	Scotland	15
15 Feb	Lansdowne Road	Ireland	12	Wales	19
15 Feb	Murrayfield	Scotland	33	England	6
1 Mar	Twickenham	England	25	Ireland	20
1 Mar	Arms Park	Wales	15	France	23
15 Mar	Parc des Princes	France	29	England	10
15 Mar	Lansdowne Road	Ireland	9	Scotland	10

1987

7 Feb	Parc des Princes	France	16	Wales	9
7 Feb	Lansdowne Road	Ireland	17	England	0
21 Feb	Twickenham	England	15	France	19
21 Feb	Murrayfield	Scotland	16	Ireland	12
7 Mar	Parc des Princes	France	28	Scotland	22
7 Mar	Arms Park	Wales	19	England	12
21 Mar	Lansdowne Road	Ireland	13	France	19
21 Mar	Murrayfield	Scotland	21	Wales	15
4 Apr	Twickenham	England	21	Scotland	12
4 Apr	Arms Park	Wales	11	Ireland	15

1988

16 Jan	Parc des Princes	France	10	England	9
16 Jan	Lansdowne Road	Ireland	22	Scotland	18
6 Feb	Twickenham	England	3	Wales	11
6 Feb	Murrayfield	Scotland	23	France	12
20 Feb	Parc des Princes	France	25	Ireland	6
20 Feb	Arms Park	Wales	25	Scotland	20
5 Mar	Lansdowne Road	Ireland	9	Wales	12
5 Mar	Murrayfield	Scotland	6	England	9
19 Mar	Twickenham	England	35	Ireland	3
19 Mar	Arms Park	Wales	9	France	10

1989

21 Jan	Lansdowne Road	Ireland	21	France	26
21 Jan	Murrayfield	Scotland	23	Wales	7
4 Feb	Twickenham	England	12	Scotland	12
4 Feb	Arms Park	Wales	13	Ireland	19
18 Feb	Parc des Princes	France	31	Wales	12
18 Feb	Lansdowne Road	Ireland	3	England	16
4 Mar	Twickenham	England	11	France	0

4 Mar	Murrayfield	Scotland	37	Ireland	21
18 Mar	Parc des Princes	France	19	Scotland	3
18 Mar	Arms Park	Wales	12	England	9

1990

20 Jan	Twickenham	England	23	Ireland	0
20 Jan	Arms Park	Wales	19	France	29
3 Feb	Parc des Princes	France	7	England	26
3 Feb	Lansdowne Road	Ireland	10	Scotland	13
17 Feb	Twickenham	England	34	Wales	6
17 Feb	Murrayfield	Scotland	21	France	0
3 Mar	Parc des Princes	France	31	Ireland	12
3 Mar	Arms Park	Wales	9	Scotland	13
17 Mar	Murrayfield	Scotland	13	England	7
24 Mar	Lansdowne Road	Ireland	14	Wales	8

1991

19 Jan	Parc des Princes	France	15	Scotland	9
19 Jan	Arms Park	Wales	6	England	25
2 Feb	Lansdowne Road	Ireland	13	France	21
2 Feb	Murrayfield	Scotland	32	Wales	12
16 Feb	Twickenham	England	21	Scotland	12
16 Feb	Arms Park	Wales	21	Ireland	21
2 Mar	Parc des Princes	France	36	Wales	3
2 Mar	Lansdowne Road	Ireland	7	England	16
16 Mar	Twickenham	England	21	France	19
16 Mar	Murrayfield	Scotland	28	Ireland	25

1992

18 Jan	Lansdowne Road	Ireland	15	Wales	16
18 Jan	Murrayfield	Scotland	7	England	25
1 Feb	Twickenham	England	38	Ireland	9
1 Feb	Arms Park	Wales	9	France	12
15 Feb	Parc des Princes	France	13	England	31
15 Feb	Lansdowne Road	Ireland	10	Scotland	18
7 Mar	Twickenham	England	24	Wales	0
7 Mar	Murrayfield	Scotland	10	France	6
21 Mar	Parc des Princes	France	44	Ireland	12
21 Mar	Arms Park	Wales	15	Scotland	12

1993

16 Jan	Twickenham	England	16	France	15
16 Jan	Murrayfield	Scotland	15	Ireland	3
7 Feb	Parc des Princes	France	11	Scotland	3

7 Feb	*Arms Park*	Wales	10	England	9
20 Feb	*Lansdowne Road*	Ireland	6	France	21
20 Feb	*Murrayfield*	Scotland	20	Wales	0
6 Mar	*Twickenham*	England	26	Scotland	12
6 Mar	*Arms Park*	Wales	14	Ireland	19
20 Mar	*Parc des Princes*	France	26	Wales	10
20 Mar	*Lansdowne Road*	Ireland	17	England	3

1994

15 Jan	*Parc des Princes*	France	35	Ireland	15
15 Jan	*Arms Park*	Wales	29	Scotland	6
5 Feb	*Lansdowne Road*	Ireland	15	Wales	17
5 Feb	*Murrayfield*	Scotland	14	England	15
19 Feb	*Twickenham*	England	12	Ireland	13
19 Feb	*Arms Park*	Wales	24	France	15
5 Mar	*Parc des Princes*	France	14	England	18
5 Mar	*Lansdowne Road*	Ireland	6	Scotland	6
19 Mar	*Twickenham*	England	15	Wales	8
19 Mar	*Murrayfield*	Scotland	12	France	20

1995

21 Jan	*Parc des Princes*	France	21	Wales	9
21 Jan	*Lansdowne Road*	Ireland	8	England	20
4 Feb	*Twickenham*	England	31	France	10
4 Feb	*Murrayfield*	Scotland	26	Ireland	13
18 Feb	*Parc des Princes*	France	21	Scotland	23
18 Feb	*Arms Park*	Wales	9	England	23
4 Mar	*Lansdowne Road*	Ireland	7	France	25
4 Mar	*Murrayfield*	Scotland	26	Wales	13
18 Mar	*Twickenham*	England	24	Scotland	12
18 Mar	*Arms Park*	Wales	12	Ireland	16

1996

20 Jan	*Parc des Princes*	France	15	England	12
20 Jan	*Lansdowne Road*	Ireland	10	Scotland	16
3 Feb	*Twickenham*	England	21	Wales	15
3 Feb	*Murrayfield*	Scotland	19	France	14
17 Feb	*Parc des Princes*	France	45	Ireland	10
17 Feb	*Arms Park*	Wales	14	Scotland	16
2 Mar	*Lansdowne Road*	Ireland	30	Wales	17
2 Mar	*Murrayfield*	Scotland	9	England	18
16 Mar	*Twickenham*	England	28	Ireland	15
16 Mar	*Arms Park*	Wales	16	France	15

1997

18 Jan	Lansdowne Road	Ireland	15	France	32
18 Jan	Murrayfield	Scotland	19	Wales	34
1 Feb	Twickenham	England	41	Scotland	13
1 Feb	Arms Park	Wales	25	Ireland	26
15 Feb	Parc des Princes	France	27	Wales	22
15 Feb	Lansdowne Road	Ireland	6	England	46
1 Mar	Twickenham	England	20	France	23
1 Mar	Murrayfield	Scotland	38	Ireland	10
15 Mar	Parc des Princes	France	47	Scotland	20
15 Mar	Arms Park	Wales	13	England	34

1998

7 Feb	Stade de France, Paris	France	24	England	17
7 Feb	Lansdowne Road	Ireland	16	Scotland	17
21 Feb	Twickenham	England	60	Wales	26
21 Feb	Murrayfield	Scotland	16	France	51
7 Mar	Stade de France	France	18	Ireland	16
7 Mar	Wembley, London	Wales	19	Scotland	13
21 Mar	Lansdowne Road	Ireland	21	Wales	30
22 Mar	Murrayfield	Scotland	20	England	34
4 Apr	Twickenham	England	35	Ireland	17
5 Apr	Wembley	Wales	0	France	51

1999

6 Feb	Lansdowne Road	Ireland	9	France	10
6 Feb	Murrayfield	Scotland	33	Wales	20
20 Feb	Twickenham	England	24	Scotland	21
20 Feb	Wembley	Wales	23	Ireland	29
6 Mar	Stade de France	France	33	Wales	34
6 Mar	Lansdowne Road	Ireland	15	England	27
20 Mar	Twickenham	England	21	France	10
20 Mar	Murrayfield	Scotland	30	Ireland	13
10 Apr	Stade de France	France	22	Scotland	36
11 Apr	Wembley	Wales	32	England	31

ROLL OF HONOUR

Grand Slams – England 11, France 6, Wales 6, Scotland 3, Ireland 1
Triple Crowns – England 18, Wales 11, Scotland 5, Ireland 4

HEAD TO HEADS

England *won*	36	France *won*	27	Drawn	7
England *won*	44	Ireland *won*	27	Drawn	7
England *won*	48	Scotland *won*	22	Drawn	8
England *won*	33	Wales *won*	35	Drawn	10
France *won*	42	Ireland *won*	23	Drawn	5
France *won*	34	Scotland *won*	33	Drawn	2
France *won*	30	Wales *won*	37	Drawn	3
Ireland *won*	39	Scotland *won*	36	Drawn	2
Ireland *won*	29	Wales *won*	43	Drawn	5
Scotland *won*	32	Wales *won*	45	Drawn	1

TABLE OF TABLES

	Played	Won	Drawn	Lost	Points	% Won
England	304	161	32	111	354	53.0%
Wales	303	160	19	124	339	52.8%
France	279	133	17	129	283	47.7%
Scotland	302	123	13	166	259	40.7%
Ireland	302	118	19	165	255	39.1%

RECORDS

ENGLAND

Team records against other countries:

	At home	Away
Biggest score	60 v Wales in 1998	46 v Ireland in 1997
Biggest winning margin	37 v France in 1911	40 v Ireland in 1997
Highest score against	27 v France in 1975	37 v France in 1972
Biggest losing margin	13 v Ireland in 1964	27 v Scotland in 1986

Most points scored by the team in a season: 146 in 1998

Most points conceded by the team in a season: 100 in 1986

Most all-time appearances: Rory Underwood 50, Rob Andrew 40, Will Carling 40, Peter Winterbottom 37, Peter Wheeler 36 and Jason Leonard 36

Top all-time points scorers: Rob Andrew 185, Paul Grayson 182 and Dusty Hare 178

Top all-time try-scorers: Cyril Lowe 18, Rory Underwood 18 and David Duckham 9

Most points by a player in a season: 67 Jonathan Webb in 1992

Most points by a player in a match: 24 Rob Andrew in 1995

FRANCE

Team records against other countries:

	At home	Away
Biggest score	47 v Scotland in 1997	51 v Scotland and Wales in 1998
Biggest winning margin	35 v Ireland in 1996	51 v Wales in 1998
Highest score against	39 v England in 1914	49 v Wales in 1910
Biggest losing margin	26 v England in 1914	37 v England in 1911

Most points scored by the team in a season: 144 in 1998

Most points conceded by the team in a season: 100 in 1999

Most all-time appearances: Philippe Sella 50, Serge Blanco 42, Jean-Pierre Rives 39, Roland Bertranne 37, Jean Prat 35 and Michel Crauste 35

Top all-time points scorers: Didier Camberabero 113, Serge Blanco 106 and Jean-Pierre Romeu 104

Top all-time try-scorers: Serge Blanco 14, Philippe Sella 14, Christian Darrouy 13 and Philippe Saint-André 13

Most points by a player in a season: 54 Jean-Patrick Lescarboura in 1984

Most points by a player in a match: 24 Sebastien Viars in 1992 and Christophe Lamaison in 1997

IRELAND

Team records against other countries:

	At home	Away
Biggest score	30 v Wales in 1996	29 v Wales in 1999
Biggest winning margin	24 v France in 1913	18 v Scotland in 1953
Highest score against	46 v England in 1997	45 v France in 1996
Biggest losing margin	40 v England in 1997	35 v France in 1996

Most points scored by the team in a season: 71 in 1983

Most points conceded by the team in a season: 141 in 1997

Most all-time appearances: Mike Gibson 56, Willie John McBride 53,

Fergus Slattery 49, Phil Orr 46, Tom Kiernan 44 and Moss Keane 44

Top all-time points scorer: Michael Kiernan 207, Ollie Campbell 182 and Eric Elwood 135

Top all-time try-scorers: George Stephenson 14, Brendan Mullin 11 and Joseph Quinn 9

Most points by a player in a season: 52 Ollie Campbell in 1983

Most points by a player in a match: 21 Ollie Campbell in 1982 and 1983

SCOTLAND

Team records against other countries:

	At home	*Away*
Biggest score	38 v Ireland in 1997	36 v France in 1999
Biggest winning margin	28 v France in 1912 and Ireland in 1997	23 v Ireland in 1984
Highest score against	51 v France in 1998	47 v France in 1997
Biggest losing margin	35 v France in 1998	28 v England in 1997

Most points scored by the team in a season: 120 in 1999

Most points conceded by the team in a season: 132 in 1997

Most all-time appearances: Jim Renwick 42, Sandy Carmichael 41, Scott Hastings 41, Andy Irvine 39, Alastair McHarg 37 and Colin Deans 37

Top all-time points scorer: Gavin Hastings 288, Andy Irvine 194 and Peter Dods 144

Top all-time try-scorers: Ian Smith 24, Arthur Wallace 11, Andy Irvine 10 and Arthur Smith 10

Most points by a player in a season: 56 Gavin Hastings in 1995

Most points by a player in a match: 21 Gavin Hastings in 1986

WALES

Team records against other countries:

	At home	*Away*
Biggest score	49 v France in 1910	34 v Ireland in 1976 and v Scotland in 1997 and v France in 1999
Biggest winning margin	35 v France in 1910	25 v Ireland in 1976
Highest score against	51 v France in 1998	60 v England in 1998

Biggest losing margin   51 v France in 1998   34 v England in 1998

Most points scored by the team in a season: 109 in 1999

Most points conceded by the team in a season: 145 in 1998

Most all-time appearances: Gareth Edwards 45, JPR Williams 44, Ken Jones 41, Gerald Davies 38 and Ieuan Evans 36

Top all-time points scorers: Neil Jenkins 284, Paul Thorburn 166 and Phil Bennett 142

Top all-time try-scorers: Gareth Edwards 18, Gerald Davies 16 and Ken Jones 16

Most points by a player in a season: 64 Neil Jenkins in 1999

Most points by a player in a match: 22 Neil Jenkins in 1999